SHANLEY · DARREL ASCHBACHER · WILLIE WEST · MEL RENFRO

KEN WOODY · BOBBY MOORE · TOM GRAHAM · TOM DROUGAS

L ELSHIRE · GARY ZIMMERMAN · MICHAEL GRAY · DON PELLUM

EIL · CHAD COTA · RICH RUHL · ALEX MOLDEN · JOSH WILCOX

AKILI SMITH · SAUL PATU · RASHAD BAUMAN · JOEY HARRING

CHUGH · JACK CRABTREE · NORM CHAPMAN · JIM SHANLEY ·

BOB BERRY · DENNY SCHULER · BOB NEWLAND · KEN WOODY ·

STEVE GREATWOOD · VINCE GOLDSMITH · NEIL ELSHIRE · GAR

EWMAN · J.J. BIRDEN · BILL MUSGRAVE · DANNY O'NEIL · CHAD

CH MOORE · PETER SIRMON · MICHAEL FLETCHER · AKILI SMITH

N CLEMENS · NICK REED · JACK PATERA · PHIL MCHUGH · JACK

WEST · MEL RENFRO · LARRY HILL · DAVE WILCOX · BOB BERRY ·

· TOM DROUGAS · DAN FOUTS · DON REYNOLDS · STEVE GREAT

Y · DON PELLUM · CHRIS MILLER · ANTHONY NEWMAN · J.J. BIR

N · JOSH WILCOX · KENNY WHEATON · DIETRICH MOORE · PET

JOEY HARRINGTON · KEENAN HOWRY · KELLEN CLEMENS · NIC

SHANLEY · DARREL ASCHBACHER · WILLIE W

N WOODY · BOBBY MOORE · TOM GRAHA

ELSHIRE · GARY ZIMMERMAN · MICHAEL GRAY · DON PELLUM ·

WHAT IT MEANS TO BE A DUCK

WHAT IT MEANS TO BE A DUCK

MIKE BELLOTTI
AND OREGON'S GREATEST PLAYERS

ROB MOSELEY

TRIUMPH
BOOKS

Library of Congress Cataloging-in-Publication Data

Moseley, Rob.
   What it means to be a duck: Mike Bellotti and Oregon's greatest players / Rob Moseley.
      p. cm.
1. University of Oregon—Football—History. 2. Oregon Ducks (Football team)—History. 3. Bellotti, Mike. 4. Football players—Oregon—Biography. I. Title.
   GV958.U553M67 2009
   796.332'630979531—dc22

                              2009017229

This book is available in quantity at special discounts for your group or organization. For further information, contact:

Triumph Books
542 South Dearborn Street
Suite 750
Chicago, Illinois 60605
(312) 939-3330 • Fax (312) 663-3557
www.triumphbooks.com

Printed in U.S.A.
ISBN: 978-1-60078-159-9
Design by Nick Panos
Editorial production and layout by Prologue Publishing Services, LLC
Photos courtesy of University of Oregon unless otherwise indicated

CONTENTS

FOREWORD

What It Means to Be a Duck

For 14 years I had the distinct pleasure of leading the Oregon football program. Getting a chance to work alongside my fellow coaches and with the players who suited up for the University of Oregon could not have been a more enriching experience.

A number of different men have coached the Ducks over the years, but there are certain traits that have defined the program throughout the generations. Hard work. Doing more with less. Exceeding expectations. Whether it was Len Casanova, Jerry Frei, Rich Brooks, or any of the other great coaches to have graced the sideline in Eugene, those characteristics have always defined what it means to be a Duck.

Coming up through the ranks of lower-division NCAA football earlier in my career, I too learned to embrace those values. Whether it was at Chico State in Division II or at Weber State in Division I-AA, you rolled up your sleeves and went to work, trying to get the most out of the resources you had. When I joined the staff at Oregon in 1989, I found that the exact same way of doing business was employed by the men working under Coach Brooks.

There are other schools across the country that might be perceived to have an edge over the Ducks due to location or tradition or what have you. Oregon is special because some kids who were overlooked by some other places came here, had success, and played with chips on their shoulders. They felt like they had something to prove. The program has come a ways in the last few years, but we still embrace blue-collar values. We worked our way up and paid our dues, building facilities and reinvesting in our success probably more than anybody in the Pac-10 Conference.

As head coach of the Ducks from 1995 to 2009, Mike Bellotti had a 116–55 record. His teams won two Pac-10 championships, a Rose Bowl, and a Fiesta Bowl.

Our program has received a lot of attention recently for facility improvements we have made, and the aggressive, creative approach we take to recruiting. And we're proud of those developments. But all those things have really done is helped close the gap between Oregon and some other schools across the nation. No facility I know of ever made a play to win a football game. What's going to separate us, and keep us one step ahead of the pack, remains "old school" values like hard work and overachieving.

I always wanted my players to carry that underdog mentality, to feel they had something to prove. The thing I really like is outperforming peoples' expectations. Among the seasons I'm most proud of during my time as coach of the Ducks are 2005 and 2008. Both years featured injury problems at quarterback, and yet they are two of the four 10-win seasons in school history, both ending up at the Holiday Bowl. That 2005 team came within a play of beating Oklahoma, which has got to be the best team in the history of college football that didn't make a BCS bowl game.

In terms of pure success, the steady improvement of our program from 1996 through 2001 was extremely gratifying. Winning six games in 1996, seven in '97, and so on and so on until the 11-win Fiesta Bowl season of 2001 was very special. We had a great group of seniors led by quarterback Joey Harrington, and they took the Ducks to new heights.

Those teams, like the one I first took over in 1995, had inherent chemistry due to strong senior leadership. But sometimes the leadership you need to be successful doesn't come naturally. That's what made the end of the 2005 season so awesome, to lose a great leader like quarterback Kellen Clemens but still win 10 games, including a blowout over the Beavers. We weren't necessarily a great team at that point, but the kids worked together and achieved greatness.

I've often said the 1996 team was the best coaching job I was ever involved with, and it was for similar reasons as that 2005 squad. We lost a lot from the 1995 team, guys who had been key to the Rose Bowl season of 1994. And after 1995 I lost both my coordinators, so I had to hire new offensive and defensive coordinators for the second year in a row. Perhaps it would come as no surprise, then, to hear that the 1996 team wasn't always on the same page. Team chemistry was an issue, and we entered the month of November with a 3–5 record, having lost five in a row. I met with all my players over the course of the season, individually and in small groups, to find a solution. Ultimately, we got quarterback Tony Graziani and Saladin McCullough back healthy, and we cured the psyche of the team. We went on to finish with a three-game winning streak, including another convincing win over Oregon State. By working together and fostering team chemistry and unity, we proved that year that you can overcome a tremendous amount of things.

Sometimes that means being tough on the players. Tough love was a hallmark of the great coaches at Oregon, from Casanova to Brooks to all the rest. They were different people, but the bottom line is that they were deeply respected. We'd all love to be liked by everyone, but you can't always worry about that. The bottom line is to be respected, and to teach lessons that guys may not fully grasp until they leave the program. And then three or five years down the line they realize, that's what coach was trying to get at. It's not just about being tough in order to get through football practice or even a game, it's teaching a work ethic that will help you get ahead in life. That's a huge thing.

—Mike Bellotti

ACKNOWLEDGMENTS

Fɪʀsᴛ ᴀɴᴅ ꜰᴏʀᴇᴍᴏsᴛ, ᴛʜɪs ʙᴏᴏᴋ ᴡᴏᴜʟᴅ not have been possible without the generous contributions of all the players involved. Each gave of his time to provide me, and in turn the legions of Oregon fans, with treasured insights into his experience as a Duck.

Thanks as well to Mike Bellotti for writing the foreword to this volume.

A number of the players involved in this project helped me track down former teammates. In particular, Ken Woody and Norm Chapman helped me make tremendous progress.

I'd have been unable to complete this project without the help of Ross Concillo, who transcribed nearly every interview conducted for the book.

This project was completed on top of my full-time job covering the Ducks for the *Register-Guard* newspaper in Eugene. Many people were extraordinarily understanding of that, notably the sports editor at the paper, Ron Bellamy.

And, of course, Lynne was there for me every step of the way.

Finally, this being my first ever chance at publishing an acknowledgment: thanks for everything, Mom.

INTRODUCTION

THERE IS EVERYTHING THAT TOOK PLACE FOR OREGON football before October 22, 1994, and then everything that came after Kenny Wheaton's interception against Washington.

Without Wheaton's game-changing 97-yard interception return for a touchdown that gave the upstart Ducks a 31–20 victory over the mighty Huskies, there would have been no 1995 Rose Bowl. Without the credibility of that season, Rich Brooks might never have been offered an NFL job, and the Mike Bellotti era, including the 2002 Fiesta Bowl and the national championship flirtation in 2007, might never have come to pass.

These days, Oregon is synonymous with lavish facilities, flashy uniforms, wide-open offense, and a near permanent foothold in the national top 25. Since Wheaton's interception in 1994, those traits have defined what it means to be a Duck. You can read the accounts of Joey Harrington, Rashad Bauman, and other modern-era Ducks in this volume for a taste of what competing at college football's highest levels is all about.

As Bellotti notes in the foreword, playing football at Oregon has always been about putting in the hard work necessary to overachieve in relation to other programs nationally. In the years since Wheaton's interception, the Ducks haven't just sat back and enjoyed the luxury of their facilities and their uniforms. With few exceptions, Oregon football has continued to overachieve, consistently ranking among the nation's best despite a local recruiting base that is almost nonexistent.

Prior to Wheaton's interception, expectations were different, but the results were no less compelling. Oregon has a proud tradition of football that goes well beyond the last two decades. The Golden Age was the Len Casanova era, from 1951 through 1966, and the likes of Jim Shanley, Mel Renfro, and Dave Wilcox have painted vivid pictures within this book of what it was like to play for the man known as "Cas."

Casanova was followed directly by the five-year tenure of Jerry Frei, whose players still remain bitter that such a profoundly good man could have been dismissed. Ahmad Rashad, who played for the Ducks as Bobby Moore, and Dan Fouts are among the players who have shared the experience of playing for Frei in this volume.

The 1970s were a difficult decade for Oregon football, but running back Don Reynolds conveys the spirit the program still possessed. As an undersized back once doubted by his own coaches, Reynolds is the perfect man to illustrate the obstacles that the Ducks faced, and occasionally cleared.

When Rich Brooks took over the program in 1977, there was still a sense that Oregon was treading water, as players like Vince Goldsmith related for this project. The Ducks always seemed poised to become a consistent winning program, but could never quite string it all together. Among the players in this generation of Oregon football were Steve Greatwood, Don Pellum, and Michael Gray, all of whom went on to serve as assistant coaches with the Ducks. There can be no greater statement about the family atmosphere fostered in Eugene, even under the tough-as-nails Brooks, that so many who gave of themselves for Oregon on the field decided to come back and continue on the sideline.

Followers of the program point to the emergence of Bill Musgrave in the late 1980s as the true turning point for Oregon football, from plucky, regional underdog to consistent national heavyweight. Musgrave relates his version of that era in these pages. From there, Danny O'Neil picks up the narrative, as the Ducks experience a hiccup in 1991 before their crescendo into the 1994 campaign.

Even that most historic of seasons was not without hurdles for the program to overcome. Oregon began the 1994 season 1–2, and was only 4–3 entering October 22, 1994, when Washington visited Autzen Stadium. But then came O'Neil's dramatic fourth-quarter touchdown drive.

And then, just when the Huskies were poised to answer, the neighborhood bully in position to crush the Ducks' dreams once again—well, you know how it goes.

Kenny Wheaton's gonna score! Kenny Wheaton's gonna score!

Those, of course, were the immortal words of Oregon radio announcer Jerry Allen. For another version, read Wheaton's personal account of "The Pick," and the rest of his experience as a Duck, right here.

At this writing, Oregon has announced the first change in the football program's leadership since Bellotti replaced Brooks, with offensive coordinator Chip Kelly taking over as head coach, and Bellotti moving to athletics director. The next chapter of Oregon football will thus be written in the coming years by players with their own voices.

But the spirit of hard work and overachievement that has defined Oregon in decades past will continue to define what it means to be a Duck. I'm sure you'll enjoy the stories you'll find here.

WHAT IT MEANS
TO BE A DUCK

The
FIFTIES

JACK PATERA
LINEMAN
1951–1954

I WAS THE FIRST ONE IN MY FAMILY TO GO TO COLLEGE. I didn't even start thinking about it until after my final high school football season, at Washington High in Portland. I really wasn't recruited by anybody but Oregon; some of the smaller colleges had a few people come through, but that was about it. When the Ducks offered me a scholarship, I thought it was great, partly because I had a girlfriend who was going to Oregon. It was completely unexpected.

On my first trip to Eugene, there was a member of the alumni who took George Shaw, Ron Pheister, and myself down to Eugene. Jim Aiken was still the coach at the time, and the three of us high school players met him in the basement of McArthur Court, where the football team normally dressed. We were shown around, and Jim Aiken, in his froggy voice, shook my hand and said they could give me a job for 70 bucks a month, and then 35 bucks for books and tuition. I just thought it was great. Then, he put his arm around George and Ron, and I followed behind. And they carried on a conversation for about 10 minutes, and then the alumnus came down and took the three of us to lunch. It was funny because I sat there with these two guys that had been talking with the head coach, and here I was just delighted that he had even said a few words to me. And that was how I became a Duck.

I graduated high school in '51, so this was early in 1951. I had gone to Oregon State for senior weekend, and I never got to talk to any coaches because nobody was interested. So that was basically how I went to Oregon. I had no plans to go to college until my senior year, and people started to tell me I might get a scholarship because that was about the only way that I was going to go to school. Everything fell into place, and I became a Duck.

I was thinking about it the other day, that I must have really been brainwashed because I've been in the state of Washington since 1976 and I still hate the University of Washington. There must be something that they do to you. I don't think I even knew what the University of Washington was when I went to Oregon.

Len Casanova came on in the spring of 1951. I don't remember exactly when Jim Aiken was fired, but Cas was there in the spring and he came and talked to our high school team, so he was there before I graduated. I remember Cas' speech and, of course, I thought he was talking directly to me even though our whole football team was there.

I suppose that I was a little full of myself when I got to Eugene. I had been selected to play in a high school all-star game, and I was competing against these guys that I didn't really know, but you'd read articles about how they were the biggest, toughest guys you'd ever see. I played pretty well in the game, and had a great deal of fun, and at that time it was the greatest experience I'd ever had. So I felt I was a pretty good player, and I went from the Shrine Game a couple weeks later to Eugene.

We were there for about three weeks as a football team before the student body got there. It was all a new experience to me. I was walking around with my head in the clouds, wondering what was going on. It was exciting for me. I wasn't familiar with anybody who had gone to college. My family just wasn't involved with that kind of deal. I liked football, and I enjoyed playing. I got knocked around a few times in practice, flat on my back, and I remember thinking, *Holy mackerel, that hasn't happened before*, but I just got up and figured I had to learn how to do it. I wasn't over-awed or anything like that. It was a learning process, and that went on for four years. I guess the only trouble I had was when Cas told me they weren't going to pay for the books. I reminded him that they had promised me, and he said, "All right, this one time, I guess."

Cas was someone whom everybody on the team felt the same way about. He was delightful. He was a person who seemed to like you the best, even though you knew he made everybody feel that way. He was very personable. As the years went on, I ended up feeling like I was a very, very good friend of Len Casanova.

3

I think we all kind of just thought he was bluffing when he got mad at us. We respected Cas, but when it was all over, we always thought he never meant it. I don't think I was the only one. We all loved Cas, and when he got mad at us, for the most part, we didn't think that he was really that serious. There was always some forgiveness in the background.

I remember one day at practice I got hurt, a guy threw a blocking dummy on my knee, so I was kind of limping around practice and something happened, and Cas said, "If you don't want to practice, start running until I tell you to stop." So I was running around Hayward Field, and I ran around it all practice. After practice Cas sent everybody in, and Jack Roche came over to me and said, "Cas says you can stop," and I said, "I'm not stopping until Cas tells me to stop." And Roche said, "Come on, just come on in." But I wouldn't stop until Cas came out, and after about half an hour Cas came out and he said, "All right, come on in," and he was really grumpy and didn't say anything. And I thought, well, I stood up to him, and now maybe we're friends. I guess I was a little tough to get along with, hard-headed—I was called a lot of different things. But I would have run all night and all day if Cas hadn't told me to stop. It was little things like that, whether they made us closer, or that's how we connected, I can't explain it. It was part of the program that made me like Cas and the coaching staff. I liked the rest of the coaching staff, too.

The team that we had wasn't very good at first. I think we had 19 freshmen letter in 1951. That was the year they made freshmen eligible. A lot of them were from Pennsylvania, guys whom Aiken had recruited. By the time we were seniors, there were only three of us left—Hal Reeve, George Shaw, and myself. So we had a lot of people go through that program, but we continued to improve. We were a better team each year.

About the only play that I really remember well was when we played USC as juniors, in 1953. They had a guy named Lindon Crow, who was a wingback in the single wing they ran, and I saw the play develop and I took Crow down. It was probably only for about a one-yard loss, but in my head it was more like 10 or 12 yards. I just remember that play well, like it happened yesterday.

I just really loved to play the game. Against Cal our senior year, I think I was playing both ways, and Cas sent someone in for me. So I went over to Cas and said, "Cas, what is he doing in there?" He said, "Well, we gotta get some guys some playing time." And I said, "This is the first time we have a chance to really beat Cal," so I put myself in the next play, and he didn't say

Before going on to a distinguished career as an NFL head coach, Jack Patera was an all-conference lineman for the Ducks.

anything. Later in the game, Paul Larson was fielding a punt for them and didn't call for a fair catch. I was running down there and getting closer and closer, and when he didn't call a fair catch, I smacked him. That was one of my better hits in four years at Oregon.

A few weeks after that we got beat real bad by UCLA in Los Angeles. I remember what Cas said: "Every once in a while, you're going to have a game like this. Just go out and forget about it." And, you know, I think that was the best suggestion we could ever get. You don't really recall what coaches say after you win a game, but how you react to losses is important, and that's when guys like Cas did some of their best coaching.

It never entered my mind at first that I might take that path myself. I was going to graduate in education. Somebody asked me if I was going to be a coach, and I told him, "No way." On Saturday after a game you go by the athletic department, the coaches are meeting. On Sunday, the coaches are meeting. They work seven days a week, 20 hours a day. Who would want a job like that? The fellow said, "That's good thinking. Coaching is the hardest way to make an easy living there is." I thought about that, and knew I didn't want to be a coach.

So I went off to Baltimore and played a couple years, and then Cas called me. He said, "All right, you've had your fun. It's time to get into your life's work. I want you to come home and be on the coaching staff." And I told him I wasn't really interested, and he said, "Come on, you can't play forever." At that point I was thinking to myself maybe I could. I was thinking I could play until I was 50. I had no idea that I would ever become a coach. It was the furthest thing from my mind. I saw John McKay the year he took over at USC. I had become very good friends with a USC alumnus who had the coaches over for a cocktail party. John saw me and told me that when I got through playing he wanted me to come and coach for him. I told him the same thing: that I wasn't going to be a coach. So I knew firmly in my mind that I would never coach. There was just no way.

Finally Don Heinrich, whom I played with in Dallas, he called me in the spring of '63. He said, "I know you told me that you weren't going to coach, but our camp needs a line coach." I finally broke down and told him I'd do it. I wasn't more than three months into that job before I just knew I was going to be a coach forever.

Jack Patera was an All–Pacific Coast Conference lineman in 1964 and was invited to play in the East-West Shrine Game, the Hula Bowl, and the College All-Star Game. He was a fourth-round pick in the 1955 NFL Draft and played seven professional seasons with Baltimore, Chicago Cardinals, and Dallas. As a defensive line assistant, he coached Minnesota's "Purple People Eaters" in the 1970s, and Patera was the inaugural head coach of the Seattle Seahawks. After coaching Seattle from 1976 to 1982, Patera remained in Washington state, where he currently resides.

PHIL McHUGH

TIGHT END

1954–1956

I STARTED MY SENIOR YEAR IN HIGH SCHOOL with a class in which the teacher had us write a paper on what our aspirations were. I wrote that I was hoping to go to the University of Portland because it was a Catholic university, and it was at home, and I figured I'd have to work to get some money to go to school. That year we won the state championship in football, and so I got an invitation to go to the University of Oregon, and all of a sudden my plans changed.

It was such a total change of environment. It isn't like I had been planning on going away to school all through adolescence. Today the kids are exposed to so much more. They're so much more aware of what's out there. Most of us those days were not nearly as tuned in to what college life was going to be like. It was a whole different world. It was my first time being away from home, for one thing. It was not anywhere close to the recruiting and the exposure to the press and the publicity that the kids today go through. The simple act of choosing a school to attend wasn't that big of a deal. I just think it was a much simpler time. The complexities of today's world were not there.

Once I determined I wasn't going to the University of Portland, it mainly came down to Oregon or Oregon State. I had taken a visit to Seattle, but that just seemed too far from home.

Ultimately, after meeting with Len Casanova and getting a chance to visit with him, that's what convinced me that I should end up at Oregon. Even at that early time in our relationship, I was just very impressed with what a gentleman and a good man Cas was. My relationship with Cas went on a little longer than the four years I played for him in school. I joined his coaching staff and was with him for about 13 years after graduation. So my memories of Cas are kind of mixed up, both as a player and as a coach with him. But it wasn't as if he treated me any differently. It was a totally different role for me, so in that respect it was certainly different. It was different being a coach than being a player. But not in the way Cas treated me or the way we interacted.

We had four freshman games my first year. I broke in with the varsity as a sophomore, in 1954. We had two senior ends, but I would substitute for both of them, and ended up playing probably as much time or more than they did. George Shaw was the quarterback then. I caught something like 22 passes that year, which was a pretty good performance for those days, and which was also more than I caught the next two years, after George had graduated. There were some pretty good quarterbacks around in those days, and George was probably the best in the entire country. He was a great athlete, although not a particularly big guy. I would guess he was 5′11″, never more than 170 or 175 pounds, but very fast, and an outstanding baseball player as well.

8

As an end, I don't think I ever got more than three feet away from my tackle. We never used a split end during the years that I played. If you were an end, you were a tight end. They actually started using the split end the year I graduated, which is probably just as well because I didn't have the speed that you look for in a split end. The split end is a little more of a combination of a back and an end, and I'm afraid I didn't have those kinds of skills.

I ended up playing with a pretty talented group of guys. Dicky James, Jim Shanley, Jack Crabtree, they came around my last couple of years. Ron Stover was a great player, and Lon Stiner was a tackle who was a year older than me. Those were all pretty outstanding athletes.

You played both offense and defense in those days, which is hard to imagine now, with what you see in college football. The pace in which the game is played now, it would have taken us a couple of games to get that much offense. The game today is just dramatically different. The thing I think is still the same is you still get nervous and very excited on game day, get very pumped up. The emotions about all the players are still the same. Listening to the Oregon kids talk about the win over Oregon State in 2008, that's no different than what we felt. Our class never lost to the Beavers. We had a tie my senior year when they went to the Rose Bowl, but we never lost, and that's something that not a lot of classes can say.

I was very proud that I was able to balance everything, not only going to school and getting my degree, but at the same time being able to participate in both football and basketball. I don't know that you could do it today. For one thing, with all the pressures on the kids and the coaches, I don't know that they could afford missing time in one sport to play another.

My senior year I was chosen to play in the East-West Shrine Game, which in those days was the biggest all-star game. Steve Belko had just taken over the basketball coaching job, and I figured I was not going to be able to go to the Shrine Game because of basketball practice. But when Steve found out I had been selected, he came and told me, "No way in hell are you missing that. This is a once-in-a-lifetime opportunity. You've gotta go play." I think the attitude was, if you did everything you could and played as hard as you could, you deserved the reward. That was certainly one of the highlights, to get to do that. My favorite little story about the Shrine Game was that the two quarterbacks were John Brodie and Paul Hornung, who played both ways. At one point in the second half, I caught a pass inside the 10-yard line, and I thought sure as hell I was gonna score a touchdown, but Horning tackled me just short of the goal line. I figure that made for some quality name-dropping, even though I didn't get the score.

Coming back to Oregon and getting a chance to coach, that was very special. The coaches that were there, Jack Roche, John McKay, Jerry Frei, and Bill Hammer, all those guys were still around. The first year, I had the freshman coaching job, so I was involved, but not to the same degree as the rest of the staff. I sat in on the meetings, but it wasn't until the following year I got a little bit more involved as a member of the varsity staff. A year before, those guys all were my coaches, guys I looked up to. To listen to Roche coach his defensive plans and Johnny and his offensive plans, as a player it was very exciting. And then to be suddenly sitting in the meetings and hearing how all these things came about, it was wonderful.

Phil McHugh was a team captain in two of his three varsity seasons, and a two-time All–Pacific Coast Conference selection. He also won two letters in basketball and was that team's captain as a senior. McHugh finished his Oregon football career with 37 receptions for 468 yards and a touchdown, and he served as an assistant coach with the Ducks from 1958 to 1968.

JACK CRABTREE

QUARTERBACK

1955–1957

FINDING AN OFFENSE THAT WAS THE RIGHT FIT for me in college was really important. I was a T-formation quarterback, and so I didn't belong in other kinds of offenses. UCLA wasn't a T formation, and USC ran a little of everything, and I just wasn't comfortable with that. Oregon ran the T formation with George Shaw a few years before I got there, and Len Casanova coached that system. In the end, it was going to be either Oregon or Washington, which ran a similar offense.

Once I left San Bernardino Junior College, I still wasn't sure which place I would end up. I had scholarship offers from both, so I got into my car, started driving north, and told my folks I'd call them when I stopped. I stopped near Eugene in Glenwood and got a hotel room. I went over and saw Cas and John McKay and told them I liked it so much I was going to stay. This was where I wanted to be.

Cas, of course, is the second father-figure type. McKay was really a charismatic type of person. By the time I was a senior, I was pretty in tune with what McKay wanted to do on offense. He was in my brain, and I was in his. In those days, nobody gave signals from the sideline or came in to give the play. If you went out, you could only go out once a quarter. If you went in, you had to stay back in. That's why you played defense also. So I called all the plays at the line of scrimmage, unless there was a timeout or an incomplete pass, in which case we would huddle. Otherwise, all the plays

11

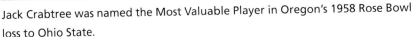

Jack Crabtree was named the Most Valuable Player in Oregon's 1958 Rose Bowl loss to Ohio State.

were called on the line of scrimmage. McKay had to trust me to do what he wanted, and I think he just grilled that into me. He was in my brain. We had a great connection.

I was one of two quarterbacks in 1955 and 1956, the other being Tom Crabtree. He and I pretty much split the plays, switching off within the games. My sophomore year, we were playing Arizona, who was not in our conference at the time, and I had a very good game, good enough that I was the player of the game. Except they thought I was Tom Crabtree. He got the credit for it. We were considered a passing team for those days—liked to throw the ball—although I bet I never threw more than 15 times a game. Nothing like you see these days.

I would love to play today and get to focus on offense. I had a great back behind me, in Jim Shanley, and John McKay was in love with him. He was the halfback, period. And when we would be practicing offense, as soon as Jim got hit by somebody, McKay would say, "Okay, we're going to defense." He didn't want him getting hit too much. I played defense because I had to, and I don't think I was a bad defensive player, but that's just the way it was.

The great part about our team is that every single player on our team graduated. We were pretty sharp and responsible. I think every single one of them, as I recall, has gone on successfully to whatever career he went into.

That's the group that was seniors in 1957, when we went to the Rose Bowl. I don't think the tone was much different than any other year, as we went through the season. We knew we would have a good team, and a team on which everybody knew everybody else and was comfortable playing together. There wasn't anybody coming on board who was going to beat out anybody else. Other than that, I don't think there was any particular thing. What happens, happens. Some good players come in and make a difference. We were experienced. We knew what to do.

We lost the last game of the regular season to Oregon State. I threw a pass to Shanley for our first touchdown, and it looked like he was going to score again late in the game. He scored on a running play but fumbled after crossing the goal line. Today that would be a touchdown, should have been the game winner, 14–10. Instead they ruled it a fumble. But we still went to the Rose Bowl, so it wasn't too disappointing.

When we got down to the Rose Bowl, I remember the press being on us terribly. They said we didn't belong there, and we were probably the worst team that had ever gone to the Rose Bowl. You don't know how good a team is until you play them, that's what I thought. The parity around college football is unbelievable, so it's just hard to call. Ohio State was the old three-yards-and-a-cloud-of-dust type of team. As long as they keep the ball out of our hands, they don't lose. Nowadays, usually whoever has the ball last wins. It would be a lot of fun to play today, not that they would recruit me today. But I'd like to think so!

As we went along, they scored right off the bat, and then we came back and just held on to the ball and scored. They ended up winning 10–7, but we gained more yardage, and I was named the game's MVP even though we lost. It was an honor that I appreciated and certainly didn't expect and never even thought of until it happened. They handed it to me when I was already in the locker room, but it had never crossed my mind. I completed 11 passes, and I suppose that was a lot in those days.

Going to Oregon, I ended up at the right place. I would guess 99 percent of the football players come to play football. They get an education, and they want that, but primarily they come to play football. But it turns out that you get an education, too, and that's great. I put that to use and had a great career. It wasn't in football, but it was a great career.

Jack Crabtree was just the third member of the losing team ever named Rose Bowl MVP when he earned that honor in the 1958 game. Crabtree completed 55-of-99 passes for 624 yards and four touchdowns as a senior, earning honorable mention all-conference honors. He was chosen in the 12th round of the 1958 NFL Draft and played one professional season after spending two years in the army. Crabtree worked in the athletic apparel industry following his retirement from football and currently resides in Eugene.

NORM CHAPMAN

LINEMAN

1955–1957

MY TIES TO OREGON FOOTBALL GO BACK A LONG WAY. I went to Medford High, and some friends of mine had gone to Oregon. I was recruited by a couple of other schools, but I chose Oregon because I liked Len Casanova and the people here. So that's how I ended up here.

Casanova was always approachable, but not a guy who throws his arm around you. Not a real outgoing guy, but a guy you knew was honest and told you what was true. He was very tough on us on the football field, but you probably wouldn't have realized that if you knew him off the football field, because he was a very well-mannered gentleman, highly thought of amongst the coaching ranks.

The players, I don't think we can say we loved Cas until we got away from the situation and looked back and said, "Man, he sure did a lot for me. Aren't I lucky to have passed through the university at his time?" I think every one of the players would say that, in all. It was a great experience, and we're lucky that Cas and his assistants made it a great experience. I know there are players from other schools whom we have talked to who said it wasn't any fun, the coach was an angry guy. I'm not saying it was all fun and games for us, but after we were gone, we appreciated it more.

Back in those days, when I started at Oregon in 1954, freshmen didn't play on the varsity. You played freshman football. You went down and scrimmaged, and the varsity beat up on you, but you only played three games against other schools, and that was it.

There were about 45 guys on the varsity team at that time. It wasn't easy for a lot of us, being away from home the first time. I'm sure for players today, there are a lot of distractions for guys coming onto campus, there's a little better grip owing to that experience. They have so many counselors that are hired by the university. Our coaches did all the counseling at that time, and it wasn't a very big coaching staff. Not like now, where they have all kinds of people.

Things seemed a lot farther away then, just by the nature of the transportation system in those years. A lot of us were from Oregon, but for guys who were from California, it wasn't a matter of just getting on a plane and being home in an hour. I'm from Medford, and it took four hours to drive to Medford then, and you probably couldn't get a ride if you wanted to find one, anyway. It was a big adjustment, but Cas and his assistants did a great job helping us adjust to college life. We got through it together, living in the dorms, eating all our meals together.

That first year we played two games with the Oregon State rooks, and we beat them once and they beat us once. Then we went and played Grays Harbor Junior College up there in Aberdeen, Washington, and we beat them real bad. That was it for the three games. We also went down and scrimmaged the varsity, and you can figure out how that went. We didn't have much luck against guys like Jack Patera, who was a great football player, and many others.

My sophomore season, in 1955, I started part of the time. Art Weber was a senior, and he was the starter, but I got some chances. Fall of '56, as a junior, I became a starter. We had a good team. We ended up being average with our record, but we had a good team. We went and played Colorado and beat them 35–0, and went on to win about half our games, but Colorado went on to win the Orange Bowl, so they were a great team. Why they started so slowly, I don't know. Colorado had a bunch of guys who went on to play pro ball.

The tie against Oregon State was in the first year that Parker Stadium was opened up. They went to the Rose Bowl that year. And then we went the next year. When you're playing, you don't remember much about the game, I guess, but to me it was a much bigger rivalry than it is today, and I'm not degrading the rivalry or anything. I think a big reason was there were a lot

A blocker for some of the best backs in Oregon football history, Norm Chapman later became a respected assistant coach for the Ducks.

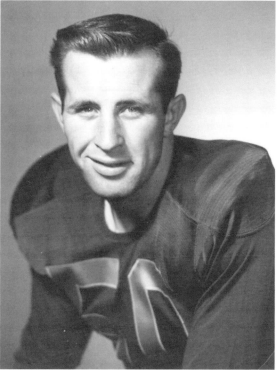

more guys on the team from the state of Oregon—on both teams. I considered Oregon State when I was coming out of high school, but, again, it was a matter of Cas. There was a new coach at that time at Oregon State. And then I had a couple close friends who were a year older than me who were here. Bill Bowerman, the legendary track and field coach at Oregon, had a big effect on that, too. He was from Medford, and he came in as a track coach. He was such a big name in Medford that it made a difference.

My senior year, I think we really felt we had a good team, but I don't think anybody projected a Rose Bowl in the future of that season. The year before we weren't even close, but we had some really good leadership. Two of our running backs, Jack Morris and Jim Shanley, were not only great runners but complete football players. They blocked, they played defense. Those guys transcend the years, I think. They could have played today. Jack Morris, for example, was a 9.5-second 100-yard dash guy and a great hurdler. Dick James, who finished up in 1955, played in the pros for 10 years, and Jim Shanley was maybe the best runner of them all. They weren't real big guys, but they were extremely good football players. I think the strength of the team was in those runners. We always remind them that they had to have people block for them, but they were outstanding players. Willie West was a sophomore that year, and he was another really great football player.

Of course, things didn't end up for me as I might have hoped. A little past the midway point of the 1957 season, I broke my leg and dislocated my ankle in the Washington State game. It happened on a punt play. I snapped the ball on extra points and punts, and if you were uncovered, you were expected to go down the field and try to make a tackle. The guy caught the ball and made a move, and I lunged one way, and my left ankle just popped out and broke that outer bone. The cleats on my shoe were facing me. It was that kind of a dislocation. I remember it vividly, and it was a pretty serious injury.

But even knowing that's how things were going to end up, I would still have done it all over again. I really treasured being with that group of people in my growing years. I tried my best to be around the team as much as I could after the injury. I always went to practice on my crutches. Fortunately, I got to go on trips with the team. I would just try to encourage them. A couple of the coaches would have me do some statistics for tackles or something like that. There weren't 14 sportswriters upstairs doing it like there are these days. I would have done anything to be a part of the team. Fortunately, I think they accepted me. The coaches were very aware of that and wanted to make sure I was a part of it.

So I wasn't able to play in the Rose Bowl game, but the trip was still special. Just before we went down there, I had a hip-high cast, and I got it taken off, so I was able to get around a little bit. The dinners and the parties they would take us to were great. Back then there was one bowl game, you didn't go to any others. As a player, I wished like hell I could have played. Every player who has encountered that type of thing would say the same thing. It would have been great to finish my senior season. Fortunately, I went into coaching afterward, so I was able to stay close to it.

Playing and coaching football at Oregon was the most wonderful experience of my life, obviously. It means more to me, other than my family, than everything else. I have teammates that I still get together with to this day. We have a little golf tournament every spring over in Black Butte, in Central Oregon, for 20 years. We get guys showing up there who played all the way back into the '50s, like myself. These days it's getting to be a younger group, and starting to include some guys from the '70s now.

It's great camaraderie. When we're reminiscing, people pretty much all say the same thing of their wonderful experience at Oregon, and much of it was due to the coaches. And not only Len Casanova. There were some other wonderful guys on the staff, guys like Jerry Frei, Jack Roche, Bill Hammer, and Johnny McKay. It was an honor to follow them and coach for the Ducks.

Norm Chapman was a cocaptain of the 1957 team that reached the Rose Bowl, along with Jack Morris and Jim Shanley. After his playing days were over, he served as an assistant coach for the Ducks from 1967 to 1971. He retired in 2002 and still lives in Eugene.

JIM SHANLEY

RUNNING BACK

1955–1957

M Y FOLKS MOVED TO OREGON WHEN I WAS in fifth grade, and it was a time when I was just getting interested in athletics. In those days, we didn't have television, so we'd turn the radio on. When I was in the fifth grade, I just got captivated by the sports announcer who would talk about the Oregon Ducks. "Here comes the green and gold," he would say. "Here come the Webfoots." So, even as a youngster, I was already a Duck.

As I got older, then the university started showing some interest in me. I just knew that's where I wanted to go. When I was a junior at North Bend High School, they started having us up to Eugene. Every once in a while our team would be in that area playing a high school game and they would get tickets for us. I guess I just grew up being a Duck. My high school coach was a Washington State graduate, and he was trying to push me to go to Stanford or Washington, but those places just seemed like they were too far away to even think about going. When the coaches started talking to me, John McKay and Len Casanova, I was just extremely impressed and excited about being a Duck.

John McKay was a guy I just thought the world of. When you would cover stuff in chalk talks and on the field, it just seemed like he made everything so simple—I couldn't understand how people didn't understand what to do. Consequently, John McKay liked me a lot. I know that. Coach McKay was one of those guys who might not pay a ton of attention to you, but you couldn't take that personally. And then when he did pull you aside and deal with you one on one, it just meant the world to you. John McKay was a big guy in my career because he coached me directly.

Yet I knew Cas was the guy. He was the guy who set the tone for things and chewed on you when he had to. Every year, starting with my sophomore year when I became a starter, Cas, in reviewing the film, would always chew on you a bit. "Come on, Shanley," he'd say. "A good back would run through those arm tackles."

And what was really meaningful was the way Cas made such an effort to keep in touch with you even after you had graduated. I couldn't believe how close in touch he stayed with me over all those years. Wherever I went, whatever I was doing—coaching, selling insurance—Cas would always call me and keep up with me, or occasionally ask me a question about insurance.

Even after coaching, he stayed in touch and encouraged me to be close to the Ducks and make contributions and so forth. I've done it periodically over the years, though probably never to the extent he would have liked. I remember one time, his wife had friends in Spokane, so they would come up to Spokane and visit, and whenever they were there, I would have lunch with Cas. One day after they'd been there, these friends had driven him up to the house where I lived, but we missed each other. Later on, Cas sent me a letter that said, "Drove by your house. Based on the house you have, you should be contributing at much higher levels to the University of Oregon than what you are!"

Then they would have all these events in Eugene honoring Cas, and I think every time they did, they felt like it was going to be the last one, and then Cas would live for another 15 or 20 years. He just kept going. He was an amazing man. I always tried to be there for him. It was just part of what you did as a Duck.

We were a pretty good team, because we played in the first Rose Bowl since 1920, so that was a big deal. The Rose Bowl of course stands out in my memory because of the bigness of it, and how we were such underdogs and came very close to winning it. Close only counts in horseshoes, they say, and when you run into Ohio State people, they tell you that. That memory will live on forever, because every year there's a Rose Bowl and you get to recollect being there as a young guy.

There were other games. My sophomore year, maybe the most exciting game was the one against USC. I scored our first touchdown on a 70-yard run against USC. That was an exciting thing for me, to be playing in the

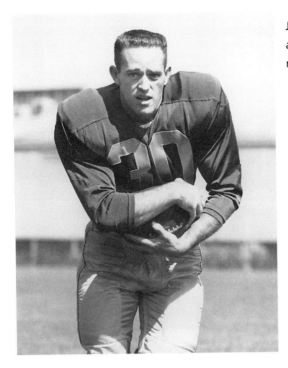

Jim Shanley finished his career as Oregon's all-time leading rusher with 1,887 yards.

Coliseum and to take off on a 70-yard run for a touchdown. There were some other long runs from those days that got called back, which we joke about now whenever we get together for reunions. Spike Hillstrom seemed like he was always the guy that got called for the clip. We liked to give Spike a hard time about that.

The guy I was closest with was probably Norm Chapman. Norm and I were roommates, and then we played together for the full four years. Both of us started as sophomores. And then over the years we talked probably every week on the phone at least once. He'll come up and stay with me and go to the Oregon–Washington State game, or I'll come down to Eugene and stay with him and go to a game. We have a place down in Depot Bay where we'll go and play golf. We get together a lot.

I felt so sorry for Norm when he got hurt our senior year. It was in the Washington State game that he dislocated and broke his ankle. Norm would snap that ball as a center on punts and was always the first guy down the field. I was lined up as a halfback and, if nobody was coming, I would take off and be right behind him. He had just taken a block so I was in pretty good position to see him actually get hurt, and it was the worst looking thing I'd ever seen, so I felt really bad for him. You knew, right then, that the season was over for him. But we always made sure to keep including him in all the events. He was one of the cocaptains that year, was out there for the coin toss in the Rose Bowl. It was sad seeing that happen, but I didn't look at it like he was no longer part of it.

There wasn't really any secret to my success. First of all, you had to have the physical ability to play the game, and that doesn't equate to the physical abilities of athletes today. At the time we played, we didn't have a guy on the team that was heavier than 220 pounds. I think the thing that I always felt about myself was I was coachable. Whatever they told me to do, I was really going to try and do it that way. I didn't have the blazing speed I wished I did, but I was quick, and I could get through the 40 faster than most anybody else. So I could get out in front of guys, and generally in a 70- or 80-yard race going for a touchdown, somebody was going to catch me, but not always. I didn't run a straight line all the time. Sometimes I'd run 100 yards to gain 80. I'd be zigzagging all over the place.

I guess I'm most proud of the fact that I played there for three years, and made such close friendships that were maintained over the years. John Robinson was a very close friend, and Dicky James, I just admired the heck out of him. That was a great class of seniors that were there with Dick James, like Lon Stiner and Harry Johnson. Jack Crabtree, he came on his senior year. He didn't start and play too much until his senior year, but he had a great senior year. I've been close with all those guys. We used to have a golf tournament every year at Black Butte. It got so big that some of the older guys among us broke off into a couple foursomes at a different time and place and did the same thing. That was always great fun.

23

Jim Shanley was a three-time All–Pacific Coast Conference selection who started on both sides of the ball all three seasons. He ranked 10th in the country in rushing as a sophomore with 711 yards, and finished his career as Oregon's all-time leading rusher with 1,887 yards. Shanley played one season with the Green Bay Packers and later became an assistant coach at Washington State. He retired from coaching in 1970 and became a life insurance executive in Walla Walla, Washington.

DARREL ASCHBACHER

LINEMAN

1957–1958

I GREW UP IN PRINEVILLE. MY BROTHER, Ron, was an All-American tackle at Oregon State. And so I was headed for Oregon State, too. Had I gone to college right out of high school, that's where I would have ended up. My dad had owned his ranch since 1920, so I grew up around agriculture. It seemed pretty logical that I would follow my brother and play for the Beavers.

But my plans changed when we started a family. I was real young when our son came, and 14 months later my daughter was born. So right after that I stayed on my dad's ranch and worked to support the family. When I finally was ready to go back to school, I went to Boise Junior College, which happened to be the No. 1 junior college team in the country at that time. When it came time to transfer, it was between Oregon and Oregon State again. By that time I had gotten to know Len Casanova, and I was really, really impressed with him. He was such a great father figure and a super coach.

The first time I met Cas was in about 1954, when I was still just out of high school. Then I went to Boise, and the coach there, Lyle Smith, was a real close friend of Cas'. They were in the navy together as officers in the Second World War. Joe Schaffeld and myself kind of came to Oregon together. We played against each other in high school in the state playoffs, and then together at Boise. That's really why I went to Oregon, because I really liked Cas.

Our first year, 1957, was the Rose Bowl season. I didn't know at the time that the year before they had burned Cas in effigy, people were so frustrated with him. They sure turned it around. Joe and myself were pretty much relegated to holding bags at the early part of the season. They didn't let us play much. At Boise, I was an end and Joe was a tackle, but at Oregon they tried to make a tackle out of me and put Joe at guard. We always played together on the same side, even at Boise, but not at those spots. We got kind of tired of that and started to think about leaving. I was going to go up to Willamette, and Joe was going to follow me.

Well, somebody told us we couldn't do that because we had accepted scholarships. Luckily the next day we got a chance to make an impression. They called the second string the Ugly Ducklings in those days. They gave us a chance to scrimmage the varsity, and we just about tore them apart. Everybody on that Ugly Duckling team was a real good defensive player. If we could have had platoons, we all would have started on defense. They didn't substitute as much in those days, but every chance he got, Cas would put us in on defense. That included the Rose Bowl, when we played Ohio State.

I think the most poignant memory I have from that '57 season is when Norm Chapman got his leg broken up at Washington State. That bothered me a lot and also motivated me. He was one of the guys I tried to emulate, he and Ron Stover. That was a great team. Along with Norm and Ron, we had Jack Crabtree, who was named the Most Valuable Player of the Rose Bowl. It was a super honor to be able to participate at Oregon and be on that Rose Bowl team. Ohio State just barely beat us.

Coming from a small town like Prineville, even though we played the whole season in big stadiums, there was nothing like the Rose Bowl. I remember Harry Mondale, when we were walking out, one of the Oregon band members said, "Go get 'em, Ducks!" And Mondale said, "Well, you get their band, and we'll get their team." And we did. I do know the whole week when we were down there, we were completely discarded. The press was against us, and after the game Cas wouldn't let them into the dressing room. They just didn't give Oregon anything, not any chance. They didn't realize how well-coached and good that team really was. Ohio State was lucky to even walk out with a win. It was just a great experience, especially coming from a small school, to be able to walk into the Rose Bowl our first year at Oregon. That was a great experience.

The next year we were the No. 1 defensive team in the nation. We had a total of 50 points scored against us. Cal scored 23 of those, so we should have had another Rose Bowl season, but we just couldn't score. We had a new quarterback, Dave Grosz, and we'd get down to the 10- or 5-yard line pretty easily, but we just couldn't put it in the end zone. We had better statistics than almost everyone we played. We played Oklahoma, and lost 6–0. I remember walking off the field and Bud Wilkinson putting his arm around me and saying, "You guys played a heck of a football game." I'll always remember that. We finished the season against Miami and lost 2–0. That was another great game, and we had two touchdowns called back. Our defense was just really playing well.

We never felt like underdogs. Everything was different then. It was just a different football game. I'm having an awful hard time adjusting to all the crap that goes on on the field now. The players are always trying to get the people to yell and scream, drawing attention to themselves, all of that. That's what they have cheerleaders for. I'm not alone because I know a lot of the old guys feel that way. That was just our era, our time, things were just different. We played for the University of Oregon and Cas and our families. Nothing more than that.

I went on to play in Philadelphia with the Eagles. Buck Shaw was the coach there, and he was good friends with Cas, so that helped me out quite a bit. And Norm Van Brocklin was really in my corner. He said I could come and play for Philadelphia, and it happened—yet another reason I'll always be thankful I was a Duck.

It was just a really, really good bunch of kids that I got to play with. And everyone on that Rose Bowl team got their degree. What a great deal that was. It's pretty unusual. We felt lucky to get the chance to play together for Oregon, and we felt lucky we had a chance to go to the Rose Bowl. When people ask me about it now, I like to tell everyone it was the '94 Rose Bowl team that I was on, not '58. I get a kick out of that.

Darrel Aschbacher played on two of the four Oregon defenses in the modern era that allowed opponents fewer than 10 points per game. The Ducks allowed 8.8 points per game in the 1957 Rose Bowl season and 5.0 points per game in 1958. Aschbacher appeared in 11 games at guard with the Philadelphia Eagles in 1959. He currently resides in his home town of Prineville, Oregon.

WILLIE WEST

HALFBACK

1957–1959

IARRIVED AT OREGON ALONG WITH MY FRIEND and high school teammate from San Diego, Alden Kimbrough. Early in the fall of 1956, we went down to Coos Bay with the freshman team to play Oregon State, and it was a sea of mud, ankle deep. Alden and I were looking at each other like, "What is this?" Being a couple of Southern California boys, we were a little puzzled, a little doubtful, I guess. The following January it must have rained 30 days out of 31, and we counted every one of them. We were wanting to go home, and we called home, and of course the folks said, "What's the matter? Are they mistreating you? Are you doing badly in school?" We told them no. "Then what's the problem?" We told them it rains too much, and they said, "Well, not good enough. I think you better stay." They wouldn't let us come home. Had it not been for them, we probably would have made a mistake. Because we both enjoyed our entire four years of school at Oregon.

We were recruited by John McKay, who was an assistant at that time, and later went on to USC. We were invited on a trip up here, which is the normal procedure, of course. Once we got here, it was one of those beautiful Oregon fall days, about 70 degrees, blue skies, sunshine, no rain. Green, and beautiful. We really liked that because it was somewhat different from where we grew up. We liked that a lot. The people were friendly when we got here. We liked the campus and the atmosphere around here, so we went back home and talked about where we might go. Both of us had received scholarship offers from several schools, and we had pledged to go to school together somewhere. So, for various reasons, we eliminated all the other colleges except for Oregon. Sometime midsummer we decided that Oregon was the school we wanted to come to, so we declared, and came up here. We discovered later, on that trip to Coos Bay, that the weather we experienced on our visit could change dramatically.

The racial climate in Eugene was still sort of evolving at that time. There were some places you had to be careful about what you were doing. I think blacks had not been allowed to move into Eugene not too long before we came to school here. I don't know the exact year, but I know it was not too many years before we got up here. Of course, we didn't know anything about that when we came up here on our recruiting visit. It might have affected things perhaps, but we got by okay. I had a few incidents, but we worked it out. It's gotten better every year since. I think there were only 20 blacks on campus at that time, and even that might be high. It was a transition that we were not accustomed to, when you grow up in a pretty racially diverse area. You notice it when that situation changes. I think Eugene has had its racial problems, and those were evolving, but as I said, other than a couple incidents, there were no problems.

Alden and I remained close the whole way. As a matter of fact, there were several of us from San Diego High School that came up here. I'm from the San Diego area, and Alden and I were the first out of there, and we helped to establish a nice connection to other football players from San Diego. I think there might have been a total of 15 or 20 San Diego–area players that came up here.

McKay was my position coach. I was pretty close to him, but Len Casanova was just a one-of-a-kind person and human being. He was just a renaissance man, a multifaceted guy, not only a father figure, but a counselor. He was much more than a coach. He would call you into his office and you'd think, *Oh, what'd I do this time?* And he would just want to talk. Or he'd say, "Hey, I talked to your parents the other day, and they wanted to know how you're doing, so I better ask you how you're doing." Of course, he already knew. He was that type of person. He would establish contact with people, and stay in contact with his players long after they had left school. He was just phenomenal. I think it was the relationship much more than the Xs and Os. His assistant coaches, I felt, did much more of the Xs and Os. He was involved in it, but they all had autonomy, and he was a guy who set the tone and kept things together.

In those days, I always felt I could play with anybody. I don't recall having had any problem with the transition to college ball at all. It was more getting used to being in school and the changing circumstances in terms of adjusting to a new environment, one pretty much unlike where I had come from. But I never had any problem on the field.

I loved offense, mostly. It was more fun. It wasn't that I disliked defense. I just wanted to carry the ball and score the points. I enjoyed defense, it was just that I wanted to run the ball. In the pros, I was considered to be too small to do that. I did my first year and got injured, and there was no choice after that. It was just more fun to run with the ball.

When I joined the varsity in 1957, we had Jim Shanley, who was a phenomenal halfback. I played with Joe Schaffeld and Jack Morris, Jack Crabtree and Ron Stover. Those were some of the guys who were stalwarts my sophomore year, the year we went to the Rose Bowl. Those were the guys who were the leaders of the team at that time.

Getting to play in the Rose Bowl, it was phenomenal, of course. It was the dream of everyone that plays in the Pac-10 to reach the Rose Bowl. And then you go down there in the sunlight again, which was nice. Those of us from Southern California knew what that was like, but for the people from Oregon, it was probably more of a factor to be in that type of climate. But all the hoopla and things like that surrounding the game was fun. That's what stood out.

It was a close game. I think we were a 21-point underdog to Ohio State, or something, and it ended up a 10–7 game. Late in the game we actually had a shot to win. As a player, if somebody is saying that you're an underdog, you don't feel that way. You play, and I guess it's like some coach said, "That's why you play the game. You really don't know what's going to happen." I was splitting time with a fellow named Charlie Tourville at that time, but I started that game, which was special because I had all my friends and family there.

We might have been able to go back the next year if our offense had been at the level of our defense. We only allowed more than seven points one time in all of that season. Jack Roche was a phenomenal defensive coordinator. The guy's mind for defense was so impressive. We felt like he could set up defenses to stop anybody. We had lost some key guys from the Rose Bowl team and went 4–6, but we lost five of those games by a total of 24 points. None of those teams were that much, if at all, better than us, but we just weren't able to prevail.

Willie West was a versatile athlete who led Oregon in both rushing and receiving in 1958.

We only lost twice when I was a senior, and wouldn't you know it, those are the games I remember best. We lost to Washington on a fluke. One of their players tricked our guy! Don McKeta, their receiver, and Bob Schloredt, the quarterback, kept throwing this little out pattern late in the game. We were leading 12–7 at that point, and they would throw this little out pattern for five yards, and go out of bounds, and then they'd run another play for two or three yards and throw this little out pattern again. They started from, like, the 20 or so and started marching down the field. Then about the third or fourth time they threw that little out, McKeta faked going out of bounds, and our defensive back on that side relaxed, and then McKeta turned up the field and ran something like 60 yards for a touchdown. They went up 13–12. Then they kicked the ball off to us, and we got a fairly sustained march down the field, but we only had about one or two minutes left, and we got down pretty close before they buckled down and stopped us. We had been in command of the game, and then we had no trouble getting back down into scoring range, but they pulled it out.

We had a much improved offense in '59. I don't know what the dynamics were in that '58 year. We had a fairly decent line, and backs and receivers. I just don't know. Breaking in new linemen might have been the factor. I really don't recall why our offense was not as quite as productive, but I do know it was the same guys in '59 that went 8–2 and probably should have been 9–1.

Willie West led Oregon in rushing and receiving in 1958 before being voted the team's MVP in 1959 along with tackle Tom Keele. West was a first-team All–Pacific Coast Conference selection as a junior and an All-Coast pick in 1959, when the Ducks were an independent, as well as an honorable mention All-American. West was a fourth-round pick in the 1960 NFL Draft and participated in two Pro Bowls during his nine-year pro career. He returned to Eugene to raise his family after retiring from football.

The SIXTIES

MEL RENFRO

HALFBACK

1961–1963

MINE IS A VERY UNIQUE AND DIFFERENT type of story, because I was headed to Oregon State. Terry Baker, who won the Heisman with the Beavers, was my high school teammate and the quarterback when I was at Jefferson High in Portland. I was recruited hard by Amos Marsh and the Beavers, and I really liked their program. Then, two weeks before I was getting ready to report in Corvallis, my dad came up to me and said, "Melvin, you're going to Oregon." And I said, "Oh?" And he said, "You're going to Oregon." And that was that.

Evidently, Len Casanova, Max Coley, and, I guess, Bill Bowerman had been wooing my parents for some time, and they overruled my decision. I liked Oregon and the coaches there, but I felt a strong pull because Terry Baker was down at Oregon State, and I kind of wanted to follow him. But I was the type of guy who was going to do what my parents told me to do. I just obeyed their wishes, and the rest is history.

That was quite the high school team, as you might have guessed. In my years there we won 35, against one loss. My brother Ray was an even better ballplayer than I was. He didn't go on to play college or pro, but he was 6'3" and 210 pounds and could run the 100 in 9.6 seconds. And we were just unstoppable. Together with Terry Baker, we won two state championships, and we should have won it my senior year, if not for some questionable officiating.

When I arrived in Eugene, John Robinson was the freshman coach. We only played four games, but we just massacred everybody. We beat the little puppies up at Washington about 51–12 or something, and I scored three back-to-back touchdowns. We had some good ballplayers in my years. Doug Post was the quarterback—Bob Berry came in later—and Dave Wilcox came my junior year. Steve Barnett and Ron Snidow were just two tremendous linemen. Larry Hill was the other running back. Bruce Snyder, Dick Imwalle—we just had a great bunch of players and enjoyed playing together.

Racial tensions were an issue some places you went in those days, but in Eugene I was treated well and with great respect. There were a lot of business owners in Eugene who were very kind to me. Not that they did anything illegal. But for instance, I needed furniture for my apartment when my wife and I got married and never encountered any problems. The chancellor of the school invited me to his house for a party, which doesn't really happen. It was just great, and I enjoyed that atmosphere.

That's not to say the transition from high school to college wasn't tough for me. I was kind of a C student in high school, and college took hard work. You've got to study, and you spend so much time in athletics. I didn't graduate. I think I left halfway through my senior year and signed my NFL contract with Dallas. I just remember spending many nights after practice in the library studying and getting tutoring, and I ran track also. There was no down time for me. I was kind of worn out by the time my career ended at Oregon. I had a lot of success in track. I was actually training for the Olympic decathlon my senior year when I decided to go pro. But I decided I had had all these years of hard work and studying and it was time to move on.

35

The important thing was how the coaches at Oregon treated me. They kind of looked after me and made sure that I went to class. They were like a second group of parents. Being away from home for that long, and being away from your family—to have people that stepped up and were there to encourage you was important. We spent a lot of time playing sports, and you don't get to go home as much as other students. You're always there—during vacation times, when other students go home for a week, we were still in town working out. One year, the NCAA championship track meet took place after school got out, so we had to stay there until the track meet. After that you got to go home for a couple weeks, and then you could have a summer job for a month or so, but then it was time to come back early for football

36

Mel Renfro competed for two of the giants of coaching in the history of Oregon athletics, football coach Len Casanova and track coach Bill Bowerman. *Photo courtesy Getty Images.*

again. Under those circumstances, just the fact that the coaches were there for us if we needed something made a big difference.

Running track meant I got to compete for both Len Casanova and Bill Bowerman. The thing about Cas was he was tough. He had great coaches and he let them do a lot of the coaching, but he was the guy in charge, and if he needed to tell you something specifically, he would bypass the position coach and come and tell you directly. The other thing was, off the field, you could always talk to him about your issues and how you were doing, and he kept track of how you were doing academically. If there were situations or areas where you needed help, he would always recommend somebody who could help you.

The same was true with Bill Bowerman. He was a workaholic. He had us doing some incredible things, just running, running, running, all the time. There's no mystery why he had such successful athletes, and had so many records and championships. It was because he worked hard and had guys that were committed to working hard for him. The results just speak for themselves. I remember he spent time developing the prototypes for what would be the Nike company, and we used to wear those shoes and pants and shirts, and he developed the raised surface for the broad jump pit. Many innovative things—he was always a step ahead of everybody else. It was a joy performing for him. He'd have us run to the golf course, run at the golf course, and run back to the university. It's what made us successful. He just wore us out.

My first season with the varsity, in 1961, I thought it would be a big jump, but on my second play of the first game, against Idaho, I ran 80 yards for a touchdown and had a great game. I think that sophomore year was probably my best year. We were quite explosive. We played Ohio State, and they were supposed to just run all over us. But they only beat us 22–12, and Woody Hayes was just livid. I saw him on the sideline, and even after the game was over, he was just screaming and hollering. I remember reading an article a little bit later after that game, and I hadn't realized I had 15 unassisted tackles and 10 assisted tackles. So I had quite a game on defense, and I suppose I had a fairly good game on offense.

Playing both ways was a challenge. I probably would have set a lot more records and done a lot more offensively as far as yardage and touchdowns had I stuck with offense. I was on the field all the time—offense, defense, special teams—and I played hard every play. You make a stop on defense, and then you field a punt and run it up a ways, and then you're on offense running the ball; that can wear you out. They'd platoon us in and out, but you couldn't always give 100 percent even though you wanted to. Your body just wouldn't let you.

But playing both ways ended up helping me in the NFL. I went to Dallas as a running back and wide receiver, but I got to camp and there were four or five very good running backs. And they had tremendous wide receivers. So Tom Landry decided to get a good athlete on the field and they put me at free safety, and I also returned punts and kickoffs. I just started intercepting passes right away, and led the league my rookie year in punts and kickoffs. That year I intercepted seven passes and went to the Pro Bowl, so it was good to have that background of playing defense as well as offense.

In 1962 Bob Berry returned to Oregon, and so we had the "Firehouse Four." It was a great group of players. Berry could throw the ball extremely well, and he was a fiery guy. Just explosive. I had the speed and change of pace and could catch the ball well, and Larry Hill was a remarkable running back. Many times I'd be blocking for him, and I'd turn around and he'd be gone down the field. Of course, Lu Bain was a good fullback. But Bob was a tremendous quarterback and leader. We'd do anything for him. When you've got so many guys that can play so well and contribute, I think you've got something.

On defense, we added Dave Wilcox that year. Dave was just a big old country boy, and you just didn't mess with him. He was like a bull rider, big and tough, and part of the reason for our success, with how he handled himself out there. We had Larry Hill on the corner, I played safety. I probably made as many tackles as our linemen and linebackers, and I would force the run because I studied film so well. I was always up making tackles. But we had great personnel across the defense and we all played well together.

We played two games in Texas in 1962, which was special for me because I was born in Houston. The first was against the Longhorns, and that was disappointing to lose because they were No. 1 in the nation that year, and we had them beat. We had them down in the third quarter, and I think one of our kickoff return guys fumbled a kickoff, and they recovered inside the 10-yard line. It was hot, too. We weren't used to that kind of heat, and we just ran out of gas late in the third quarter. They were too good of a football team, and they came back and beat us. But we had them on the ropes.

A few weeks later, when we played at Rice, we prepared ourselves for the heat. We knew what it was going to be like, got the proper rest and fluids,

I knew Lu Bain from my freshman year living in the dorm

and I just had a remarkable game. I had about 20 of my relatives there who I could only see from a distance. Back then with the segregation policies, they wouldn't let blacks into the stadium, but because of me, they roped off an area right on the 50-yard line, and my grandfather got to see me play. I had never met him before. I saw him up in the stands and I got to wave at him as we were leaving the field. I had a remarkable game, offensively and defensively, and I guess the news report read, "Renfro Runs Rice Ragged." When I got back to Oregon, a lot of my classmates who listened to the game on the radio, said, "Wow, from the way the guys described the game, you were just all over the place." That was probably the highlight of my whole college football career.

On the other hand, I had an Achilles' heel with Oregon State. My sophomore year, we were on the 2-yard line, and it was cold and snowy, and if we score, we win. They give me the ball on a sweep. Of course, everybody in the world knew I was going to get the ball, so they stacked that side and we didn't make it, and Oregon State won it. That was a big disappointment, because after the game I felt like a piece of broken glass I had played so hard and gotten beat up so bad. It took a day or two for the pain to go away, not just the mental pain, but the physical and emotional pain.

Both of Terry Baker's years, 1961 and 1962, he beat me. The second year, my junior year, we played in Corvallis, and it was my Achilles' heel again. I was fielding a punt in our territory and I misjudged it. It hit my knee, and they recovered. Later in the game, Terry Baker juked me on a fake throw to the wide receiver, and I bit on it. The halfback was circling out of the backfield, and Baker threw it to him, and they ran in for a touchdown. I still wonder what would have happened if we had played on the same team.

We had a great year my senior year. We ended up going to a bowl game, of course. I cracked my rib against Washington returning a kickoff, but actually didn't miss a game. I came back the next game against Washington State. It was painful. I remember the Stanford game well. I always had great games against Stanford. My sophomore year, I had a chipped bone in my ankle, and I hadn't played for a little while. But I came back and I was in on four plays and was responsible for three touchdowns. I caught a pass for a touchdown, I returned a kickoff, and I threw a halfback pass for a touchdown.

My career ended under difficult circumstances. The 1963 Civil War [the Oregon–Oregon St. game] was pushed back because of the Kennedy assassination. I was emotionally distraught. I was sitting around my apartment drinking beer and banged my hand up against the mirror in the bathroom out of frustration, and it unfortunately cut my wrist really bad. It bled pretty bad. I had to go to the hospital and get it sewn up, so I was unable to play the next week. That's kind of the way my college career ended.

But, overall, my Oregon career was wonderful. I've lived a blessed life, and that was a major part of it.

Mel Renfro is one of the great two-sport athletes in Oregon history. He was named a football All-American in 1962 and 1963, and finished second in the NCAA 120-yard high hurdles in 1962. Renfro finished his Oregon career with 1,540 yards and went on to play 14 seasons in the NFL, participating in 10 Pro Bowls and four Super Bowls. He is a member of the college and professional football halls of fame.

LARRY HILL

HALFBACK

1961–1963

I GREW UP IN ASTORIA, OREGON, and my sister was a Duck, so it seemed natural that I'd probably end up there. And coming out of high school, I originally wanted to go to Oregon. But the Ducks didn't initially offer me a scholarship. They could only hand out 25 per year, and they were pretty selective. I was up visiting Washington when I found that out, and my first reaction was, "Well, screw Oregon." So I actually committed to the Huskies first.

I was all set to start attending classes there, and then my father was killed in a truck accident. He owned a beer distributorship in Astoria. So family concerns started to take over. That made me grow up quite a bit. Oregon not offering me a scholarship at first had burned me, but then I thought, *To heck with pride, go where your heart is.* Bottom line, at the last minute I changed my mind to go to Oregon. It was a tough call to make, to call Jim Owens at Washington and tell him I was going to Oregon. But then I called Len Casanova and told him the same thing, so it ended up being a fun day.

Cas was super. He was an outstanding coach and gentlemen, and had a big influence on my life. One thing you didn't want to do was disappoint Cas. If you got in trouble or did something, the worst thing would be having Cas pull you into his office and talk to you. That would be the ultimate tough deal to confront. He was a classy guy, and just a legend. I used to respect the hell out of him, and still do. When he left this world, I was disappointed, deeply disappointed.

When I started at Oregon, the good thing about those days was that they had a freshman team, so you had the chance to get kind of oriented just playing with guys your own age. And John Robinson, who of course went on to be a famous coach, was our freshman coach. That was quite an experience.

Robinson at that time had a heck of a speech impediment. He really just stuttered terribly. Our group would start laughing, which was bad, I know. But I was also so impressed in later years when I would see him on TV and he would be so articulate. It was just amazing that he overcame that, but it was funny at the time.

I believe we just played Oregon State and Washington and Washington State that first year. I prefer the format of having a freshman team to what they're doing now, letting guys play with the varsity their first year. It gave us a chance to adjust to the college level in both athletics and academics. And going through it together, that's how those freshman guys all turned into such great long-term friends.

Bob Berry, in fact, is still one of my best friends. Bob and I keep in really close contact. I lost my wife in 2008, and it's just amazing how many of those guys from the team came up to the funeral. Mel Renfro, Monte Fitchet, Dave Wilcox, guys that went on to play in the pros. It's amazing how you keep those contacts through the years, and sometimes it takes bad news to get you together. But it sure meant a lot to me.

One thing that was unfortunate about my playing days was that we were not in a conference. We were independent, which was good and bad. We played some tough teams in those days, Texas, Ohio State, BYU, and of course always the Northwest schools. I guess the good news is that I don't think I ever played USC!

Berry, Renfro, Lu Bain, and I were known in those days as the "Firehouse Four." The thing that was neat about that group is that it wasn't an individual thing. It was for the team. You might be the guy with the ball in your hands on one play, but if you weren't on the next play, you had to get down the field and throw a block for the other guy. We had formations called Flanker Left and Flanker Right, and in one of them I was split out as the receiver with Mel in the backfield, and in the other I was the running back with Mel at flanker. Lu was the fullback, and Bob was a heck of a quarterback.

No doubt about it, Renfro was the best football player I've ever been around. He was fantastic. I played against him in an all-star game in high school, and he was just unbelievable. He touched the ball three times and scored three times, or something close to that. I was glad to have him on my side once we got to college. I remember in that high school game I had to tackle him a few times, and that was one of the things that Oregon said they liked. I recall someone saying, "It looked like you had pretty good speed, you could catch up with Renfro." And I said, "I had the angle. I was lucky." Because he was a helluva lot faster than I was.

I started my junior year at Oregon, and I think the first time I touched the ball was against Texas, and I went over 30 yards for a touchdown. That was down in Austin. It was just an off-tackle play. Ron Jones was the pulling guard and came around and took his guy out. The end came down, it was probably Wilcox, and there was a big hole that I went right through. That was a highlight for me because it was the first time I got to play on offense.

As a sophomore, I played just defense. In those days, you could substitute one or two in on defense, but otherwise you had to play both ways. I played corner or safety. I really enjoyed playing defense, especially intercepting a pass and taking it back. That was the most thrilling thing, even versus scoring from the line of scrimmage on offense.

43

Beating the Huskies in 1961 was another highlight of my career because they were tough. Of course, the rivalry against the Beavers was always a big one. We had a tough go there because they had Terry Baker. I will always remember that Oregon State when the Beavers had Terry Baker was a tough go.

The Sun Bowl in 1963 was a lot of fun. I think the main thing was just getting together with guys before and after the game, and almost living with them down there at that time. I don't really have vivid memories of the game, except that it was a fun thing to get to play in a bowl game. Of course, we never played in the Rose Bowl, which would have been the ultimate. I was also able to play in the Hula Bowl after the season, which was a great experience.

The guys in my class get together every year for a golf outing over in Bend, Oregon. I've attended that for a while now. I live in Seattle, so it's quite a distance, but that's been one of the best things, because there are guys a few years younger and a few years older, and it's really formed a bond among that group. Living in Seattle and being a Duck has not been easy, although that has changed the last few years when Oregon has won its share. I love it now. I hate to tell everybody, but I do have season tickets to Huskies games, mainly because I like to watch college football. But being a Duck up here has been very interesting, because even though Oregon State was a big rivalry, the Huskies were the big one for me, especially because I almost went to Washington.

Larry Hill won the Clarke Trophy as Oregon's most improved player after rushing for 534 yards and scoring four touchdowns in 1962. He ran for 269 yards and scored three touchdowns as a senior and was invited to the Hula Bowl. Hill retired in 2008 and lives in Seattle.

DAVE WILCOX
END/GUARD
1962–1963

I ALWAYS FIGURED I WOULD END UP PLAYING FOOTBALL. After my second year at Boise Junior College, my brother John was playing with the Philadelphia Eagles. They won the championship, so I got to go to Franklin Field and watch them play the Packers when I was 18. I spent a couple days there, and I drove with him back to Oregon a couple days after Christmas. It was an experience. When I was in Philadelphia, that's when I started to think it would be great to play football as a career.

My brother John was a Duck in college, and so was Joe Schaffeld, whose family was from Vale, like ours. Our families knew each other from Oklahoma in the 1930s, and they moved out to eastern Oregon a year apart, in about 1935. Oregon State was big over in eastern Oregon, being the ag school, but the fact that my brother went to Eugene was a big deal. And he was also a big reason I went to Boise first. John went directly to Eugene out of high school, and then decided he should make a more gradual adjustment. So he went over to Boise Junior College for a year and a half, and then he came back to Oregon. I wasn't sure I wanted to do the same thing at first, but going from Vale to Eugene was a big move, while going from Vale to Boise to Eugene seemed like a smoother transition. We were farm guys coming to the city, after all. Where we were, the only traveling we did growing up was when we played football. When we were in high school, we lost two games, so we traveled all over the place in the playoffs.

But more than anything, Len Casanova was probably the biggest reason I became a Duck, to simplify it. Lyle Smith, who was my old coach at Boise, was really good friends with Len Casanova. He never told me I should go to the University of Oregon, but even though there were some other programs that recruited me, like Washington and USC, I trusted Lyle Smith, and he and Cas were similar people. I knew the Oregon coaches and also knew the Oregon State coaches, and after I went to Boise Junior College, both Len Casanova and Tommy Prothro, who was at Oregon State, visited with my parents. They really liked Tommy Prothro because he was from Tennessee and was a southern guy. But the thing was, he smoked in our house. Well, Cas smoked, too, but he went outside to do it. And while that wasn't a huge deal, it mattered a little to my parents.

Cas was just a very honorable man. I don't know if I know any bad things about Cas, other than that he smoked until he was about 98. I suppose he was just raised to handle himself well, and he expected the same of his players. If you got in trouble, whoever else you got in trouble with was the least of your worries, because you had to talk to Cas. So a lot of people decided that getting in trouble wasn't the way to go; we had to keep things straight. He was just a very classy gentleman.

After I left Oregon, I got to know Cas better because he was no longer my coach, my boss. I went to San Francisco to play football, and we lived in Redwood City. Cas had coached at Santa Clara and also at Sequoia High School in Redwood City. When I went down there in 1964, we went to this one place to eat, and the guy asked me where I was from. When I told him Oregon, he said, "Oh, yeah, Len Casanova. He used to coach here!" They all knew him down there and what a great guy he was. Everywhere you went, when you mentioned his name, it was like, my gosh, how lucky were you? Cas' second wife had some family in Idaho, near where I grew up, and every time they went to visit her family, he would always make a point to go out and stop at our house and talk to my mom and my dad and my brother. And he would also go up and visit the Schaffelds, and he would often send me a card from Vale. It would have a postmark on it from Vale. I thought, you know, for a guy to go out of his way to do that is just very classy. He did this for everybody, but he made it kind of feel like you were special.

When I got to Oregon in 1962, we played both ways. I was a backup at first. There was a guy named Milt Kanehe, who was a tackle from Hawaii who came over at the same time, and we played side by side. As the season went on and on, we played more and more because we got to know the system. I was playing defensive end and tight end at that point.

We didn't play in a conference back then. That first year, we played Texas in Austin in the third week of September. We were doing pretty good until about the start of the fourth quarter. Then the heat and humidity hit us, and all of a sudden guys couldn't do anything. They were a great program, and for us to go down there and open at them was something. Then we played Ohio State right before the Civil War.

I played almost the whole game against Oregon State. A guy named Greg Willener was the tight end I backed up, and we both played a lot. You didn't do a lot of that back then; about the only guy who ever got to come out of the game in those days was the quarterback. Whoever thought those rules up must have had too much to drink one night.

I also remember that Civil War well because the Beavers had Terry Baker and we had Mel Renfro, the old high school teammates from Portland. They were in the larger division than I was at Vale, and they would always win championships in their division while we would win in ours. To come and play against Terry Baker, and then also have Mel Renfro on the team I was on, that was pretty interesting.

Renfro was an amazing athlete. In 1962 I came over to Eugene in May after we got out of school in Boise, and I got a job. I was living with Joe Schaffeld and my brother, and worked at American Steel. The NCAA track meet was going on at Hayward Field, and I followed a little bit of track. In that 1962 track championship, Paul Warfield finished second in the long jump for Ohio State, and Mel was third. And then Mel finished second in the hurdles, too, and I'm sure he did some other things. They were just incredible athletes. We ended up playing against Warfield in 1963, and he caught about 13 passes against us.

My senior year, we had a lot of ends but had lost almost the whole line to graduation. So about 30 seconds before spring practice began, they asked me to move to guard. I said, "You gotta be kidding me." I had no idea what to do, but they told me they would work with me. So I ended up moving there on offense. I got to rush the quarterback on defense, so that was better. I didn't really like offense, anyhow. But my whole career you played both ways and on special teams, even when I went to the 49ers. I think there were just 36 guys on the roster for San Francisco in those days.

When I moved to guard, I would always end up going the wrong way and stuff. The one thing I made sure to do was stay out of Mel Renfro's way. He didn't need me in his way. We also had Bob Berry, who was such a great leader. Bob was a guy that just kind of took charge of things. At that time, quarterbacks called their own plays even though they had a game plan from the coaches. Berry was good about changing plays when he saw something. He knew what to call. Most of the time, of course, that just meant giving it to Renfro.

In 1963 we opened in Portland with Penn State. I don't know what Cas didn't like about us, to schedule all those tough nonleague games. We also went and played at West Virginia. And then we played Indiana in Portland. We went back and just crunched West Virginia and we beat the poop out of Rice because Mel Renfro had an incredible game. Against Indiana, we were behind near the end of the game, and when we came into the offensive huddle, Bob Berry started just yelling at the guys that we needed a block and we were going to go down there and score. Sure enough, he threw a pass for a touchdown, and we won. Then we beat the Beavers after the Civil War was pushed back a week because of Kennedy's assassination. That qualified us for the Sun Bowl.

Before we went to the Sun Bowl, a couple of guys from the 49ers came to town and took Mel and I out to breakfast over at the Eugene Hotel. It was the day of the NFL Draft, and they didn't want us talking to any AFL teams. The 49ers ended up taking me, and they wanted me to sign a contract right then and there. I wanted to talk to Cas first, and they tried to go along with me, but I wanted to go by myself, and it was a good thing because he told me not to sign anything or else I'd screw up my eligibility for the bowl. He knew some people with the 49ers from when he worked down in that area, so he took care of it. Houston had drafted me in the AFL, and Cas said he didn't want to make my decision for me, but he thought I should sign with the 49ers after the bowl. They were offering me $12,500 with a $4,000 bonus, and he said that was pretty good. I had never had anything like that kind of money, and I figured Cas knew his stuff, so that's what I ended up doing.

We had our practices for the Sun Bowl in Eugene, and then I flew home for Christmas the day before with another eastern Oregon guy, Larry Horyna from Ontario. The rest of the team took a charter that started in Seattle and continued down the West Coast, picking guys up before continuing on to El Paso. But Larry and I flew out of Boise to Salt Lake City.

After a hall of fame NFL career, Dave Wilcox sent two sons on to the Oregon football program, tight end Josh and defensive back Justin.

We were supposed to fly to El Paso from there, but our flight got cancelled. Larry was about four years older because he'd spent some time in the air force, so he took control of the situation. But there were no cell phones or anything in those days, and nobody knew where we were for a while. We ended up missing one practice, which we kind of thought was a pretty good deal. It didn't end up hurting us, that's for sure. We were playing SMU and got off to a pretty good start, and ended up holding on at the end to win.

Then, after the game, Milt Kanehe, Larry Hill, Dick Imwalle, and I, plus Len Casanova and his wife, all got on a plane to go to Hawaii. Cas was a coach in the Hula Bowl, and we were playing for him. That was the first time I had ever been on a jet airplane. I have a picture of us all getting off the airplane. We had leis around our necks, and everybody was wearing a coat and tie. That's one thing Cas did: helped refine us by making us dress up a little bit. Oregon must have had a wardrobe of blue blazers with the "O" on them, because when you went to school, they issued you one for road trips, and then when you graduated, you turned it in so they could give it to the next guy.

We got to Hawaii at about 11:00 PM on New Year's Eve, the same day as the Sun Bowl. It was about three days before the Hula Bowl. It was New Year's Eve, our first trip to Hawaii, so you can imagine how wild it was. John McKay was an assistant for the Hula Bowl, and he'd gone over early to prepare the other players. That team had about 26 guys, and there was Paul Warfield, Carl Eller, and I—I think about five Pro Football Hall of Famers all together. Well, I only had about two days to practice with McKay on defense—I didn't have to play offense, which was fine—and two days didn't seem like enough time to learn very much of anything. So I just went out there and played. I ended up intercepting a pass and being named defensive player of the game. After missing that first day at the Sun Bowl and then showing up late for the Hula Bowl, all I could think was, so much for this practice stuff.

Dave Wilcox was a third-team All-Coast pick as a senior in 1963 and was named Oregon's most improved player. Wilcox was invited to the Hula Bowl and the College All-Star Game, and was a third-round NFL Draft pick by the San Francisco 49ers. He played 11 professional seasons, making seven Pro Bowls and being named All-NFL five times. Wilcox was inducted into the Pro Football Hall of Fame in 2000. His sons Josh and Justin both played at Oregon. Wilcox lives in Junction City, Oregon.

BOB BERRY

QUARTERBACK
1962–1964

I T'S AMAZING TO ME ALL THE ATTENTION AND HYPE there is now surrounding college football and recruiting and everything. Back when we started, it wasn't the big deal that it is now. Guys didn't know much about scholarships, that kind of thing. My dad was my high school football coach, and by my senior year he told me I was probably going to get some scholarship offers. I had a few, and his advice to me was that he didn't care where I went or what schools I checked out, but to do him a favor and check out Len Casanova and Oregon. He had known Len personally when he was in Santa Clara; when Cas coached down there, my dad was a high school coach in the valley. I did visit Oregon, and ended up liking it, and it seemed to be a good fit.

I was recruited by John Robinson and Phil McHugh, and of course Len was the main man. They were just great people. I found a fit there. I didn't want to go to Southern California or the University of Washington, any of those other places. This was all before I entered the university and realized the Huskies were such a big rivalry. I didn't know I was picking one rival over another. Mainly, my becoming a Duck was due to my dad's respect for Cas. He thought highly of him, and I liked Oregon and Eugene.

More than his coaching style, what was impressive about Cas was that he was just a great man. I believe he could have run for governor. What you see too often in football a lot today is a win-at-any-cost attitude, and he had the moral character that I think is missing in some of today's programs. He was just a super guy. He cared about the individual first, and then the team that you were part of. He was like a father to a lot of guys. He was like my second father, really. He wasn't a hollering and screaming guy like you see some coaches these days. There's no need for that. I've played on several teams where they've had that kind of coach, and that just doesn't work. It doesn't work for me, at least. And Cas cared about all the guys. He didn't care if you were the first-string guy or the fourth-string guy. He was building young men. I remember more about that than the Xs and Os and the great games. That's what stood out in my mind. We learned lots of lessons.

You never knew what to expect your first year. I had some confidence because I was a successful high school player and played in what I thought was a pretty competitive league. But I hadn't seen anything like Mel Renfro. Actually, when John Robinson recruited me, one of his carrots he was dangling was that, "You've got to come up and be the quarterback at Oregon because we've just got the best running back in the country." And I was thinking, *Well, I've played against some pretty big guys down here.* And the guy he was talking about was Mel Renfro. When I got to Oregon, I was just flabbergasted. Mel was a world-class athlete, not just in football. So it was pretty fun.

We had a great group of guys who came in as freshmen, Mel Renfro, Larry Hill, Monte Fitchet. We still get together, the twelve of us who were freshman, every year over at Black Butte Ranch in Central Oregon. We play golf and kind of reminisce. That's pretty amazing for a group of freshmen. We still remain close, the bunch of guys I went to school with. My memories are mostly of playing and coming of age with them. We're still pals.

Like I said, I was pretty confident personally as a freshman, and that turned into confidence in the team because these guys were all good. We had some good skill guys, and so we were pretty good while playing the freshman schedule. We played the Beavers a couple times, and Washington and Washington State. John Robinson was our coach, and that was his first head coaching job. He went undefeated his first year.

Robinson is a funny guy, a great guy. There are some funny stories about him. That's when we all learned to hate the Huskies, from him. One time, we went up to play the Huskies, and they wouldn't put us on the main field, so we had to play them on a practice field down by the lake, and that made him mad. We were up I think 21–0 on them at halftime, and he came in and was ranting and raving like we were losing the game because he just hated

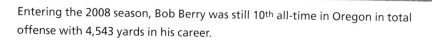

Entering the 2008 season, Bob Berry was still 10th all-time in Oregon in total offense with 4,543 yards in his career.

them so bad. He had us line up and do live tackling practice at halftime of the game. Guys lined up and just started banging into each other, full-on tackling. We went out, and Renfro ran the opening kick of the second half back, and I think we ended up winning 51–0. But Robbie was so fired up he had tackling practice at halftime. It was crazy, but that's how intense he was about beating the Huskies.

We had a great program by my sophomore year in 1962, and we played all the big guys. We were independent then, not tied down to the Pac-10. That was fantastic. We went all over the country. We played Air Force Academy at the dedication of their stadium. That was a big deal. Colorado Springs put on a big deal for us. The South back then was obviously very different. We played there twice my sophomore year, against Rice and Texas. Mel had a couple of great games down there, and as I remember it was the first time they ever cheered for a black guy.

One of the things that stands out from 1963 was the Indiana game in which we came back to beat them in Multnomah Stadium on the last second with a passing touchdown. It was a back-and-forth game, and I always had enough confidence in those situations. I figured if we had time to throw the ball, we would complete some passes and go down the field and win. On the final drive, Mel caught a little swing pass, and even though it was a muddy game, and I threw not the greatest of passes, he was able to reach back with one hand and keep the drive going. We plodded down the field, and H.D. Murphy caught a pass in the corner of the end zone to win the game. That was fun. Those kinds of wins are always fun.

I was one-for-three against Oregon State in my career, and the one I like to remember is the one we killed them in Eugene, to end the 1963 regular season. That was right after Kennedy had been killed, and they had put the game off for a week. Mel didn't play, but I had a pretty good day throwing the ball, and we were ahead 31–0 before we knew it. We ended up winning 31–14, and then got to go down and play in the Sun Bowl.

My senior season we had a young team, after losing Renfro and Hill and Dave Wilcox. We were a bunch of overachievers, but we found ways to win. Of course, I wish we could have found a way to win that last one against Oregon State, and maybe go to the Rose Bowl. But we battled hard.

There were challenges in my Oregon career, but just the usual, nothing bad. I never really got hurt bad. I stretched some knee ligaments and separated a shoulder, which didn't keep me out of many games. Actually, the jump from high school to college, for me, wasn't quite as difficult as the jump from college to pros. I could still run the ball a bit in college. But when I got to the pros, I realized I better just stay in the pocket and throw the ball.

Bob Berry quarterbacked Oregon to three consecutive winning seasons and victory in the 1963 Sun Bowl, a landmark run for the program at that time. He finished his UO career with 4,297 passing yards and 39 touchdowns and was named the team's MVP and an All-American in 1964. Berry was invited to the East-West Shrine Game and the Hula Bowl after his senior season, then was drafted in 1965 by the NFL's Philadelphia Eagles and enjoyed a eleven-year pro career. Berry was a member of Oregon's inaugural athletic hall of fame class in 1992.

DENNY SCHULER

RECEIVER

1967–1968

THESE DAYS, OREGON GETS A LOT OF ATTENTION for all its various uniforms. Well, I'm almost embarrassed to say that I think probably one of the biggest reasons I chose Oregon, 40 years ago, was because of the uniforms. They had the Green Bay Packers–style uniform at the time. I still wish they had it because I always was attracted to that. It's such a great uniform. So rather than education or what was I going to play, that sort of thing, it was the uniforms.

My father also had a lot to do with it. Len Casanova at that time was really known for his wide-open offenses, and my father always envisioned that I would have a better chance playing in an offense like that. I'm from Snohomish, Washington, originally, and rather than the Jim Owens pound-it-out sort of thing the Huskies were doing, my father always saw me doing more what Cas was doing with the Ducks. Actually, my father passed away during the whole process. I'm sure that he would not have let me choose Oregon because of the uniforms, but I knew he wanted me to go to Oregon for other reasons.

I was actually being recruited by Washington State at the time, too. Jim Shanley was recruiting me, and he was one of my heroes growing up, so it was really tough for me because I liked him a whole bunch, too. Washington really was my first choice. In those days if somebody really wanted you, they offered you a four-year scholarship. Nowadays, it's a one-year renewable scholarship, but in those days if they really wanted you, they'd offer you a four-year scholarship, and if they only kind of wanted you, they would offer you a one-year scholarship. For example, the University of Washington and Washington State, they both had maybe 150 kids on their freshman team. Most of those kids were on one-year scholarships, and then they'd take the best ones and advance them to another three-year scholarship. Well, Oregon offered me a four-year scholarship, so that was another big factor for me.

John Robinson was recruiting me for the Ducks, and I fell in love with him. I don't remember a thing about him in the recruiting process, other than that I was always laughing. He'd always make me laugh, and when you're a kid, a kid will see a school through the coach that's recruiting him. I don't think you can ever underestimate how important a recruiting coach is to a kid. Those were the days when Oregon wasn't on TV, and you didn't have all the visual things that you have today. I was very fortunate that I was introduced to some great people at Oregon, certainly Cas and John Robinson. It was a tough move. I didn't know anyone at Oregon and I was homesick as hell. Luckily, my mother stayed down in Eugene in a hotel for two weeks and wouldn't let me go home, because I was ready to go home. Once you break through all that, it was a great move—a wonderful decision—and I've never had any regrets about it.

57

I got there in the fall of 1964. In those days they just had freshman football, you couldn't play on the varsity your first season. We had our freshman schedule, played Oregon State twice, played Washington and Washington State, and that was it. We usually practiced against ourselves mostly, and every now and then we'd go down and practice against the varsity, which scared the hell out of me. Playing in those games was the biggest thing in the world. That year we went back to Seattle, so going back to Husky Stadium, after watching games when I was growing up there as a kid, that was huge. There were probably about 500 people in the football stands, and about 400 of them were from Snohomish. They actually brought the Snohomish High School football team down to watch me play. So that was a big deal for me. I do remember that game more than any others. I didn't start on the freshman team. I got to play a little bit, but it was certainly a big deal. That was a great introduction. I still think in a lot of ways that was a great way to break into college football. You weren't immediately thrown through the meat grinder, and we didn't have to meet at night. It was just a good way to be introduced to college football. I really think in a lot of ways I wish they did that now, rather than just throwing kids in there. But it's a little different, less scholarships now and whatnot.

I'll always remember the view from my dorm window. I was in Douglass Hall, which is right across from Hayward Field. I would see all these grown people—and I'd never seen an adult in my life ever do this—but Bill Bowerman was taking all these people, I think they were recovering after heart attacks, and he was having them jog. I thought it was the funniest damn thing in the world, to look out my window and see all these grown people jogging. Now it's very common to see people jogging in Eugene, but nobody jogged in those days.

I was going to play basketball at Oregon, too, but then I got about a 1.67 grade-point average my first quarter, so they decided that wasn't the best idea. They decided I needed to hit the books a little more.

My second year was my redshirt year, and I actually broke my collarbone in practice, so I did not end up playing that year. I'm not sure how much I would have played that year anyway.

My third year I was healthy, and I got to play a little bit. I was a reserve tailback. The following spring, Cas quit, and Jerry Frei came in. I'd always enjoyed lining up as a receiver and running all the various routes, so Jerry Frei asked me if I'd like to be a receiver, and I said I'd do anything to get on the playing field. So in the fall of 1967 I got moved to receiver.

I really didn't interact with Cas that much, but the thing I always do remember was that it was always such an Oregon family. It was always taking care of each other. He was always looking after you. Luckily, I didn't really get into any trouble, except for that first quarter I mentioned.

I thought the world of Cas, had a tremendous amount of respect for him, but my playing career really blossomed when Jerry Frei came on board. I think anyone who ever played for Jerry Frei had a great deal of love for him. Those were the days when we weren't very good, but we were always being compared to Oregon State. Back then, Jerry Frei would let you have a mustache or a short beard, or your hair could be a little bit longer, and that was not the case at Oregon State. Jerry Frei was always willing to let you express yourself. Those were the Vietnam days, and we were allowed to express ourselves and say what we wanted to. I always had a great deal of respect for the fact that he was letting us grow not only as football players, but as young men as well.

If I have one favorite personal highlight, it was scoring the first touchdown in Autzen Stadium after it opened in 1967. We were playing Colorado. I like to say I caught 15 passes that day, and 14 of them were in pregame warm-ups. It might have been a couple more, honestly, but not many. I found out years later through Don James, who worked at Colorado the next year, that the defensive back I beat on that play was Hale Irwin, the golfer. It was a broken play, and Eric Olson was scrambling to his right, and I was in the end zone and happened to be coming back into the play. I actually did catch it sliding out of bounds. I was lucky, very fortunate. We made a comeback in the second half and actually made that game very competitive. That was great. The bad news was, I actually sprained my ankle in that game and didn't get to play in a number of games after that.

I had two good years where I got off the bench and played in some games, and that really says a lot to how bad we were at the time, that guys like me were playing. We weren't real good. You knew that Jerry Frei was going to recruit, and they brought in some kids in '69 and '70. In '71 Frei got fired, and that's unfortunate, because by that time they had some good players in there, like Dan Fouts and Bobby Moore, a lot of good players.

I think the one thing that's so great about Jerry Frei, a lot of people at Oregon expected a lot out of Oregon and wanted a lot of his assistants fired. And Jerry, to his credit, told them that he would make that decision if he felt it was the thing to do. He was told to go too, eventually, but he certainly got the thing going. Recruiting is the life blood of every program, and he got it going. Early on, he didn't have Joey Harrington, he had John Harrington, who was more my size. But we had a very good staff. All those guys certainly distinguished themselves over the years. It kind of became a hotbed of coaches. A lot of good coaches came through.

59

Unfortunately, he had too many kids that looked like me, about 5'10", 155 pounds, and not enough kids that looked like Bobby Moore, who came in a few years later. It's all about recruiting, and we had some good kids, but we didn't have a large amount of great players, especially in '67.

In '68 we had a better year. In those two years we played very well on defense. O.J. Simpson's two worst games of his collegiate career were against Oregon. We did some good things, but all in all we didn't win enough games.

After starting at receiver his final two seasons at Oregon, Denny Schuler began a career as an assistant coach that lasted three decades. He served as a coordinator at Weber State, Utah State, California, Oregon, Oregon State, and Northern Iowa. Schuler was Oregon's defensive coordinator from 1986 through 1992, when the Ducks consistently finished in the top half of the Pac-10 in total defense and began a tradition of regular bowl appearances that continues to this day.

BOB NEWLAND

RECEIVER

1968–1970

IDIDN'T PLAY FOOTBALL UNTIL THE NINTH GRADE because that was the first year I was big enough to be with the rest of the guys. I started every year in high school, but I almost stopped playing football my sophomore year because I was a total string bean. I was the fastest guy on the team, but wasn't very big compared to a lot of the other guys.

Going to Oregon was an easy decision because in my heart I was always a Duck. My best friend was a runner named Bill Keenan, and he and I had decided we were going to go to the same school. One of the places we looked seriously at was Stanford. Keenan had taken both physics and chemistry at North Eugene High School, but I had taken only physics. The coach at Stanford offered me assistance to get my chemistry out of the way at a junior college. Had I done that, I would have gone to Stanford. But I didn't want to go to junior college for a year. I had been down there two or three times, and I really thought about it, but not getting into the school really sealed the deal. I had some other options, but pretty much it came down to Oregon or Stanford, and Stanford was a no because I couldn't get directly into school. So Bill Keenan came to Oregon with me.

My first year at Oregon, the freshman team's coach was George Seifert. That was his first coaching job. He had traveled out here from Iowa. One of the assistants was John Marshall, who went on to coach in the NFL. This was the freshman staff! John Robinson was the offensive coordinator my

Despite Oregon's prolific offenses of the last two decades, Bob Newland's 1,123 receiving yards in 1970 remained a school record four decades later.

junior and senior year, and he was a great offensive coordinator, a great offensive mind.

The head coach was Jerry Frei, who was a great man and a great coach. People loved to play for him. I actually wasn't recruited by Jerry Frei. I was recruited by Len Casanova, who then about two weeks before the recruiting season was over decided he didn't want to be the head coach anymore. He was succeeded by Jerry Frei, and for a moment I wasn't sure because I didn't know him. He had been the line coach. But he was a great guy, great to his players, very fair. It was a very controversial time with civil disobedience, hair length, and all sorts of stuff like that. He let guys be themselves. Back when some football coaches were telling some black players they couldn't have Afros, or telling players they couldn't have mustaches, he didn't let that bother him. He felt like young men should be able to make their own decisions. He wasn't easy on people. He just gave kids a little more of a leash to figure out what they thought about things. He is the coach that impacted me the most at Oregon.

There was a lot of unrest on campus at the time. I actually was on the student senate at the time too, and I was against the war in Vietnam. I went on a couple marches for that. I remember going on one in which some of the people got out of control and the police had to be called. It was an interesting time. It was pretty rare for athletes to be involved, but there were a few football players who were on the senate. That year, the student senate was trying to take away the incidental fees from athletics. And this is almost humorous: I think the students gave $100,000 to incidental fees, but had that not gone to athletics, it would have really hurt athletics because of how low the budget was back then. So I ran for senator and won, was an active participant. We had no Phil Knight to support athletics. Before him there were guys who were amazingly solid all the time, but now with what Phil gives, it just changes the landscape of everything.

I also joined a fraternity, Phi Delta Theta, right across from the library. There were lots of football players in the house, and some great lifelong friends. Dave Walker, Keith Sherman, Jack Rust. I wasn't a real crazy guy. I was more sort of a quiet guy, but there were some crazy things that took place. I just lived in the house for two terms and then moved away. One of the funniest guys ever was a guy named Mike Kish, who went on and did some standup comedy and became an investigator for the D.A.'s office. We just had a ball. When I moved out of the house, I lived with Rust and Kish for a term of my sophomore year. My junior year, I lived with Rust and Kish and Dave Walker and another Phi Delta who wasn't a football player, and Mike Johnson, who was a football player. It was his dad's rental house at 22nd and Kincaid. Then my senior year I lived with Donnie Frease, who was a defensive back from San Jose and had been Jim Plunkett's receiver in high school. Donnie was a great guy.

I had a really good freshman year. I used to enjoy having the chance to go down and run with the varsity. They had a cornerback named Jimmy Smith who was a first-team All-American and a first-round draft pick, and I used to go against him from time to time, and that was really fun. I had a pretty significant year my freshman year. I guess my m.o. when I was a player was that I was always in the best shape of anybody. I was a real steady guy. I always did extra work, and I was here in the summer working out.

Prior to my sophomore year, I was picked as one of the five best incoming sophomores in the United States. That was a *Sports Illustrated* preseason deal.

63

And then I proceeded to tear ligaments in my ankle on the first play at Colorado when I was a sophomore, so I missed five games. I came back at the end of the season and ended up catching about 20 balls, but it was a disappointing year.

I'll never forget Dan Fouts' first pass in 1970, up in Portland at Civic Stadium. He came in after Tom Blanchard had hurt his knee tripping over a seam in the artificial grass, and the first play they called a streak to me. I was able to get wide open, as I generally was. But it was a night game and it was played on a baseball field, so the lights were not in the right place. I turned to look back at the ball and couldn't find it because of the lights. I'm wide open, and the ball hits me right between the numbers, and I dropped it. I couldn't see it. So I dropped the first pass Fouts threw, and I have heard about that forever. And, honestly, I don't know if I dropped another pass or two my whole career, because I was known for having great hands. So that always bugged me a little bit. I went on to catch 10 balls for 175 yards or something and I had two touchdown catches, and we won the game by a touchdown. Of course, that drop becomes infamous, because Fouts went on to be one of the greatest quarterbacks ever, and it's such a great story. This tall, skinny kid from San Francisco comes in and just uncorks one, which I drop. So I guess even if things are pretty good, you can be humbled.

64

I always had great confidence in myself, and I thought I could do just about anything, that there weren't many limitations. But I could clearly look at Ahmad Rashad and know that he had physical skills beyond what I had. He could throw the football 70 yards down the field. If it had been 20 years later, he might have been a quarterback. He could do everything. His sophomore year, he had a marvelous year as a wide receiver, but he was so good, and there were other good wide receivers, that they put him at tailback. He was unstoppable, which allowed Leland Glass to move to wide receiver and get more athletes on the field. Ahmad was unstoppable at tailback. He could have been a linebacker, a safety, a corner, he just had it all.

I played with some of the greatest players who ever played at Oregon. Ahmad Rashad, he and Mel Renfro were two of the greatest football players to ever come out of U of O. Tom Graham was a great middle linebacker. He didn't have good eyesight, and so it was remarkable how well he played without good eyesight. Great athlete, huge guy. He weighed about 240 pounds and he could run like a deer. I believe we had 12 guys that went on to play in the NFL over a three-year period. We didn't have great depth, and we were better on offense than we were on defense, and part of the reason was there were no scholarship limitations back then, and so you could go about five deep and stack players like cords of wood, and USC and UCLA would do that. They would take guys so that they couldn't go somewhere else, and leave us only one or two deep. My good friend Dave Walker, who started for three years for the Ducks, he probably would have never had that opportunity at a place like USC. His engine ran hard all the time, and he just played like crazy, but he wasn't going to dominate many guys with his size. He just did it with big heart.

We finished tied for second my senior year, which I think is about as high as the Ducks finished for a long stretch, and there was no bowl to go to because there was only one bowl, the Rose Bowl. That year it was Stanford, and they had only lost a couple. We played Stanford midseason, and they beat us by two or three touchdowns. We ended up 6–4–1. We beat USC. We beat UCLA. We beat Air Force, who was undefeated at the time. We lost to Washington by two points, and had a bunch of turnovers. It was a horrible Washington team; we never should have lost to them. The Beavers beat us. They just wanted it more, and beat us, which happened for about eight years straight during that era.

65

I caught a long ball against USC that took us down to the 3-yard line, a catch that set up our only touchdown in a game we won 10–7. I caught 11 passes against Air Force for 170 yards or so, which was a big win, and that was a game that came during a stretch when Bobby Moore [Ahmad Rashad] was suspended for a couple games that year. That was a big aerial matchup because there was a kid named Ernie Jennings from Air Force, and he and I were kind of neck and neck among the top receivers in the country, and I kind of won, so that was pretty fun. I had a big game against Illinois where I ended up with 225 yards, which was a school record for a long time, and in that game Blanchard and I hooked up on the longest touchdown pass in school history, 95 yards, which was a big deal. That's still a record at Oregon, although I expect it will be broken one of these days.

Bob Newland graduated as Oregon's career leader in receptions (125), receiving yardage (1,941), and receiving touchdowns (13). He led the Pac-8 Conference with 67 receptions for 1,123 yards in 1970 and was voted the Ducks' team MVP. Newland was a seventh-round NFL Draft choice in 1971 and played five professional seasons. He now lives and works in Eugene.

KEN WOODY

PLACE-KICKER/DEFENSIVE BACK

1968–1970

MY EXPERIENCE COMING OUT OF ROOSEVELT HIGH SCHOOL in Seattle wasn't like most guys' experiences because I wasn't initially offered a scholarship. Bruce Snyder was recruiting me for Oregon and it was always, "You're going to come down on your own and pay your own way." But I felt like they wanted me. I was a football coach for many years afterward, and I know the power of a letter from a big-time team showing interest, what it can mean to a guy who's not quite recruitable.

I was originally attracted to Oregon for three things. One, they had cool unis. I loved the uniforms. And they had little guys on their team. Cleveland Jones, who was from Portland, I think he was only 5′6″. I was only about 5′9″, and I said, "Hey, little guys can go there." Coaches hate that, because every little guy wants to come to your school. And third, they also had a very good journalism school. So those things sealed it for me, and I came down in 1966.

I spent that first fall on the scout team. Back then, the guys on scholarship also had jobs, and Dane Smith, this linebacker from Medford, would tape ankles before practice. I came in for my first day of practice, and here was this guy who looked like he was 28 years old. He had two days of beard growth. He was married with two kids, taping ankles, and he was going to be the linebacker tackling me in running back drills. It was a rude awakening.

The freshman coach back then was Norm Chapman. We played Oregon State twice that year, and Norm just hated those guys. We played the first game up in Corvallis, losing 3–0. Norm was walking around at halftime, smoking a cigarette, saying, "Tom Blanchard, you're an All-American? Horse shit! Andy Maurer, you're an All-American? Horse shit!" Then he takes a drag off his cigarette, jumps onto the taping table and screams, "I hate these people!" I was so fired up. We had to punt right after that, and I was on the punt team. The Oregon State guy called a fair catch, and I just went in and leveled him, and there's, like, four penalty flags hitting me. I remember getting off the field, and Norm said, "Great hit, great hit." Obviously getting late hits against Oregon State was okay in his book.

The second time we played the Beavers that year was at Hayward Field. I didn't start that day, and the reason they didn't start me is because they had a scholarship guy they had to start. But I ended up coming in and playing in the second quarter, and playing most of the game after that. I got a field goal that helped us win the game. After the kick I came off the field, and Norm Chapman came up and hugged me, and that hug meant more to me than anything. It was like I was one of the guys, and coming from a coach that we idolized meant even more.

The next year I redshirted, which wasn't unusual in those days. For most guys, however, it was because the coaches saw promise in them. For me, it was because I wasn't good enough to play yet. But I ended up kicking the next three years. They gave me a half-scholarship after the 1968 season, and a full ride after the 1969 season.

67

There were some really good times. Beating the Huskies 3–0 in '68 was great. Kicking a field goal to help beat 'SC 10–7 in 1970 was great, and I had an onside kick against UCLA when we beat them that same year. And there were other times when I was booed by about 34,000 people at home, including my mother. When we played Washington State my senior year, I missed two extra points and two field goals. The more intense I was, the worse I did. I never drank during the season. Maybe I should have. I think it would have helped me.

That Husky game was particularly satisfying just because I'm from Seattle, and they should have recruited me. I was all-city running back, and if they had done just the same thing that Bruce Snyder had done—sending some letters showing interest in me as a walk-on—I would have gone to Washington. I'm proud to say that I played them four times and I personally outscored them three out of four of those games. My freshman year, I blocked a kick and got a field goal. My sophomore year, I got the field goal to win it 3–0. My junior year, I got three field goals, and they only scored a touchdown. But my last year I had a field goal blocked, and they won that one 25–23. That kind of hurt.

The week that we played the Huskies, I could never sleep. I would just tremble in bed, I hated them so much. I wanted to prove them wrong. The Huskies were not very good the first two years, and we kind of took advantage of that. The first year, 1968, we played in Seattle and we had trouble getting there. Our plane got screwed up, so we had to take a bus to Portland and then fly into Seattle. Husky Stadium had no lights for our walk-through, just a car in the east end zone with its headlights on. The Huskies provided shoes for us that first night because our stuff hadn't arrived yet. We were out there in the dark, running around, doing drills, and just going, "This is big time football?"

The next day, it was just miserable weather. It was still scoreless in the fourth quarter, and we got down there, and I tried a field goal. It was wide. But this guy, Otis Washington of UW, came in and, as he went by, he threw his elbow and smacked me right in the jaw. I remember falling over and looking at the official, and he threw a penalty flag for roughing the kicker. So we got a couple more plays, and I got another chance. I got what was, at that time, a school-record 42-yard field goal. Now everybody looks back and says, "Great kick, you won the game." But they forget, too, that Washington got the ball first-and-goal from the 2-yard line and couldn't score in four plays. The fourth-down play, they had a tight end wide open and overthrew him just a little bit. So our defense played a huge part in that game, obviously. But I got carried off the field after the game, which was thrilling.

And it was even better because I worked for the *Seattle Post-Intelligencer* newspaper in the summer as a sportswriter. The Monday after the game, one of the guys from the paper asked Washington's coach, Jim Owens, "Coach, did you ever think you'd get beat by a sportswriter?" So they had some fun with that.

The next year, against USC, we had planned to throw it about 70 times. But as I remember, there were a couple interceptions early on, and so we started running the heck out of it. Bobby Moore went for 168 yards that day. We started out by kicking off to USC, so they went on offense first. Our nose guard was Dave Walker, who was about 5'6". The coaches told him to play two yards off the ball so he could read the plays at the snap. But it was boom, boom, boom, like the Germans through Poland. The Trojans took up

Ken Woody provided versatility for the Ducks as a player and later was involved with the team as both an assistant coach and television analyst.

about half the first quarter driving down the field, and scored a touchdown. Walker said, "Screw this." He got up on the center's nose and after they scored the first time they never scored again, largely because of him adapting to what needed to be done.

In the third quarter, it was still 7–0, and Jerry Frei sent me out to attempt a field goal. We had this guy, Jack Stambaugh, who was about the meanest, toughest guy on the team. Huge guy. We were down at the 5-yard line, I ran out there, and the fans were booing. Maybe it was me, or maybe they just wanted them to go for the touchdown. Anyway, Stambaugh was in the huddle, and he turned around and looked at me, and said, "Oh, great." And I said, "Hey, I didn't come out here on my own." My buddy Denny Schuler was on that team, and he will swear today that the team wanted to punt from the 5. Anyway, it worked out, and we got the field goal.

After that play, the coaches told me not to kick it deep on the kickoff. But honestly, I could never tell where it was going to go on the kickoff. And sure enough, it went deep. I'll never forget, I kicked it and started running down the field like a mad man, thinking I was going to torpedo somebody. And right when the USC guy caught it, the rest of them looked up the field, and it was like they were looking right at me. Boom! I got run over by Sam Cunningham and the 'SC wedge. George Seifert was the coach in the press box, and he said, "Tell Woody I'm going to kill him. I say don't kick it deep, he kicks it deep." I was just trying hard.

I suppose I had a habit of that. My first few years, I got into games as a defensive back every once in a while—knocked a pass away against Washington State and made several tackles on kickoffs. On the kickoff team they originally wanted me to be a safety, but I couldn't contain myself, I'd just run in there. I was once leveled by this guy from Air Force. It's funny how things happen in slow motion. He hit me, and I remember flying head over heels, seeing the sky, and then the scoreboard, and then the grass, and then the scoreboard again. As I was laying on the grass, the guy looked over and he said, "Are you okay?" and I said, "Yeah, I'm great!" And he walked away, saying, "Man, this guy must be stoned." That kind of thing didn't happen as much once I was kicking full-time, but it sure happened that day against USC. We went on to win that game when Bobby Moore scored in the fourth quarter.

For every highlight I remember, there were also some funny moments, and some tough ones. When I was a sophomore, there was a day we were working on our kickoff return. I was the kicker, and I was thinking that I'd just whip it down the field. I came in for my approach, and it was like hitting a golf ball fat. I hit probably a foot behind the ball, and this cloud of dust came up, and the ball dribbled out. The kickoff coverage team went by, and the ball was still back there. Max Coley was a coach then, he said, "Damn it, Woody, I didn't want an onside kick." I just said, "Oh, sorry," and played along.

Any time I didn't have a great game, the next Monday there'd be, like, 10 guys out there trying out to take my job, and maybe I was lucky that there weren't a lot of other good kickers around. But my coach, Jerry Frei, stuck with me. And that influenced me, both as a teacher and a coach, for the rest of my life.

Ken Woody is a former Fox Sports football commentator who played defensive back, receiver, and kicker for the Ducks. He coached college football for 18 years, including stints as an assistant coach at Oregon, Washington, Washington State, and Utah State, and was head coach at Whitman College and Washington University–St. Louis. He resides in Eugene and contributes analysis on Oregon football to the *Register-Guard* newspaper.

The SEVENTIES

BOBBY MOORE

[AHMAD RASHAD]
RUNNING BACK

1969–1971

T HE TWO SCHOOLS I PICKED BETWEEN were Notre Dame and Oregon, and people just couldn't believe I had put those two schools in the same category. It was like, "You've got a chance to go to Notre Dame and you're going to Oregon?" But I had always liked the Oregon Ducks since I was a kid growing up. I liked their uniforms, I loved the Duck, I loved Bob Berry, I loved the whole thing, and that's why I wanted to go to school there. When I finally met the coach, Jerry Frei, I was set that Oregon was where I was going. I was going to be a Duck. I confirmed my Duckhood right there when I met Jerry Frei.

I grew up in Tacoma, Washington, so I got some exposure to the Ducks on television. I remember watching Bob Berry and Mel Renfro and those guys. I never went to a game, but I saw them on television. Notre Dame probably had television shows across the country, which helps explain the interest in them. There was also the University of Washington; they had gone to the Rose Bowl a couple times when I was growing up, and people always thought that was the natural place for me to go to school.

But I just liked the fact that Oregon was a place where you could really grow as a person. It wasn't all about football. Football was important, but it was a very socially explosive time in life, and Oregon was right on the pulse of that. That was something I wanted to explore. When I got down to Eugene, they didn't have a special dorm for the football players. I liked that. I just believed that going to college was an experience you were supposed to enjoy from every single aspect, not only athletically, but also from the scholarly aspect.

Growing up, sports were always what I did after school. I enjoyed school as much as I did sports, and I enjoyed socializing and all that stuff. Sports just weren't so important that it took up 24 hours of your day. It took up two hours, during practice in the afternoon, and then you had 22 hours to figure out something else to do. I was one of those guys who had other interests. And once I got to Oregon, Jerry Frei was a guy where, if you felt strongly about something, and maybe it conflicted with practice one time or something, but you felt very strongly about it, you could go. Jerry Frei was one of the biggest influences in my life to date, and at that point he was one of the most influential people I had ever met. He was a man committed to not only turning out excellent athletes but also turning out excellent people.

I went to Oregon during the Vietnam War. I seem to recall that there was a chemical company on campus that made napalm, and there was quite a protest, which I attended. Staying socially engaged was just important to me, in terms of never taking yourself out of society. Even though we were football players, you're still a part of society. There were a lot of places that didn't appreciate any of that. You went somewhere and you were a football player. You lived in a dorm, you ate with the football players, you took all the classes football players took. We didn't do that at Oregon.

73

When I first got to campus, there were more dogs and Frisbees than I had ever seen. There were dogs running all through the student union. I have three dogs now, so that was cool with me. It was just a really cool place. A lot of so-called hippies, sure. It was a really free-spirited place, you know? It was the Berkeley of the Northwest. I don't know if that was necessarily exactly what I was looking for, but I liked where I was. You never know what you're looking for, but that sort of fit at the time. I needed a well-rounded experience, and I certainly got that.

We had a pretty amazing freshman class in 1968. Leland Glass was on that team, and there was another running back named Davey Jones. And we had Tom Graham, who was one of the greatest defensive players to ever play. Tom Graham is one of the greatest players ever. He was so good. In my whole career, he was as dominant as any player I've ever played with, even professionally. Tom made tackles from sideline to sideline. He was our heart and soul. He was something.

Athletically I think we were a pretty advanced class, so it was a shame that we had to play freshman football because there were a lot of us who were every bit as good as the varsity. There was an excitement about what kind of potential we had. It was like we were rebuilding, we were going to do something at Oregon, put them on the map. We had a great freshman class, a lot of great players, and we couldn't wait to play. We used to scrimmage against the varsity all the time, and we'd beat them. We couldn't wait.

Jerry Frei was the most important guy to my development. Norm Chapman was pretty inspirational also, and Phil McHugh. Just great guys, great coaches. Frei had one of the greatest coaching staffs ever, if you look at all the guys who went on to become pro coaches. George Seifert was my freshman coach. He was tough, man, really tough, a great coach, though, but he was a tough guy. He was the toughest guy I think I'd ever seen at that point. Coming out of high school I'd never seen anything quite like that. I was fortunate to play for some great guys. I had a great coaching influence at that time.

I played receiver my sophomore season, in 1969. I had 15 touchdowns, and I remember thinking it felt easy. I was having a good time playing out there. I had three touchdowns against Utah, which had never been done before at Oregon. The quarterback was Tom Blanchard, who was a great player, and Bob Newland was another great receiver. At Oregon we always knew we could score points. We always knew we could put up 30 points, but we also knew that the other team could put up 35. You had to outscore us to beat us, so we were pretty cocky offensively. We rolled in thinking, *We don't care whom we're playing, we're going to put some points on the board*. That was kind of our attitude, and that's the way it was for three years.

I moved to running back in 1970, which wasn't necessarily a natural position for me. But I was okay with it. The move was made so we could get other talented guys on the field, and Jerry Frei was such a great guy, he said, "We've got some other guys that we'd like to play. We can put you at running back and still get you the ball a bunch, and that way we can have Leland Glass come out and play. And that will make us stronger as a team." I thought it was fine, if we were going to be stronger as a team, and running back was kind of cool. I had played it in high school. I remember my first couple games I wasn't very good at it, and Jerry came to me and told me if I wanted, he'd

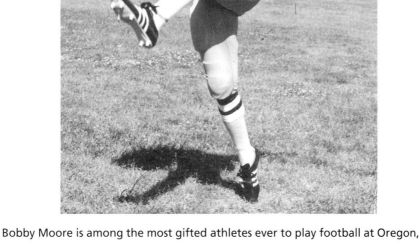

Bobby Moore is among the most gifted athletes ever to play football at Oregon, and he was a star in the NFL as Ahmad Rashad.

move me back to wide receiver. I just said, "No, I'll stick with this," and I got it down pretty much after that.

Blanchard was still playing quarterback at that point, but then Blanchard got hurt, and Dan Fouts came in and just blew them away, man.

Both of them played in that miraculous comeback against UCLA in 1970. I was friends with a lot of guys at UCLA, including a couple of the basketball players, Sidney Wicks and Curtis Rowe. And they all left the game before it was over. The place was almost empty by the time we won, because we scored all those points in a hurry. But that has to be one of the best comebacks of all time. I remember Leland Glass making a huge play. We needed a first down, and he caught a ball, a simultaneous catch to keep the drive alive. I had two touchdowns in the fourth quarter. On one of them, I caught a pass in the flat, and I think about three guys thought they had me tackled, but I sort of spun out and jogged in for the touchdown. That might have been one of the coolest plays I've ever been involved in.

I scored a touchdown to beat USC that season. USC was like the pride of our conference. Really, every game we went into we were the underdogs. Idaho I guess we weren't. But every other game, we had to wear our hearts right on our sleeve. We had to play well or else get killed. We had a lot of 215-pound linemen that were up there trying to block 260-pounders at USC, so we took a lot of pride in being Oregon, and having an attitude about us, that we were every bit as good athletically as the other guys. That was kind of the way we saw that.

We also tied Army that year, when I ran for a late touchdown and then also the two-point conversion. Bobby Knight was coaching basketball at Army then, and he still comes up to me to this day and says, "I was on the sideline that day, and that might have been the single greatest play I've ever seen." I think I ran through everybody on the team. It was just a play straight up the middle, and I must have run through nine guys. And then, to tie the game, they ended up giving me the ball for the two-point conversion. It was like, *Jesus, I'm about to die here!*

Senior year, we had one of the hardest schedules in the country. As I recall, Nebraska was No. 1, Texas was No. 2, Stanford was No. 4. There was probably somebody else in the top four or five teams.

No matter who we played, we still felt like we could score, and I felt like I could run the ball. Jim Figoni was the center, and he was really a small guy, didn't weigh much, but he was really good technically. He never missed blocks, one of those kind of guys. Tim Stokes was a tackle, Tom Drougas was another tackle. John McKean was one of the guards. It was a good group to run behind.

I was hurt for that last Civil War. I got a thigh bruise a week earlier, and I spent the whole week at the infirmary trying to get my thigh to loosen up, but I just couldn't run. To not be able to play in that game was really one of the biggest disappointments in my athletic career. It still bugs me that I was never able to beat Oregon State. That was the toughest thing for me. But, man, those guys, I've never been keyed on any more in my life, I'm telling you. They used to just beat me up something terrible. Whatever our differences were, Oregon and Oregon State, they took it out on me. They were a pretty conservative bunch, and I was the most liberal guy at a liberal school, I guess.

I think not beating Oregon State probably put a lot of pressure on Jerry Frei, because that Civil War game became kind of a watermark at Oregon. From what I understood, they asked him to fire some of his assistants and he wouldn't, so they fired him. That's the kind of man he was. He was a great coach.

It's one of the most important things in my life, having been a Duck. They call me "Big Duck." To all my friends, I'm "Big Duck." I look back at my years at Oregon with a tremendous amount of pride and respect, and there is a fraternity among all of us who played at Oregon, that once you're in the family, you're always in the family. Phil Knight and I talk all the time about the Ducks. I come out every year to go to a basketball game or a football game. It's just what college should be. It's what college is all about, and I don't think anybody can look back at their college career at any school and be more respectful and proud than I am about my university.

Bobby Moore, now Ahmad Rashad, left Oregon with school rushing records for yardage in a game (249), a season (1,211), and a career (2,306), and for receptions in a season (54) and a career (131). He was a three-time first-team all-conference pick, a two-time team MVP, and a 1971 All-American. Moore was invited to the East-West Shrine Game, the Hula Bowl, and College All-Star Game after his senior season and was the number-four overall pick in the 1972 NFL Draft. He played in four Pro Bowls and a Super Bowl during his 10-year NFL career. He was inducted into the College Football Hall of Fame in 2007.

TOM GRAHAM

LINEBACKER

1969–1971

INITIALLY I WASN'T EVEN GOING TO PLAY FOOTBALL in college. I was going to play baseball. The Los Angeles Dodgers had drafted me out of high school. But Oregon was appealing to me, which was an odd circumstance. I grew up in a housing project, and my mom bought a set of encyclopedias from these two nuns that went door-to-door. I think she paid 25 cents a month for them. She might still be paying them off! I took those encyclopedias and I think I read every one, and what fascinated me the most was reading about all the different states. And when I came to Oregon, I just loved reading about the outdoors, the rivers and trees and mountains.

Coincidentally, my football coach had sent out a few letters to different schools, one of them being Oregon. And he told me that he got a response back from Oregon and that I could go play football, and they would let me play baseball as well. I figured if I could go up there and play football and baseball and be near the rivers—I just love to fish—that's the place I wanted to go. I don't think I even looked at any other offers. I don't even know if there were any other offers, to be honest. But I wanted to be a Duck.

I was a winter high school graduate and headed up to Eugene from California in early 1968. School ended in January, and spring quarter at Oregon began in March. Rick Akerman was another early high school graduate, and the coaches hooked us up to make the trip north together. My cousin took me over to meet him, and we headed off for Oregon in Rick's car. At one point, I looked over and saw that the gear shift was a three-speed on the column. Well, I didn't know how to drive a three-speed. I was scared to death to try, so I was hoping Rick would be able to drive 18 hours straight. After about three or four hours, he told me it was my turn, but I said I didn't know how to drive it. He said, "That's all right. There's not many cars out on the road right now." So he taught me how to drive a three-speed on my way to Oregon.

They didn't have spring ball at that time, so I just went out every day and watched the team work out. They had a separate team for freshmen, but even my freshman class hadn't come in yet, so even though I was on campus and they were playing, all I could do was watch. I couldn't participate yet. Rick and I were the only two on campus from our class.

It was a strange time because I was 17 years old, hadn't even turned 18 yet. In those days you had to register for the draft when you turned 18, and I didn't have a clue of what to do, so I went to my coach, Norm Chapman. Norm was the linebackers coach, and a great guy. He became a first father figure to me, along with Jerry Frei. Now, Norm had these beady eyes, and back then it was no big deal to smoke. So Norm was smoking, and he said, "You don't want to go to war, do you?" And I told him, "No, coach, I don't want to go to Vietnam." And he said, "Will you go to war for me, if I keep you out of Vietnam?" I said, "Yeah, coach, I will." He gave me this name of a guy down at the recruiting station, and I went down to see this guy. They had all these guys lined up in their underwear, getting examined and whatnot. I was sitting there with this note, and I told them I was supposed to find this guy Norm knew. Some of the guys looked at me and said, "Oh, you're Norm's boy." I found the right guy, he wrote something on a piece of paper and said, "Okay, get going," and that was it. I didn't get sent off to Vietnam.

There were three black players on the team at that time. That was Claxton Welch, Stan Hearn, and Dave Roberson. Well, maybe three and a half. There was Warner Wong, who was Hawaiian, but he was darker than Claxton or Stan, so we figured he was black too. But that was it during that first spring I was in Eugene. In the fall, when my class came in, I think the African American population in Oregon increased by 400 percent. But I didn't have a problem with that. The high school I went to had about the same level of diversity, and that wasn't an issue for me.

Well, I should say it wasn't an issue in football. My first fall, I made a decision whether I was going to be a football player or a baseball player. And that's

Tom Graham set records for tackles at Oregon that may never be broken before moving on to a 10-year NFL career.

80

where diversity did come into play. I was the only black baseball player who was there, while on the football team there was 20 or 25 guys, and so it became a social decision. These were the guys I hung out with, went to class with, and so I kind of evolved from playing baseball as well as football into just being a football player.

On the football field, I didn't find the adjustment from high school to college that difficult. It just seemed like playing on an all-star team. We weren't playing with the varsity. Guys today go into college and a lot of them think they're ready to go against players 21 or 22 years old. And maybe some are. But we didn't have to face that. It was no big deal. It was like an all-star game with a bunch of guys your own age.

We played Washington, Washington State, and Oregon State twice that first season. And that was when it started to get built into your head that you just hated the Beavers. I didn't understand that at the time. You had to become a varsity player there, I think, to really understand that passion—unless you grew up in-state, of course.

I started playing right from the start in 1969, and I remember it well because our first game was against Utah at their place. And that's when I first learned about altitude. The coaches tried to tell us and prepare us for the fact that the air is thin. I tell you what, either we didn't listen or they didn't prepare us well enough. You thought you were going to die out there. You could not breathe. But we won, and Bobby Moore got Pac-8 player of the week offensively and I got it defensively. It was quite an introduction.

The thing that made the greatest impression on me early on was how amazing an athlete Bobby Moore was. That was the thing that stood out to me. The year was a blur. You're still learning your way. The other game that stands out is Oregon State, which we lost. That was our season, and we were highly favored, and we lost. That was one you weren't supposed to lose. That's when I started to get a better grasp on the significance of the rivalry. They called it the Civil War, and there really was this imaginary line between us and them, and they did not have the athletes or the squad we had, but they beat us, and they beat us again and again.

81

I guess the only consolation I have about it is I ended up playing in the NFL with a lot of USC guys, and they never beat us. It was something, because we always got up for those big games, but then some games we should have won we didn't. I remember the games against Sonny Sixkiller, Jim Plunkett, the games against USC and those guys. Those were big. And we won our share, and we lost too many. Then again, we went in and beat UCLA on that great comeback in 1970. We had Dan Fouts and Bobby Moore at that point. We felt like we could beat anybody with those two guys. Personally, I don't think I learned the game of football until I got out of the game of football, and it was one of those things where if I could go back and play, I think I could have been a really good ballplayer!

My last game as a Duck, the Civil War of 1971, I was credited with 41 tackles. I know that seems outlandish, but I had the bruises to prove it. Dave Schilling was the running back for Oregon State, and I recall just continually running into that guy. At that point I was just a little bit quicker than their offensive line. They ran the triple option, but you knew Schilling was going to get the ball more times than not, so I just said, "Hey, I'm heading for you." As a linebacker, it was fun playing a running team, and I made a lot of tackles, but it was disappointing because evidently I didn't make enough of them on the other side of the line. They beat us 30–29.

I tell you how important it was to me, my experience in Eugene—I tried to get my twin sons to go there. But I was undone in part by my last college roommate, Jim Anderson, who was one of our fullbacks. Jim, if you can believe it, had become a Husky booster. I have to tell on him, because he was my competition when I was trying to convince my boys, Daniel and Joshua, to go to Oregon. He's telling my twins, "You don't want to go there. It's just a bunch of hippies, just like when your Dad and I went there." I'm trying my best to tell them that Jim doesn't know what he's talking about. On our 25th wedding anniversary, my wife and I scheduled a visit to Eugene. It was a trip down memory lane for us, but we also brought our twins because it was their senior year of high school, and I wanted them to come to Oregon and play football.

We went up to Seattle first and spent some time with Jim, and then drove down to Eugene. While we were up in Seattle, Jim was telling the boys to come up to Washington. I was like, "Jim. You are nuts. What has happened to you?" Jim and I were getting into it over this. Then we went down to Eugene, and I had scheduled a reunion with some of the guys at a pizza place. They told me the address, and we were trying to find this place, but I was having trouble. We saw these two people standing on a corner, and so I pulled up next to them to ask for some directions. Immediately they were like, "Ohh, duuude, you're lost!" And the other guy said, "Oh, here, dude, here's where you go." They started going back and forth: "No, dude, this is what you do…No, dude…Here, dude." It was unbelievable—exactly the picture of Eugene that Jim had given the boys. I looked in the rearview mirror, and my twins were looking at each other like, "What is this?" And that's when I knew I'd lost them.

Daniel went on and played at Colorado, which was Oregon's opponent in the Fiesta Bowl in 2002. Here was the deal on that one. I let it be known— I told him it was nothing personal, but if he lost, I wasn't going to feel sorry for him. Don't come to me for consolation if you lost, because I'm a Duck, and he knows that once a Duck always a Duck. I don't compromise that allegiance for nothing or nobody. I am very proud to have been a Duck. When I see people here in Colorado with the green and yellow on, I make sure to stop and talk with them. If I see an Oregon license plate, I pull up to them and ask them, "Duck or Beaver?" And if they tell me Beaver, I don't even say anything. I just roll up the window.

Tom Graham still holds Oregon records for tackles in a career (433), season (206), and game (41). Graham was a first-team All-Pac-8 selection in 1970 and was a fourth-round draft pick of the Denver Broncos in 1972. Graham played seven seasons in the NFL and still lives in Colorado.

TOM DROUGAS

OFFENSIVE LINE

1969–1971

THERE WAS DEFINITELY A FAMILY HISTORY that contributed to me playing at Oregon. My father played a little football for the Ducks before he went to World War II. He wasn't able to continue as a result of his injuries from the war, but a number of his friends did, guys he stayed very good friends with throughout his life. So the Oregon football tradition was always a part of my youth.

I guess I never really contemplated playing for the Beavers or anything like that. For a while I was thinking maybe Ivy League or something, but they didn't have the financial aid programs I needed. I also had an early adolescent experience where I ended up going to summer coaching camps down in Eugene. Len Casanova had a summer coaching camp for kids, so I went down there and had an opportunity to hang around the athletic department—Mac Court and Hayward Field—and spend time with these coaches, people like Jerry Frei, Phil McHugh, and John Robinson. So there was also this little taste of it that gave me a feeling for it, since I hadn't grown up in Eugene.

It took me two years to get on the field. I played with the freshman team in 1967, and then sat out in 1968 as a redshirt. It was a pretty interesting time, because, besides just trying to get a handle on the normal freshman experience of getting on your own, there was also a cultural revolution going on. There was the election of Richard Nixon, the year Bobby Kennedy and MLK were assassinated, and Vietnam. I just remember it was so full of tension.

It was mind-expanding, discovering that there was a big world out there. Football still had a very big place in my life, though. I was very focused on it.

And academics were important to me, as well. The toughest thing was the schedule, getting the classes you wanted to fit your schedule. I just worked that around. As it turned out, I ended up getting my major because of a scheduling conflict. I just needed a class to fill out my schedule, and I ended up taking this class called Comparative Religions 101, which was just a world religions course, and I ended up taking the whole series through the year. I was so intellectually inspired by it that I ended up majoring in religious studies. I just found it so fascinating and engaging. I really enjoyed the academic part of it. It wasn't a drudgery in any way.

My freshman football coach was George Seifert, and he was definitely a huge influence as my first-year coach. I was still growing into my body the first couple years of college, so they saw good reason to let me continue to mature for another year. That's why I redshirted. Once I actually started playing in games, besides Jerry Frei, who was a great mentor, John Robinson was certainly an inspirational guy. I took a lot of inspiration from him.

My first offensive line coach was Eddie Johns, and he was a unique character. He had a background of being a Marine drill sergeant. We ran an offense back then, which was kind of like an option-type offense, but it involved a blocking technique called the crab block, where we would actually be in a four-point stance, blocking like a Dungeness crab. The idea was that you'd be low to the ground, and get into guys' legs and hang them up. It was a bizarre kind of technique, and during training camp we used to do that after practice, doing wind sprints, going sideline-to-sideline at Autzen, on all fours, to develop the endurance in the shoulders. I have less-than-fond memories of that, and the motivational techniques of Eddie Johns being a drill sergeant. It was character-building.

Early on, I traded a starting position a little bit with a guy named Ralph Pettingell, but then I moved into being a starter more consistently. My college career kind of took off in my junior year, playing against teams like Nebraska or Cal with All-American players that I stood up well to. There was a guy named Larry Jacobson from Nebraska, and Sherman White from Cal. He was a heck of a player.

My junior year, 1971, Dick Enright joined the coaching staff, and the offense changed. We were no longer doing the crab block. It was kind of like evolution, the primate getting up from all fours. It was more compatible with

Tom Drougas was one of two first-round NFL Draft picks out of Oregon in 1972, along with Bobby Moore.

my 6'4" frame, I can tell you that. It allowed my athleticism to grow. As a drop-back pass blocker, you have to have good feet, and then all of a sudden I was able to match up with these better players.

We played well that year, too. We were in contention for a title. We lost to Stanford, but we came back and we were right in there for a Pac-10 championship. That was the year we beat USC in this game that was kind of a rain bowl at Autzen. It was unbelievably rainy, and we beat USC. I played well in that game. And, of course, that was the year that we had the amazing comeback in the Coliseum against UCLA, a three-touchdown comeback. Bobby Moore had an amazing game that day. Bobby, whom I was good friends with in school, was just such a game-changer. Every once in a while the ball would be in the air, and as a pass blocker you're supposed to say, "Well, I guess I can run down the field 60 yards and block for him," but there's a moment where you're just watching what happens. You couldn't help it, you had to watch Bobby try and make a play. I'd had enough experiences of knowing we could pull out a play, whether it was Tom Blanchard or Dan Fouts throwing the ball to Bobby. We had this guy out there that was in the same league as O.J. Simpson in Bobby Moore, where at any given moment something could happen that was great.

It seems like we had a couple others that we should have won. The two-point game with Washington was one that was definitely a big disappointment because we played really well that day. And I remember there was a play where there was a miscue on a hand-off to Bobby when we were down in the red zone getting ready to go ahead. It was just one of those things where you say, "Hey, this is the guy that's gotten us here," so you don't blame anybody. That play could have been a season-changer.

After my junior season, in spring, I was starting to hear that the NFL scouts were taking notice of my play. That honestly had never occurred to me prior to that. It just wasn't on my radar. I was going to school and had a family already. It was exciting, because I was still very much into playing the game. So at that point I really dedicated myself to training. I went on a big spring and summer weightlifting campaign working out at the YMCA in Eugene. I got into this routine with a couple of track guys, Neil Steinhauer and Mac Wilkins. Neil was the NCAA shot-put champion, and Mac won an Olympic medal in the discus. So I just started working out with these track guys that were just maniacs, and I gained about 20 pounds that spring—I went from about 235 to 255, eating nothing but one of those smorgasbord

87

restaurants that were all you can eat. I was just working out like a bandit and eating like crazy. I remember going into that season and feeling like I could dominate people, and that is kind of the way I felt most of the season. There were some days where I just thought, *Man this is a cake walk.* Sounds bad, I know, but it was the honest truth.

Tom Drougas was a first-team All-American in 1971, when he paved the way for Bobby Moore to lead the Pac-8 conference in rushing. In 1970 Drougas was an academic All-America choice. He was the 22nd player taken in the 1972 NFL Draft and played professionally for Baltimore, Denver, Kansas City, and Miami. He has worked in real estate in Sun Valley, Idaho, since 1975.

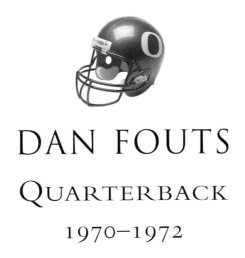

DAN FOUTS

QUARTERBACK

1970–1972

THE HIGH SCHOOL TEAM I PLAYED WITH in San Francisco had 11 guys who got college scholarships. So we were good, and that helped my adjustment to the college level. St. Ignatius is a Jesuit school, and very proud, and in San Francisco we had a pretty good reputation as being a bunch of tough guys. I think that background helped prepare me. It gave us an edge that comes from expecting to do well, and not just hoping. You are expected to perform at a high level by your coaches, and in return you expect it out of yourself.

I was kind of recruited by Cal and USC, but when the letters of intent came, there was just one, from Eugene, Oregon. I was part of a group of guys that were kind of recruited, but when the letters came out, that's all that was in my box. Jim Figoni was my center at Oregon, and he was on my high school team. He was a year ahead of me, and the Oregon coaches, Jerry Frei and John Robinson and George Seifert, were looking at our team the same weekend that they were playing Stanford down in the Bay Area. We were playing nearby in a title game, and I had a good game. That was my junior year, and I think I made an impression on the Oregon coaches that were there looking at our seniors. We had several guys that played in college football, like I said.

For whatever reason, though, we didn't have a great first year. The problem was, we didn't have many guys on scholarship, so we didn't have a very

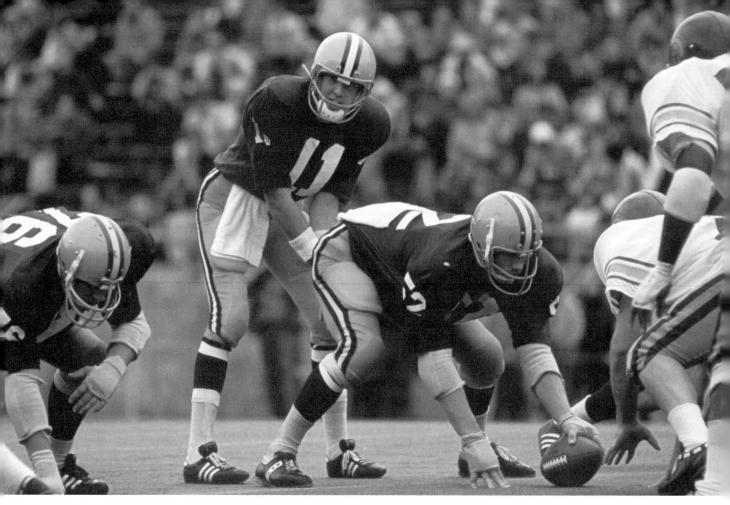

Dan Fouts was the first Oregon quarterback to surpass 2,000 passing yards, and he is one of a handful of Ducks in the Pro Football Hall of Fame. *Photo courtesy Getty Images.*

good team. It was a real lean year. The year before was an outstanding recruiting year. I don't know what the deal was with our class, but we were not a very good freshman team. We lost all our games.

That first year wasn't an easy time. You play four games against other freshman teams, and then you go and you're fodder for the varsity after your freshman season is over. I enjoyed the whole experience—I mean, I was playing ball in the Pac-8 and living the dream. I played against Sonny Sixkiller, and that was always a treat because he was always such a great player and a charismatic leader. That matchup was made especially compelling by the fact that he was from Oregon and going to Washington. I think the people of Oregon wanted him to go to Oregon. When he didn't, they were stuck with a guy from…where? California? That was me.

Still, I formed some strong bonds right off the bat. Harvey Winn was a great friend, and of course Ahmad Rashad [Bobby Moore], all the guys. We had a great group of guys I played with. I hate to name names because I don't want to leave anybody out.

My sophomore season, in 1970, I was the backup. I had competed for the job in the spring. Tom Blanchard was our quarterback, and he was really good. We had high hopes for that season. Our first game was against Cal up in Portland. One of the assistant coaches, John Robinson, was talking to our offense in a meeting before the game, and he said he was counting on everybody contributing in the game, and that everybody in the room was going to play except one guy. Everybody's looking around, and he said, "It's Fouts. He's not going to play, because Tom's going to play the whole game." And it was to boost Tom's confidence because he'd had some knee problems, and I guess it was to ease my mind. I wasn't expecting to play anyway, so that was fine with me. But then Tom trips over the turf in the second quarter, and I go in and play. We ended up coming from behind to win 31–24.

Tom was able to come right back the next week at Illinois, but his knee just didn't hold up. I finished that game, too, and then I started the next game, against Stanford at home. Playing Jim Plunkett and that great team that they had in 1970 was an experience. It was a hot day in Eugene, and we were on the artificial turf, and I remember we didn't have a marching band at the time, we had a rock band. They were in the stands with electric guitars and everything. They would have made Jimi Hendrix proud. I don't know why we had that instead of a normal marching band. That lasted until the rains came, of course, and you couldn't plug in the electric guitar. I think we had the lead at halftime, and then Plunkett came out and started running the option and killed us. I just remember getting beat up pretty good.

Two weeks later was the 41–40 comeback against UCLA. The biggest surprise of the day right up until the finish was my quarterback sneak from about 15 yards out in the first half. I got a block from the umpire and went in untouched. We went toe-to-toe with them, and then they wore us down and got a big lead. I scored on another quarterback sneak, and we were going for another when my buddy Figoni snapped the ball between my legs and I got knocked out looking for it.

Tom Blanchard came in and led us to two touchdowns, but then he separated his shoulder. Tom actually threw a pass to Leland Glass with a separated shoulder that was ruled a simultaneous catch down to the 5-yard line. The ironic thing about that was Leland got poked in the eye coming off the line of scrimmage, and said he saw two footballs coming at him. Luckily he caught the right one! So I went back in the game, and a couple plays later we hit Greg Specht for the winning touchdown. There was great drama in that game.

We beat 'SC that year too, 10–7, and that was pretty good. But the drama of coming from behind against UCLA with very little time and Tom getting hurt and playing great, and guys making plays, recovering onside kicks, that was hard to top. There were probably only about 40,000 people left in the Coliseum by the end, and the lasting memory is just the screams of disbelief as we were going off the field from the UCLA people. It was just wonderful.

It's funny what you remember, but it was raining cats and dogs for that USC game, and they had to bring a helicopter in to dry the field before the game. Just to see that was a little scary. And then 'SC comes out and goes 80 yards on the opening possession for a touchdown, and we're going, "Uh oh, here we go." It was an 'SC team that was one of the best in the nation, but Ahmad scored a touchdown to put us ahead in the fourth quarter, 10–7.

Bobby Moore, as Ahmad was known then, was about as fantastic an athlete as you could ever imagine. But I think what I came to respect more than his athletic ability was his toughness. People don't realize the pounding and sacrifice he made for us. He was an All-American wide receiver, and we needed a tailback so he took that responsibility and became an All-American running back. In those days, it was five yards and an Astroturf burn, so a position change like that was a lot to ask. But he took it on.

We played Army at the end of that year, and we were sleepwalking through the game. We should have beat Army pretty good, but they were a scrappy bunch, and we were behind by eight. Ahmad ran a blast play right up the middle, and he ran through the entire Army football team. Everybody on that team had a shot at him. He either bounced off, ran away, or stiff-armed every one of them. So he gets in the end zone from about 60 yards, and we still need two to tie. I threw him a little flat route, and he's got nothing left. But he gets it at about the 1- or 2-yard line and he's got just enough muscle and toughness and strength to break the plane and get the two-pointer. Back-to-back two of the most incredible plays I've ever seen.

The last game of 1970 was a loss to Oregon State, and the following season ended the same way. Partly because of that, Jerry Frei lost his job as head coach. That decision was brutal, absolutely brutal. I'll leave it at that. Jerry

Frei was one of the finest, classiest men I've ever met, running a program in which we had great pride.

Jerry's last game was a 30–29 loss against the Beavs. There was a fourth-down play, the last play for us on offense. I turned the wrong way and missed the hand-off and got tackled. I got to the sideline and I was close to tears. I just went up to him and told him I was sorry. And he said, "You're not the reason we lost. Don't you worry about it."

My last season, with Dick Enright as the head coach, was difficult, but I finally managed to get a win in the Civil War. The bad news was, I broke my foot in the game. We were up 30–3 at the 5-yard line going for more with about four minutes left. Sort of a questionable decision, when you look back on it. In reality, we pretty much won the game on the first play. Donnie Reynolds went right up the middle for about 60 yards, and it was 7–0. It was all over from there.

To this day, I'm a Duck, you know? People say, "You're a former Duck," and I say, "Nope, I'm a Duck." That may be a silly nickname, but to me it means a lot, because they took a chance on me. They gave me the opportunity. I think George Seifert was instrumental, because the Bay Area was his recruiting area. What a great coaching staff we had.

I look back on the recruiting process and at that time in my life, I was only 18, and I didn't even know where Eugene, Oregon, was. I grew up in San Francisco, but I was determined to give it a shot and play Pac-8 football. Oregon gave me a chance, and I never went back home. I went home for vacation breaks, but I never lived anywhere else but Oregon after that.

93

Dan Fouts was a first-team all-conference pick and Oregon's team MVP as a senior in 1972. He graduated as the first quarterback in school history to surpass 2,000 career passing yards. Fouts was invited to the East-West Shrine Game and was selected in the third round of the 1973 NFL Draft by the San Diego Chargers. After setting numerous NFL passing records and being named the league's MVP in 1982, he was inducted into the Pro Football Hall of Fame in 1993.

DON REYNOLDS
RUNNING BACK
1972–1974

COMING OUT OF HIGH SCHOOL IN CORVALLIS, I had a choice to make. Oregon recruited me as a baseball player, and Oregon State recruited me as a football player, but neither one of the schools recruited me to do both, which I thought I could do. I have to believe that, had Oregon State recruited me as both a baseball player and a football player, having grown up in Corvallis I would have had very little choice but to go to Oregon State and be a Beaver. That would have been unfortunate, but luckily they didn't do that. The baseball coach at Oregon back then was Mel Krause, and it was really Mel who encouraged me to go play football and walk on to the freshman team, even though I had signed as strictly a baseball player.

Oregon's excuse for not recruiting me in football was that I wasn't big enough, which I never believed. Well, my first year, freshmen still weren't eligible to play with the varsity, so I was playing with the best of the best as far as all the recruits were concerned. And I played both ways that year, so I was going against the first-team offense and the first-team defense every day in practice. I think one of the most memorable things was John Marshall singling me out after our third week of scrimmages or so and saying, "If any of you freshmen had the heart of this guy here, we would have the greatest team there was." That really inspired me.

When my sophomore year began, I was about fourth or fifth on the depth chart. One of the guys ahead of me had been on the freshman team with me, and I had played in front of him the whole time. But now he was ahead of me, which I didn't understand. It really upset me. I went to Mel Krause, the baseball coach, and said, "You know, I think this is probably the last year I'm going to play football. I did all I could as a freshman, and if I'm going to be behind these guys and have to start all over again, it's just not worth it."

I was determined to at least stick it out through the end of that year. We made it through training camp and were getting ready to go play at Missouri in the season opener. I found out later from Jesse Branch, who was the defensive backs coach then, that I almost didn't make the trip. Steve Sogge was the offensive coordinator and was going over the travel squad for the game during a meeting. Jesse said, "What about Reynolds? Are you taking him?" And Sogge said, "No, he's not good enough to be a running back for us." So, Jesse said, "Then I'll take him as a defensive back. He can be a defensive back tomorrow." And Sogge said, "Well, wait a second now…" The next day they took me to Missouri, and I played on special teams. Midway through the season I started at slot back against Washington State, and I had a long run for about 33 yards, which was the longest play we had from scrimmage. Dan Fouts was playing quarterback, and I dropped one of this passes that year. He never forgets to remind me that he would have had one more touchdown pass in his career if not for me.

95

Fouts had an amazing presence in the huddle. You hear about guys who are field generals, and that was Fouts. He was extremely in control, a dominating presence in the huddle. It was very impressive. There were some great players during my years at Oregon. Tom Graham and Leland Glass, Tom Drougas and Russ Francis, George Martin and Steve Donnelly. There were a lot of guys on that team, and I know I've left out many of them. We usually had a lot of good players at the skill positions, we just didn't have the depth, and the Pac-8 was good at the time. I think USC was No. 1 in the country my junior and senior year, so we played against some pretty good talent.

Like I said, I was playing slot back halfway through my sophomore year, and then I switched to tailback for good. They had another guy playing running back, but we couldn't get a rushing game going, and I was having some success whenever I touched the ball, so I guess they just figured it would be better if I was touching the ball more. Maurice Anderson had been playing tailback, and I was in the slot, and they just switched us, which turned out to be a pretty good move. The next game was against Stanford, and I had an 85-yard run, which was a record for a long time. It was an option run with

A talented two-sport athlete who also excelled on the baseball diamond, Don Reynolds was just the second Duck to run for 1,000 yards in a season.

Fouts to the short side of the field, running to our own sideline. Ron Hunt, a big tackle for us, was coming across, and I cut in front of him. I'm not a surfer, but I remember feeling like there was a wave of Stanford and Oregon guys up the field, and I was in the curl, cutting right through all of them. It was a surreal moment. I remember the Stanford coach saying he didn't know how I could do it, because they had some state sprinting champion on defense who couldn't catch me. I don't know, fear does a lot for you, I guess.

That was the most impressive Civil War for me, in 1972. I remember the ride up to Corvallis, on the bus. I always rode alone, and I remember this odd mix of people, some of them yelling at me, some of them saying hello. For two years Parker Stadium had been my home field in high school, but now I was coming in wearing a white Oregon uniform. It wasn't the first time I had come back, because I had come up the year before to play a freshman game, but this time it was with the varsity and the stadium was full. It was interesting, because I felt very self conscious. It was my home field, but yet I was coming in as the enemy.

The Beavers had some impressive guys at linebacker, Butch Wicks being the scariest. Butch Wicks I was mortally scared of because he was the kind of linebacker who would get low to the ground and deliver a blow. The first play from scrimmage was amazing. All we did was run a straight dive, and I hit the hole as quick as I could and popped through. I made a cut to avoid a linebacker, came upon a defensive back and gave him a little head fake, and then I was just running into the end zone. I remember all the Oregon fans just coming out of the end zone and just mobbing me. It happened so quickly and unexpectedly on such a basic play. There wasn't any trickery to it, just a straight dive play. A couple of my friends who were staunch Oregon State fans said they saw number 22 hit the hole and break free, and they started cheering because it was something they had done for so many years, until they realized, "Hey, that's Donnie, but he's in the wrong uniform!" That was always enjoyable. My friends from home were always pulling for me, but they didn't want to see the Ducks win.

Going into 1973 I was feeling fairly confident. I came into camp late because I was up in Alaska playing baseball. Our first game was against Arizona State, and we didn't beat them, but I rushed for 128 yards that game. I think they were ranked No. 4 in the nation at that time, so I felt like I got off to a good start. It was a night game, and pretty high-profile, and I had a pretty amazing game, and Rick Kane had a pretty amazing game, too. I liked and enjoyed sharing time with Rick Kane because it gave the team a good two-tailback system. Our styles were a little different because he was more of a power runner and a slasher, and I was more of a guy who kind of just darted and would break things. I didn't have a problem in all honesty sharing the football with him because it was about team. It was about going 115 miles per hour, and when I couldn't give any more, then he came in and gave that.

That was a great year, though it ended in pretty disappointing fashion, which I won't forget to this day. I had hurt my ankle up at Washington State with about a month left in the season. There was something about the turf there that was weird, and my ankle hit the ground and it just popped. After that, I could only play about half of each game before it would start hurting again. I was leading the conference in rushing by quite a bit, and then I couldn't go except for half games for the next three. Then, the last carry of my junior year, in the Civil War, I reached 1,000 rushing yards. After the carry, I hit the ground, and one of the Oregon State players grabbed my ankle and kept rolling over and trying to twist it, because he knew I was already hurt. I kept trying to roll with him as much as I could, but I couldn't keep up and finally it just gave, and it really hurt. I heard him jump up and say, "I got him, I got him!" That made me as mad and as angry as anything ever has in my life. You always think that somebody would want to compete against you without trying to hurt you, so that one hurt a lot, and not just physically, but emotionally. For somebody to hate you enough to really try and hurt you, I didn't get that. I was getting carried off the field, and I remember this because I saw a picture later, where I was crying because I was so upset. Not because of the pain but because I always thought sports were supposed to be honorable.

There's no easy way to say it, my last two years were pretty rough for the team. Both seasons, we went 2–9. I had a decent game against Air Force as a senior, and played with sore ribs against Utah. I ran for a bunch of yards against Northwestern even though I had turf toe. The injuries were tough, but I never stopped fighting. I was proud of that.

Academics were important to me, along with football. Playing two sports and trying to stay up on school work took some effort. One of the things I tried to do was really stay on top of the basics I needed to graduate. I tried to stay ahead. Going to high school in Corvallis prepared me for college I think more than I realized, because college was not that difficult. You have to take notes, attend class, and pay close attention to your professors to see what they're really trying to pass along. Being able to manage my time was a critical part, and I stayed on top of that pretty well.

By my last year, I was on my third head coach. My freshman year it was Jerry Frei, and then it was Dick Enright for two years, and then Don Read became head coach. With Frei, we ran kind of an 'SC offense, with the I formation and a passing game set up for Fouts, and then with Enright we tried to run the veer. There were a lot of different changes, and we really hadn't settled on anything consistent, so it made it a little difficult. I don't remember having a problem dealing with the different personalities. As far as coaching styles, it was certainly different dealing with Dick Enright going through what he was going through at the time, and then to Don Read, who was a real believer in fairness. He thought that all players were created equal, and it's not true, sad to say.

My biggest football influences were Jesse Branch, Fred von Appen, Joe Wade—the assistant coaches were who I ended up getting closer to. You dealt with the head coaches some, but the assistants were who you spent most of your time with. And I'm still close with a bunch of guys I played with. There was Bobby Green, who became a county commissioner in Eugene. I helped recruit Bobby, and I don't think he could put a sentence together in English back then. He was always saying how fast he was going to get out of Eugene once he got out of school, but I don't think he's left yet. I love Bobby. He was great. A lot of the memories I have there are of specific guys and of specific things we did. Being a baseball and football player, I probably spent a little less time with the football players because I switched over in the winter to baseball. But we would sometimes go over and play basketball at Mac Court after Dick Harter's guys came off the court. Those are good memories.

Don Reynolds became just the second player in Oregon history to surpass 1,000 rushing yards, following in the footsteps of Bobby Moore. In 1972 he was honored with the Len Casanova Award as the Ducks' top first-year player, and in 1973 teammates voted him Oregon's most valuable player. As a sophomore, Reynolds was awarded the Higdon Trophy, given to the top sophomore in all of Oregon athletics for achievements in athletics, scholarship, and citizenship, and as a senior he shared the Emerald Athletic Trophy as the athletic department's top senior under the same criteria.

STEVE GREATWOOD

OFFENSIVE LINE

1977–1979

AFTER I GOT DONE PLAYING AT CHURCHILL High School in Eugene, I did not have a lot of choices as far as playing in college. I probably would have been a Beaver if they had offered me the chance, quite honestly. When I was growing up in Portland, my best friend's big brother played at Oregon State, and I was pretty enamored of that. I was hearing from Oregon State a bunch, but then Craig Fertig took over for Dee Andros, and I never heard from them again. So it was pretty much the Ducks and Portland State after that. Don Read's wife was my home ec teacher at Churchill, and she was a great woman who had a lot of influence on me. I figured if he was married to her then he must be a pretty good guy, and I think deep down I wanted the challenge of playing at this level, so I became a Duck.

I'm still real close with a lot of the guys I came in with, and do stuff socially with them and their families. I hung out with Neil Elshire, Pat McDougall, Jeff Wood, and then later got to know younger guys like Ed Hagerty, Steve Baack, Greg Hogensen, and Greg Moser. Hazing was a little more prevalent back then, but in general the older guys were pretty decent, too. They might shave your head or something, but as long as you worked hard, you had their respect.

I was in the absolute best shape I've been in my whole life when I came to Oregon. It wasn't really premeditated, don't get me wrong. I worked a garbage route back in the old days when you actually ran from garbage bin to

Born and raised in Eugene, Steve Greatwood has spent the better part of three decades in Oregon football as both a player and a coach.

garbage bin. I was in fantastic shape, so practice didn't faze me. I didn't really notice except that I needed to get bigger and stronger. We still played a junior varsity schedule in those days. I had been recruited to play tight end, but that only lasted about a day before I was moved to guard. I believe we played the freshmen from Oregon State, Washington State, and Boise State that first year, so there were no redshirts or anything.

To be a Duck back in those days, you had to swallow your pride a little bit. It was difficult. You knew when you went out in public that you were inevitably going to hear people who were talking about how lousy you were. There was a syndicated newspaper article every Monday called the *Bottom 10*, and a big achievement for us back then was to not get yourselves mentioned in that. It was a humbling thing. Basketball guys were the kingpins on campus. I had basketball buddies, and just to see the attention and accolades they got, you felt like you were working just as hard but there was no glitz and glory in it.

My freshman year, I think loyalty was the biggest lesson I learned. That was the year Don Read got fired, and I saw a lot of disloyalty amongst players toward coaches, and vice versa. There wasn't a lot of trust there, among a core group of guys. Coach Read got fired during a break, so the campus was empty. A group of us gathered to meet with the university president in his office to plead for Coach Read's case, because he was a good man, a very fair man. And I got included because I was a local guy and around at the time when most other students weren't. There was probably half a dozen of us. That was kind of a cold reality as an 18-year-old kid to see what it was like, and then having to prove yourself again to a new coach.

The new coach, Rich Brooks, could be best described with one word: fear. It was something. It ended up being the greatest experience of my life to have him and his staff coach me. But a tough tone was definitely set right from the start. Guys were getting run out of the program left and right. We had these mat drills at 6:30 in the morning, and we had to run over to the football facilities to be on time. It was crazy. And you could do things like that back in those days that you can't do with the guys now. Coaches could do some things that would be perceived now as a little harsh.

102

As a sophomore in 1977, I started the first game, which was at Georgia. I think I was too young and dumb to even think about it, how much pressure I should have felt in that situation. I did it, and felt deep down that I could start all along. That whole winter prior to that, I was looking around, thinking, *I'm better than these guys.* I was still 225 pounds and had no business being on the field, but that just shows how bad we were. I knew that I could do it, so it wasn't a huge surprise. I suppose as a player I don't think you ever realize how bad you are.

I'll never forget that first game against Georgia. They had an All-American linebacker, Ben Zambiasi was his name. They were good. Bill Hoffman was our other guard, and he wore glasses. It was early in the game, and he came back to the huddle with his hands up underneath his face mask. I was looking at him and could hear him just muttering to himself, "Look at my nose." He moved his hands, and his nose was just split open. A guy had caught him right underneath his face mask and split his nose, and there was blood everywhere. That was the first game, and it was like, welcome to college football, kid. Getting off the bus there, there was all these little kids on top of these train tracks that go down to the locker room, and they were throwing rocks at us and waving Confederate flags, yelling "Dog meat" and all that. The phones had rung all night in the hotel the night before, and you'd answer it, and people would say, "The Dawgs are going to get you between the hedges," and hang up. So that was my first experience. It was a little different than Churchill versus Sheldon back in high school.

Beating the Beavs in Don Read's last game in 1976 was huge, and beating them Rich's first year was great, too. I don't think anyone has or ever will have the intensity that Rich brought to those games. I was proud that I never lost to the Beavers, and proud three of those were for him. He had been spurned by his alma mater for a job, and he had an intense dislike for Oregon State after that. I don't know if it's ever burned any hotter in anybody. It was something. He basically willed teams to win. Back then I think Oregon State had better talent than we did, but he found a way to get it out of us. The first year we had a young guy, Gary Beck, as a true freshman, and he actually played both ways—at running back and safety—to help us win.

Junior year, 1978, was probably the most frustrating and rewarding year of my career. Well I guess I can't really say it was all that rewarding. But that's when we really came to realize just what it could take for the program to turn the corner. We lost nine games, and it seemed like all of them were by a point or two. We were losing games by three, two, five—close games—and losing them right at the wire. It was a lot more joyous when you won back then, because it happened so rarely. Now it's just relief. That's how far the program has come. You expect to win at Oregon now. It wasn't that way when I played, not at all.

Despite all that frustration, there was a definite feeling that a winning season could happen going into 1979. Reggie Ogburn came in from junior college to play quarterback, and it was obvious how good he was just from practicing with him. He was a different kind of athlete than we had here before, and we had some decent running backs, too—guys like Dwight Robinson. We were getting some different kinds of guys. We went back to Colorado for the opener, and there was all this hype about Chuck Fairbanks making his return to college football as Colorado's coach, and we just killed them.

Then we played two very difficult games against top 10 teams, Michigan State and Purdue, played them both pretty well on the road. Everything was on the road back then. We never had a home and home deal, unless you were playing a team from a lesser conference. We beat both Bay Area teams, and that was huge. We were 5–5 heading into the Civil War, and it was so great to get that sixth win against Oregon State and finish with a winning record. But to be honest, what I will take to my grave from my senior year was the way Washington beat us on a punt return with about 1:30 to go. We had controlled the game from the outset, but they found a way to win, and we found a way to lose. That happened between the Michigan State and Purdue games early on, so there was still some of that hanging around the rest of the year, and we recovered. But that one still hurts.

Steve Greatwood entered Oregon's starting lineup as a sophomore in 1977 and won the Officer Award a year later for his contributions to the team despite physical adversity. He played in the Hula Bowl in 1980 and signed as a free agent with the San Francisco 49ers before returning to the Ducks as a graduate assistant from 1980 to 1981. He was a full-time assistant at Oregon from 1982 to 1994 before following Rich Brooks to the NFL with the St. Louis Rams. Greatwood returned to Oregon in 2000 and was named college football's top offensive line coach in 2008.

VINCE GOLDSMITH

DEFENSIVE LINE

1977–1980

ORIGINALLY, I WAS RECRUITED TO OREGON to compete in track and field for the shot put. Back in the day, I was the national high school leader in the shot put, and Oregon had one of the better programs in the country. Growing up in Tacoma, I was aware of the Ducks a little bit, and everybody knew about Bobby Moore and what he did, so Oregon was always kind of on your mind. It was always a viable option. When Rich Brooks became head coach, that's when the more serious recruiting for football started. He was a big factor in my decision to become a Duck.

It came down to Washington and Oregon. The Huskies had a coaching change the year before, and so were telling me their program was a year ahead, and the Ducks were telling me I could help start something new. But they had the same records the year before, so it actually seemed to me that Oregon was in a better position. And with the Ducks having a much better track program, it made sense to me to go to Oregon. Plus, my best friend, Vince Williams, was being recruited to Oregon, so he and I both accepted football scholarships. They agreed to let me participate in track under two conditions: one, that I participated in at least some of spring practice, and two, that I could be a scorer in track meets.

Rich Brooks was just such a professional. He was so much more serious than what I was used to in high school. I was always one of the better guys on the team, so the coaches didn't bother me much in high school. But in college, they were on your case 24/7, especially in fall camp. It was practice from sun up to pretty much sun down for about two weeks. I was a line-men, so I never had to do triple days, but some of the skill positions had to do triple days, and I was thanking God I wasn't in one of the skill positions, because I was doing all I could to get through the morning. The afternoons weren't too bad because you were awake by that point. But the mornings, they're beating on the door with a hammer to shock you out of bed, and then it was right to work.

Rich was a disciplinarian from the word go. You could never be late for anything. I got yelled at more than two or three times for being late. Even if you showed up on time, you got a funny look. He wanted you to be early. If practice started at 1:30, you had to be on the field, taped, ready to go at 1:30. You couldn't be walking out on the field putting your shoulder pads on. You were taped, helmet on, shoulder pads on, ready to go. They blew the whis-tle, you lined up and started stretching, and away you went. It's amazing how much repetition will do to you, because now it's just a natural thing. That's just how it is, with whatever it is you're doing. A new person coming into a system like that maybe can't appreciate the benefits until you get into a game where you're even with the opponent, and the only way you're going to win is to execute better. And the only way you're going to execute better is if everyone else does, and that stems from developing that understanding that, "Hey, if this guy's late, we're going to have to run," "Hey, if this guy misses his block, we're going to lose." You've got to develop disciplined practice habits that will pay off in games.

One thing about me was, I was never the biggest guy. About 5'11", 230 pounds. My thing was that I was quick and strong, stronger than most foot-ball players, and that primarily comes from the track experience. It was quickness, it was strength, and it was using your feet, which isn't a strength of a lot of big guys. It takes them a while to start and stop, but I had the quickness, the strength, and the natural leverage. I could get under a guy and straighten them up. I think learning how to use my legs in track helped me in football. Legs are about 90 percent of most sports. Once I got the under-standing of that part of the game, everything else was a quick study. Once I got my technique down, giving up some weight to a blocker didn't really matter, because if I got my hands on them I could pretty much get them off. Nowadays, with 330-pound guys playing offensive line, that would be dif-ferent. I guess the heaviest I ever was at Oregon was about 240. My first year

I reported to camp at about 224, and the first two games I was 215. It was the heat—good lord, we played our opening game in Georgia and the next game was in Texas. I sweated that weight off.

That first game in 1977, in Atlanta, it was so humid. You take a shower, you might start sweating in the shower. I wasn't used to that heat, and it didn't help that it happened to be my first game. We had half jerseys, and they tried to cut the jerseys even more, but nothing worked. I think I was just playing on adrenaline, just excited for that first game because I have some relatives in the Georgia area. That was a shock, though. Georgia had been No. 2 in the country the year before, and we were told they were going to be pretty good, and they definitely had some good players, but in the middle of the fourth quarter we were winning the game. We wore down, and they ended up winning 27–16, but it wasn't one-sided like some people thought it would be. We opened a lot of people's eyes because we had a new coach and went down "between the hedges" and played a team that everyone felt was a top-10 team. I ended up with 13 tackles, but I was so hot that I wasn't thinking about anything else other than trying to get on and off the field.

We finished that year off by beating the Beavers, which we did all four years when I was there. The first year, beating the Beavers was not a big deal to me, because I hadn't been around the rivalry long enough. Beating USC would have been a big deal, but beating Oregon State, who had about as many losses as we did, was not a big consolation. I didn't really understand the concept at that point, that you have to beat your in-state rival and that kind of stuff. As time went on, I began to appreciate that rivalry a little more. But at the beginning it was, "Okay, we beat the Beavers. We're the second-worst team in the league!"

By 1978 I think everyone around the program understood that we were a lot better team than that first year. We were still losing, but the scores were a lot closer and the games were more competitive. We knew we were a better team; it wasn't like we were hoping we got a break and didn't screw it up, and that was our only chance to win. We could go out and actually play with the other teams, but then something would always happen at the end. That was more frustrating in the second year than the first year, because we had higher expectations than going 2–9 again. I came out of a high school program where we were always winning the city championship and going to the playoffs. That first year, it was an adjustment from high school to college, and there was an excitement because everything was new. Once the "new" wore off, you're into that second year, and now you're expecting to win, and we were close, but we didn't, so that was probably the most frustrating time at Oregon, that second season.

But the good news was, we probably came together over the course of the '78 season just because we had that shared experience of being close so much and never really getting over the top. It fostered a new commitment or rededication to work harder. At that point, you really start understanding what it was going to take to win games in the Pac-10. Recruiting started to pick up, we felt like we had more talent, and to be honest it was a little shocking to feel like we could be pretty good. You're working at it, and working at it, and all of a sudden it almost scares you, because it's like, "Hey, we're actually beating people," and it's not like a guy tripped and fell down or they got some bad breaks. We just went out there and beat them for the whole game, and that was that.

We started off by beating Colorado, which was a good way to start the year, because the year before they beat us pretty good, and we went back out there and got revenge. That was another one with tough conditions—you couldn't breathe in warmups from the mile-high thin air. Rich told us not to have any excuses, that we would get used to it, and we dealt with it because we didn't want to have any excuses. The bad news was I broke my hand on about the fourth play, so I pretty much watched the rest of that game from the sideline. That actually ended up being pretty interesting, to have that vantage point and watch the way we dominated them.

I came back for the Washington game two weeks later, thanks in part to the healing powers of Rich Brooks. He would walk up to you and say, "I talked to the trainer. He says there's going to be pain, but it's recovered enough to where it's not going to bother you anymore. You just have to deal with the pain. You have to distinguish between pain and injury." Whenever he said that, you had to take off the red shirt that injured guys wore and go practice and play. I got that speech after missing a game because of my hand. I was thinking a broken hand was good for two or three games, but he gave me the "distinguish between pain and injury" speech, and I had to start practicing. The other thing he said was that if I had missed another game, he probably would have redshirted me, and I didn't want to redshirt, so I went out there and played. I wore a cast to protect it, and it healed up pretty good, so it wasn't a big issue.

Though undersized for the position by today's standards, Vince Goldsmith is among Oregon's best defensive linemen ever.

That 1979 season was memorable because we had become a respected team. People were taking note of what we were doing once we won a few games. They were blowing smoke, and we were apparently believing it because we probably could have won more games if we hadn't gotten big heads. I think our biggest problem, even to a certain degree my senior year, was that we didn't have the senior leadership that had experienced a lot of success. I was a team leader, but I think I could have been a better team leader had I dealt with the success we were having better. For instance, we had Washington beat for three quarters and 14 minutes, and lost on a punt return by Mark Lee. That hurt. After that game, I was trying to hide from the reporters because I was in the bathroom crying. But they found me and started interviewing me right there in the toilet because they wanted to talk to the guy from Washington. My father and I actually grew closer because of that game. Afterward, he came in the locker room, and we looked at each other and both started crying. I guess that's the power of sports. Man, it just hurt, and it helped to share it with someone who you knew understood.

By our senior year in 1980, we felt like a veteran group that knew what it took to win. That year was also marked by some legal problems, and disciplinary problems with both the Pac-10 and the NCAA for some issues, but it really didn't affect the guys on the team too much. When we reported to camp, it was explained to us what was happening, and that was the only time I ever really heard about what was happening or had to deal with it. Other than that, it was football, and we were eager to get on with it, because we felt we were going to have a good team.

I hurt my ankle in fall camp, and it took forever to heal. At that point, I was a preseason All-American and all that kind of stuff, and I was hating it because I couldn't just get going with the season. The first couple games were tough because I was watching, and we were struggling. I finally got my first shot against Michigan State, the third game. By then people were thinking we weren't as good as projected, because we were 0–1–1, but we came out and handled them pretty easily. The following week we went up to Husky Stadium and just destroyed Washington, who went to the Rose Bowl. That was memorable. I still like to bring that up with folks from home when I get a chance. I was glad we finally beat those guys.

We played Cal next. They weren't very good, and USC was coming up after that. At one point that week I was in Coach Brooks' office talking to him, telling him it was hard to get ready for the Cal game because I was thinking about USC. He came unglued in our next practice and made us run stadium stairs. As I was running, I was thinking, *Man, if I had known this would happen, I wouldn't have said that!* But I was being honest. It was hard to concentrate on Cal, when you're finally in a position where you think you can actually beat the perennial best team in the conference. So we went down to Cal and stunk up the place, and they won.

The following week was USC, which at that point had the longest win streak in the country. Marcus Allen was their tailback, pretty much the whole team was All-Americans. It ended up 7–7, but in our minds we actually beat those guys. It was 7–0, and we were about to go up by two touchdowns when Reggie Brown crossed the goal line. Nowadays the play would be dead right there, seven points. But while he was in the end zone, the Trojans ripped the ball out and ran it all the way back to midfield. Half of our guys were still down at the end zone with their arms in the air, signaling touchdown, and the refs say it's first and 10 for USC. We were going, "What's up with this call?" Then they scored a touchdown that we also felt was suspect, because we felt a pass had been caught out of bounds. But you didn't have the replay back then. You just had to go with what was called.

Still, even though we tied, that game was memorable in a positive way. It demonstrated that the program had turned the corner because we had an opportunity to lose that game like we had in the past. We played good for a while, but then it was time to figure out how we were going to lose this thing. It got to the fourth quarter, and they were driving for at least the winning field goal. I think they were on about the 45, and it was fourth and one, and they decided to go for it because they figured they could just run over us and get the first down. But we stopped them on fourth and one, and we took the ball and time ran out before we could score. I got double-teamed on the play, but Scott Setterlund got a good charge off the ball, and he beat his guy and got underneath him. He penetrated into their backfield and grabbed the quarterback by his foot, messing up the exchange with Marcus Allen. He had to kind of slow down to get the ball, and so that gave our guys a good chance to react and make the hit, and I think he might have even lost yards. The stadium was packed for that game, it was a beautiful day, and the only thing that would have made it better was if we had won the game. We weren't happy with the tie, but it was more proof that our program had turned the corner.

All the offensive linemen in the Pac-10 voted to give me the Morris Trophy as the top defensive lineman after that season, which I thought was significant not just for myself but for the entire program. Typically, those kinds of awards are political and go to guys on the best teams even though they may not be the best individual players. I felt good about that because it was the players, and not the coaches or the media, who voted on it. And it spoke well about the program, because at the time I went to Oregon it was pretty much a doormat, and by the time I left I think we were third in the conference and were getting respect from the media, the coaches, and also other players. They were saying that Oregon had a quality program and quality athletes. So I felt good because of that.

Vince Goldsmith was a two-time first-team All-Pac-10 selection and a second-team All-American as a senior in 1980. He was named Oregon's top newcomer in 1977 and was team MVP in both 1979 and 1980, sharing the honor with quarterback Reggie Ogburn as a senior. Goldsmith was invited to the Hula Bowl and the Japan Bowl following his senior season. He played professionally in the Canadian Football League for 10 years, and was named the CFL's outstanding rookie in 1981. After retiring, he received a master's degree in health care administration. He lives and works in his hometown of Tacoma, Washington.

NEIL ELSHIRE

DEFENSIVE LINE

1978–1979

AT SOUTH ALBANY HIGH SCHOOL, I was the first kid ever recruited by D-1 college programs. I probably had four or five total offers, but I wanted to stay in state. Coming from a small town, all my relatives are Beavers, with the exception of one aunt who was a Duck. At that time Oregon State had just hired Craig Fertig, and after going through that recruiting process, I decided that Eugene was my best option. I really respected Fred von Appen, one of the assistant coaches, and John Marshall was also involved in my recruitment. I don't think either one of those guys missed a high school basketball game of mine. I got to know them, and thought they were just incredible guys. I liked the people at Oregon. I enjoyed Eugene. It wasn't a popular decision with my family, I've got to be honest, but it's where I felt most comfortable.

I really enjoyed Don Read, but he was fired as head coach my freshman year. But the cool thing was, I got real lucky, and they hired Rich Brooks. I guess in going to Oregon, the people made a much larger impact on where I was going to go than the courses I was going to study, because I probably would have been much better off in an engineering school. I was more a math and science guy, but I figured if I was going to play football, I was going to Oregon, and I thought that at the time the facilities were a little bit better than at Oregon State.

My first fall on campus, in 1976, was awesome—it was just a great experience. We played about three junior varsity games, and you could see our recruiting class had some talented players. I got to know some really good guys, like Jeff Wood, Pat McDougall, Kevin McGill, Steve Greatwood—there were a ton of great guys and good players. Some of those guys went on to play a lot of good football over the years.

When Brooks took over, he tried to keep von Appen, who was somebody I thought a lot of, but he took the coordinator job at Stanford. The next guy in line was Joe Schaffeld, and that's when Joe and I got very close, over those next few years. Fred was highly intelligent, funnier than hell, one of the funniest guys you'll ever be around, in a witty, sarcastic sort of way—dry humor, but extremely bright. I think that's why he ended up going to Stanford, he just wanted to sit in on lectures with all the Nobel Prize winners! I really tried, and Brooks tried, to keep Fred in Eugene, but the bottom line was the draw was better there. It worked out well, though, because we formed a bond with Schaffeld. Our first defensive coordinator under Brooks was Howard Tippett, who only stuck around a couple years. He ended up coaching in Tampa for the Bucs for a few years. He was an incredible coach. We had Andy Christoff as the linebacker coach. Brooks brought in some incredible coaches. When you look back at those first staffs he had, I realize I got pretty lucky to play for those guys.

The transition from Read to Brooks was really good for the young guys who wanted to work hard. It wasn't necessarily good for some of the older guys who had been around, because, frankly, Brooks came in and changed the tone. We had a winter conditioning program, and I don't think I've worked that hard in my life. He wanted to find out who was willing to make the sacrifices to make a winning program. I thought Don Read was well on his way to doing that, but just in a different way. We all got really lucky with Brooks. Dee Andros, the legendary coach from Oregon State, was just beside himself when they hired Craig Fertig. There were two other finalists: Brooks was one of them, and then Terry Donahue was the other. Dee was angry they didn't hire Brooks. That was when the administration at Oregon State really didn't care what their football team was going to look like.

There were a lot of differences between then and now. We held training camp at Autzen. Brooks was a taskmaster, thank God. We needed it. We needed to instill some discipline to change our program around. Coaches

Neil Elshire battled injuries during his collegiate career but moved on to become one of the NFL's early sack specialists.

could do that then. Today, it's a different world. I always point out to my kids the holes in the cement as you go down the tunnel to the field at Autzen Stadium. There are some holes there, because that's where our blackboards used to flip down. That was the meeting room, right there in the tunnel. It got cold in November, let me tell you.

Prior to my sophomore year in 1977, I spent all summer shoveling gravel out of the back of a dump truck in Lane County. I put on probably 30 pounds, and it paid off right away. After three or four days of camp, I was starting, and that was after probably being number four on the depth chart when I got to camp. It was an incredible opportunity. We opened at Georgia in Athens and actually played a pretty good game, only lost 27–16 to the defending SEC champions.

Then we flew to Dallas and played TCU the following week, and it was about 115 degrees on the field for that one. It was freaking hot. TCU was just a boiler, and the carpet was just crap. It was a little bit of rug on top of cement. I realized then I had pretty strong bones because something should have broken. Well, I guess it did. The game was tied 24–24 in the fourth quarter. The quarterback dropped back in the end zone, and I broke free on a pass rush. He tried to step out, and I wanted to pull him back into the end zone. I planted my foot, and it stayed in one place. My body completely rotated, and it tore everything in my left knee. At least we got the safety and won the game.

It was absolutely worth it. It was Brooks' first win, even though it was an ugly game. That was an ugly game. It was the game where one of our safeties intercepted the ball and was running up the sideline for a touchdown, and a guy from their sideline came off their bench and tackled him. God, what a crazy game. I passed out after the injury, I was gone. The next thing I remember, a trainer's standing over me with the smelling salts. I looked up, and the first thing I said was, "Did I get the guy?" Because I didn't know. I was obviously in shock. He said, "Yes." And I said, "Okay, what's wrong with me?" And he said, "You don't want to know right now." But that play put us in the lead, at least, and we ended up winning 29–24.

That season was done for me, and I spent the next six nights in the hospital. It was nasty, but I did the rehab thing and came back the next year, made it through the whole season and had a pretty good year. That was the year we went 2–9 and lost six games by a total of 19 points. We were so close. We opened up at Colorado, which had a great team. We needed to do that in those years for the gate money, because the program wasn't pulling in a lot of money other ways. We didn't have Phil Knight giving millions of dollars back then. So we played a very tough nonleague schedule and normally had to travel quite a distance. I would have loved to have some of the nonleague games these guys have now.

We opened at Colorado again in 1979, and we had so much fun. I was Pac-10 defensive player of the week that week. Vince Goldsmith, our amazing tackle, ended up Pac-10 first-team that year. The unfortunate thing was I got hurt right at the end of that year, and that was the nail in the coffin for my college career. It was in a shorts and shoulder pads practice, and a walk-on fullback decided to cut me. He tried a little cut block, and boom. So the Stanford game that year was my last game as a Duck. At least I went out with a win.

Playing with Vince, there wasn't a lot of room to run or pass over on that side. We gave Terry Dion the easy side, he was the other end. We had a blast, and Vince was just fun to play with, and I think we helped each other out quite a bit. When you have a couple good players on one side of the ball, you're pretty confident. And it didn't hurt to have a linebacker like Brian Hinkle standing behind you, either. With us on one side, we felt like it didn't really matter who else was around. Especially in the front seven, we had some very strong players. And Steve Brown was a hell of a corner, and Mike Nolan was a kid who walked on, and he was starting by his freshman year. The biggest issue was, I think we went through three free safeties that year.

117

We were young enough and dumb enough that we believed we could turn things around, and we did by my senior year. We won six games and had a winning season. Eugene rallied behind us, which is something I had been hoping for ever since I was being recruited. I'll never forget when I was being recruited at Oregon and I attended a basketball game at Mac Court. That was the old Kamikaze Kids era, and it was just nuts at Mac Court. I just looked around and said, "Why couldn't this happen in football? There's no reason it couldn't." In '78 we got a few more fans, and there was some excitement kicking up. The wins weren't there, but it was obvious we were getting better.

Neil Elshire was honored with the Len Casanova Award as Oregon's top new-comer in 1978 following his injury-shortened sophomore season. He played six seasons with the Minnesota Vikings, from 1981 to 1986, recording 19 sacks, including 9.5 in 1983. Elshire currently lives in Bend and works in the lumber industry. His son, Erik, was a reserve linebacker for the Ducks in the 2006 and 2007 seasons.

The
EIGHTIES

GARY ZIMMERMAN

LINEMAN

1980–1983

T HERE WERE TWO MAIN REASONS why I ended up becoming an Oregon Duck. The first was that I grew up in Los Angeles, as kind of this big-city misfit, and I was looking to get away from that scene. Eugene definitely fit the bill there. I was considering most of the Pac-10, except for USC. If you can believe it, I had really wanted to go to Washington, but they didn't have a scholarship for me. Can you imagine, I might have been a Husky?

Anyway, the other key for me was that I really, really wanted to play line-backer. I played both offensive line and linebacker in high school, but in college I wanted to be a linebacker. Oregon was the only school that told me I could play linebacker, and so that sealed the deal for me. I became a Duck.

Then I showed up for my first day at Oregon. I took one look at my locker, and the jersey hanging in there had No. 75 on it. A big, lineman number. They had pulled the old switcheroo on me. At first, I was pretty upset. But I just made the best of it, and it all worked out for me in the end, so I look back on it now as one of those life lessons we all have to learn.

Coming to Eugene from Los Angeles was like being in a time warp or something, and believe it or not, I thought that was pretty awesome. Oregon was coming off a pretty good year, with Reggie Ogburn playing quarter-back, but that hadn't really been a big factor in my decision. The program also went on NCAA probation right about then, so my timing wasn't great in that regard. But it didn't really affect me much.

Playing on the line was a major adjustment for me. Andy Christoff had been the guy who recruited me. I don't think I ever so much as talked to either of the line coaches at that point. But now, all of a sudden I was in the control of Neal Zoumboukos, who we all call Zoomer. I'm not going to lie, he scared the hell out of me at first.

Our first year, Zoomer would hide in the bushes outside the dorms and try to catch people who were sneaking out. He had some creative coaching methods back then, too. He'd use all kinds of props: a hammer, a starter's pistol. He had a bit of a Napoleon complex, I guess you'd say.

My first year I played on special teams and I was a backup on the line. It was a big adjustment coming from high school, particularly because I came all the way from Los Angeles. I had to get adjusted to the rain. Also I had never played on artificial turf, and I didn't understand how hard it was. Back then, the lines were a half inch bigger than the turf because they were painted on. You had to be careful running around on that stuff. The kids who play nowadays would have no clue what we did. We used to practice behind Mac Court, the basketball gym. Oregon football has come a long way.

That first year, 1980, was the year that USC was ranked No. 1, and we tied them. That's definitely the one result I'll never forget from that season. Beating Washington a couple weeks before that was special, too, maybe because they'd passed on me in recruiting.

Off the field, we were starting to form those bonds that you never lose. All the freshman linemen kind of hung out in the same places. We were the new kids, and it was a lot of fun times. Mike Delegato, Jamey Mathews, Stuart Yatsko, and Jeff Kubitz were the veteran guys whom I was learning from. They had some fun with us, too. The older guys didn't really mess with us too much, but they kind of slapped us around to keep us in line. I also learned a lot from playing against Vince Goldsmith in practice—mainly that you didn't want to be in his way. He was crushing people. That was quite an eye-opener coming from high school, to see a guy that powerful.

As I recall, I started some games my sophomore season. Then, in spring ball, they moved me across to the defensive line, and I played there the next year. They couldn't decide on a spot for me. I guess I had good enough individual skills to play defense, so I could hold my own during drills in practice. But I just didn't have any experience on the defensive line, so when I got into games, I stunk it up. At least at that point I was comfortable with playing the line in general. Coming out of high school, you think you're good. Then

121

Gary Zimmerman went on to become one of the best offensive linemen in football history after signing with Oregon as a linebacker.

getting to the next level you realize you're not as good as you thought you were. I was a slow white guy, so linebacker wasn't really my spot. I was made to be a lineman.

The game I remember most from my junior year was playing Notre Dame in Eugene, although it kind of left a bad taste in my mouth because we tied. Regardless, it wasn't any great plays I made. That defensive line thing only lasted one season. I must have stunk at it, because they moved me back to offense.

Coming into my senior year, we all thought the stage was set for a really good year. Everyone was working hard and seemed committed to the team. We had a big crew that hung out all the time in the weight room, lifting together and working out. There were guys who worked a day job and went to school, then went in at night and lifted weights. There was a lot of team bonding and enthusiasm for the season, but I guess it didn't really carry over.

It started off on a lousy note. We opened up against Pacific, then went and got beat 31–6 at Ohio State, which was a really low point. And then that was bookended by the Civil War, which was the 0–0 tie everybody remembers as the "Toilet Bowl." I just remember that being a frustrating game. I remember one of the running backs fumbled on the 1- or 2-yard line, and we missed a very short field goal. It was just a pitiful game, and the weather was awful. We should have won, and even now that's what most people remember about me at Oregon, is that I played in the Toilet Bowl. I saw a little kid one time and even he said, "Hey, you played in the Toilet Bowl!" So the Toilet Bowl has kind of tagged people from our class. It was the most memorable game from back then. I laugh at it now. It's pretty funny.

There's no getting around it, those were some lean times for Oregon football. I was looking back on it, and saw we only won 14 games in four years. Pretty dry times. Oregon was pretty small back then. Nobody wanted to go there because it rained and we were on probation. The one thing that does stick out is that I never lost to the Beavers. I played in the Toilet Bowl, but I never lost to them. I think that's something that's gone by the wayside, because the guys now don't seem to take the rivalry as serious as we did. Back then it was kind of like the Super Bowl for us. I don't think it's looked at the same way nowadays.

Overall, I just thought there were great people at Oregon. Looking back, Zoomer was hard on me, and that's what I needed. Rich Brooks never lied to me once. I liked Rich because he told it like it was. Herb Yamanaka, one of the assistant athletic directors, has been a standup guy for all these years. He's kind of the face of Oregon for me. There's nobody better than Herbie.

To see the growth that the program has had to where it is now, it's just unbelievable. We had to dumpster-dive back in my day because they couldn't give you anything. We'd go dumpster-diving outside the athletic department to get a pair of shoes. We had connections down at the equipment room, and he would give us the heads up that they were going to dump the shoes, and we'd all go down there and dig in the dumpsters and try and find one with your number on it, snag a bunch for your buddies. We did it several years, go and fish the cleats out of the dumpster. The kids now are just given anything. I'm not sure it's better. I just think it's different.

That's the stuff I remember the best, just all the good times with the other offensive line guys. We'd just all go fishing together, simple stuff like that. Some of the pomp you see the kids involved with today, that doesn't appeal to me at all. We were real people, a bunch of good old boys who couldn't be happier than when we were just fishing and hanging out.

Gary Zimmerman was voted the Pac-10's best offensive lineman in 1983. After two seasons in the USFL, he played 12 seasons in the NFL, making seven Pro Bowls. He retired after he helped the Denver Broncos win the Super Bowl in 1998 and was inducted into the Pro Football Hall of Fame in 2008.

MICHAEL GRAY

DEFENSIVE LINE

1981–1982

WHEN I GOT RECRUITED OUT OF JUNIOR COLLEGE in California, the Ducks weren't winning as much as they win today, but the school was in the Pac-10, and I wanted to play in a good conference. I really based my decision on having a chance to play; I knew I would have a chance right away at Oregon. I thought this was a pretty solid program on the West Coast, in the Pac-10, so that was why I came.

Jim Skipper recruited me, Rich Brooks was the head coach, and Andy Christoff was here, too. Don Pellum was here at that time playing along with Steve Greatwood, and Mike Nolan was in his senior year. I got to play for some good coaches and with some guys who became pretty good coaches themselves.

Brooks was tough, a defensive guy, and I liked that. Defensive guys just have a little different mentality than offensive guys. He was stern, firm, but fair, though. We had a good program. It didn't result in a lot of wins, but we played hard, especially defensively.

Joe Schaffeld was my position coach. He wasn't easy to play for. A little bit different, a little sterner. Guys paid attention to him, the guys changed their behavior. Back then they could get away with practicing for five or six hours if they wanted. There was a different mentality. There wasn't as much media coverage. Only the big programs got on TV. Oregon maybe got on TV back then maybe three times. So you didn't get the exposure. I'm from the East

Michael Gray was a stout defensive lineman for the Ducks and later coached the position at Oregon.

Coast, and I came to the West Coast because I was interested in seeing the other programs. You'd only get to see 'SC and UCLA and maybe Washington. And when you're not on television, you don't know.

The Ducks had just started to turn the corner when I got here, winning some games. They were always looking for a chance to get to the bowl games, which I never got to experience as a player. We were just starting to recruit some bigger and better athletes, just getting ready to turn into a good team. We were slowly competing against the bigger schools. The athletes had good size up front, and the skill guys were good. Everybody still ran the ball a lot. Stanford was probably the only team that threw the ball a lot. Everybody else was a smash mouth, running type of team, which was fine by me.

The transition from junior college was tough, but I handled it. At that time I was probably 255 pounds. I came in during the winter, and that was my first understanding of defenses and how complex they could get. It was different, good. I'd never experienced it. It was a lot of learning, but I had a good spring and I was actually starting. I had come from a junior college where we didn't run stuff that was quite as complex, but I adjusted to it.

I actually hurt my knee that spring game, and I remember going to the hospital to get it checked out. That was a little scary. I got healthy over the summer, my knee was healthy. The next year I wound up starting, and I was happy about that, since that was my goal when choosing a school.

We always tried to circle the Beavers game in those days, because that was one game where we always had a good chance of winning. We had a pretty good run there, where we won eight in a row. We just kind of dominated that team. I remember Rich always talking about that game, even early in the season. We were hoping to beat Stanford and Arizona because at that time Arizona was decent, but they were not at Arizona State's level. ASU was pretty good in those days. We would always circle a few games on the calendar that we thought we had a good chance of winning.

You start to question yourself after losses, but Rich was good at being stern and telling us to stay the course. We always had a tough team, and kids played hard. Joe was a tough coach, but he was fair. We played about six or seven guys up front. It was a good time. We didn't win a lot of games, but the reward was great, getting a chance to play and graduate.

You always want to end your career on a high note, but I'm not sure I can say that. The Civil Wars were usually good games, but I played in the 0–0 game in 1983, and it's tough to say that was a great one. It was played in miserable weather. The Civil War always has miserable weather because it's late in the year, but that was really bad. There wasn't a lot of high scoring in those games anyway. It was always a battle right down to the end of the game. That was one game you always wanted to play well because you didn't want to end your season with a loss.

Not many plays stand out from my career, but I was proud that I had a sack in the Civil War here in Autzen. The games were always close, and it seemed like every play mattered. The Civil Wars were the defining games for us, because we didn't have a chance to go to any bowl games. You want to wrap it up on a strong note, because you have to think about that game for six months.

I played with Gary Zimmerman, who was a defensive lineman for a year. He was a decent D-lineman, too. I remember them moving him, and the rest is history. He became an All-Pac-10 offensive lineman. He had the athleticism and poise. He was kind of like Max Unger, more recently. He had enough aggressiveness for the defensive side of the ball, but he understood how to block people, and he was a big, strong guy, and had good leverage for being 6'6". To this day, when I talk to guys about switching sides of the ball and they fight it, I tell them about Gary Zimmerman and how a lot of time it works out for the best.

Being a Duck meant so much for me personally. You put a lot of sweat and blood into the program. Sometimes the wins come, and sometimes they don't, but you've got to stay the course. I learned that from Rich Brooks, because there were some down times as a player when you get depressed, because you want some wins. Wins were important, but you always felt like you had to have that last game, that Civil War. We left it all on the line in the Civil War. We just played harder, more focused, and they came focused, too. It was a toe-to-toe grudge match, because you want to have something to say positively after the game, to at least have something to grasp from the season that was positive.

Michael Gray was a junior college All-American who was honored with the Len Casanova Award as Oregon's top newcomer when he joined the Ducks in 1981. He finished his career with 78 tackles and went on to an eight-year professional career in the Canadian Football League. He began his coaching career in the CFL, joined the staff of the St. Louis Rams in 1996, and coached defensive linemen with the Ducks from 2005 to 2008.

DON PELLUM

LINEBACKER

1982–1984

MY PATH FROM LOS ANGELES, WHERE I GREW UP, to Eugene was about as weird as it gets. I wasn't sure if I was going to get recruited or not. I was getting a bunch of letters, but I didn't know anything about recruiting. I had a coach ask me if I was thinking about going to Oregon. I was like, "Oregon? What's in Oregon? Lumberjacks and pancakes? I don't know." That's all I thought about Oregon, which was not right, but it was all I thought.

I wanted to stay home and go to UCLA. They were calling me and talking to me, but they weren't really recruiting me, you could tell. San Diego State was recruiting me, and I was getting some letters and calls from them. Now that I really know what recruiting is, I don't think I was being recruited as much as I thought I was back then. And then one day, out of the blue, a guy from Oregon showed up. He was the quarterbacks coach, Erik Widmark. He was out scouting quarterbacks and wound up at Banning High School to watch film of our guy Mario Montgomery. Then he saw me, and asked about who I was. About that time I walked into the coach's office, and he pointed me out to Coach Widmark.

So I came up to Eugene on a recruiting trip, and loved it. It was about 50 degrees, with mist and rain in the air, and I thought that was great. A lot of people don't like that kind of weather, but I can't stand the heat. I called my mom on the trip and told her I was going to go to Oregon. It was just a different place from what I was used to in Los Angeles. I was in a convenience store in Eugene, and out of the blue a guy there said, "Hi." I looked around, thinking he was talking to someone else. You didn't really do that where I was from. I took a visit to Oregon State the next week with my brother, who was coming out of junior college, and it just didn't feel the same.

I graduated early and came up to Oregon midyear, so I was kind of in between groups. I wasn't part of the freshman guys that were already there, but those guys were pretty good at accepting me. When the fall guys came, I wasn't really part of their group either. It was a pretty close team, though. I was a wide receiver that first year, and I didn't officially redshirt, but I pretty much didn't play. I just wasn't good enough yet. At one point during recruiting I took a trip to San Diego State, and when I was in their locker room I saw how buffed all those dudes were and I was like, "I'm not ready."

That said, I was in very good shape when I got to Eugene, just not matured yet, not grown up. In the spring quarter, I ran the mile and a half, and I was about to set a record until Dennis Clay came up on me about the last 10 yards and beat me. But physically, I wasn't strong enough, and mentally the transition was tough, too. I did okay, I held my own, and Rich Brooks was pleased with me. It wasn't always easy to tell with him, because he was a pretty tough dude who didn't deal in a lot of b.s. If you weren't getting it done, he didn't really say anything. But you usually knew when he wasn't happy.

130

I was playing receiver initially. After the spring, I went home for the summer and I didn't catch any balls, or do enough workouts with other guys like that. So when I came back in the fall, I wasn't catching very many passes. Now that I look back at it, I didn't deserve to play. I was in great shape, but I hadn't been catching any balls, in particular from guys who were anything like college quarterbacks. Reggie Ogburn and those guys we had back then, they threw bullets. So I ended up not playing my first year, in 1980, which was okay. I didn't come here thinking I was going to start, like some kids do now.

The guys I hung out with as a freshman and redshirt freshman were Ladaria Johnson, Danny McCalister, and Jeff Williams. Danny and Ladaria traveled. I didn't, so I was around town when the team was on the road. Socially, I adjusted to Eugene pretty well. I came from a pretty diverse high school. I never really had any racial problems beyond one incident my first

Don Pellum was among the first players to graduate high school early and participate in spring drills as a freshman, a trend that is now common nationally.

year. We all went to a frat party after we beat UCLA, and all of a sudden I was the only guy from the team left, the only black guy. I looked around, and everyone else was gone. A guy at the party slapped my hat off, and I looked around like, I'm the only guy in here. Best not start any trouble. I just bagged it, went right out the door. That was the only incident I've ever had.

By the time I'd spent a couple years in the program, I felt better, a lot more comfortable. In my first year I had gained 20 pounds over the winter, and asked to be moved to defense from receiver. It's a move I probably should have made a lot sooner. I was a receiver at a high school that used five wide-outs, and then I got recruited by Oregon, which at the time was running the option. What was I thinking? So I asked to be moved to defensive back, and they moved me to free safety for the spring of 1981.

After redshirting that season, I started to understand what we were doing, and I got moved to strong safety. I played some on special teams in 1982. The biggest hit maybe of my whole career was at Ohio State that year. We were rushing the punter, and I ran into a guy named Vaughn Broadnax, a fullback. He just whacked me, and the whole side of my body just went numb. I hit him, and I went numb. That's how big he was.

By 1983, when I was a junior, we thought we were getting better. We were still one of those teams that could play up, or then we could play really bad. We lost badly at Ohio State in our second game, and that was really disappointing because we had some chances and didn't get it done.

After that, we went back into triple days in practice. There weren't the same rules back then about how many hours we could be with the team per week. Brooks put our asses back in triple days. It was fall camp all over again, man. There was tension about the program and the head coach, and we needed to be winning. We lost to Pacific in the opener, which was the real problem.

132

But then we came out and won the Houston game after starting 0–2. It was starting to turn a little bit. We were starting, as a team, to understand what we were doing, which was a big deal. We started to understand football. On our defense the juniors were Bob Hudetz, Todd Welch, Wendell Cason, and myself. We had a pretty good group of guys that year, all from that same recruiting class. Then that season ended with the infamous Toilet Bowl, the scoreless Civil War tie. I don't even want to know how many fumbles we had in that game. We went up and down the field and just kept fumbling and missing field goals.

That season I had been moved to linebacker, and we were very competitive at that position leading up to the 1984 season. I kept moving closer to the line of scrimmage during my career, getting bigger. I came up here at 170 or so, and we would have food-eating contests at our dorm, the University Inn, every day, myself, Ladaria Johnson, Danny McCalister, and Jeff Williams. We'd get our plate and only have one small cup of water, and then after two plates you could have as much water as you wanted, but by then you were full.

We thought we were pretty good that fall, so we were pretty confident. We got off to a good start. The big win that year was over Colorado. That was a big game because a program like ours needed to establish itself, and that sparked a pretty good rivalry. Beating Cal the next week was good, and then we got revenge against Pacific, who had caused us to go to triple days a couple years ago, so we were 4–0 for the first time.

The next week at Arizona, there must have been seven or eight guys taken out on stretchers. It was one of the most physical games I've ever been associated with. Mike Jorgensen, our quarterback, got hit so hard that he got up and went to the wrong sideline. We lost that one, and then USC came to town, and we played them tough even though we lost, so the confidence level was good. We went up to Washington, who were the Rose Bowl champs, and slowed them down on offense, but they beat us with special teams, a blocked punt, a long return, and in the end a field goal. That was the best defensive game of my career. I had about 14 tackles. I still have the coaches' tackle sheet. They tallied up our total and put it on the wall after the game, and I took it, because it was my best game ever. That was another game that gave us confidence. We played them tough, and that was when they were beginning to become a marquee program.

It was the opposite feeling a week later against the Cougars. Our plan was not good for that Washington State game. They were running the option, and we couldn't stop them. Our offense was good, but we could not stop them. That's one of the most miserable feelings in the world, when you cannot stop somebody, even when you know what's coming. That was one of those games that felt like it went on for about five days.

So now we were 4–4 with the Bruins up next. UCLA had been winning a bunch of games at the very end by kicking field goals. I remember we were playing our asses off that day. For those of us who were seniors from California, it was our last game at home. They got the ball at the end and all they needed was that field goal again at the end to win. There was a fourth down play, and they put everybody to the field side of the formation, and then they ran it to the boundary, and we just knew it was coming. We stayed home on defense and stuffed them in the backfield. Game over. They never got the chance to kick that field goal.

Then we played Arizona State, and they kicked our butt. They were really good, and better than us, unfortunately. But we finished off with a win in the Civil War. We played the Beavers up there, and they must have run the ball to my side six times in the first 10 plays. I ended up having a real solid game, although I dropped an interception. I saw that thing so clear. Man, that would have been nice. It was a great way to finish, though. We went out with a 6–5 record, and the program had started to turn.

Oregon just ended up being a great situation for me. My dad's a pretty strict kind of a guy, and so I felt real comfortable with how Coach Brooks did things. You knew what you were supposed to do, and if you do what you're supposed to do, then everything's great. If you don't, then he'd get at you.

After I got done playing, I came back as a graduate assistant coach. Being in that totally different role was eye-opening. One day you're a player, and then the next you're in meetings with the coaches finding out what they really think. I went away to Cal for a couple years, and after seeing how other people do things, I was like, "Whoa, I'm going back to Oregon." Obviously my core values came from my parents, but my understanding of how I think things should work regarding football came from being around here, being with the coaches. My roots go really deep here.

Don Pellum was a fan favorite as a player who served as a graduate assistant coach at Oregon for the 1985 and 1986 seasons, the Ducks' recruiting coordinator from 1987 to 1989, and a full-time defensive assistant since 1993. Among the players he helped develop are Peter Sirmon, Wesly Mallard, Kevin Mitchell, and Anthony Trucks.

CHRIS MILLER

QUARTERBACK

1983–1986

I MOVED TO EUGENE IN 1972, WHEN I WAS SEVEN. I went to the Oregon-Washington game with my mother two years later at Autzen Stadium, when the Huskies won 66–0. It was pouring rain, but we put plastic bags over our heads and sat there until the clock ran out. Back then, you could pretty much sit anywhere you wanted, there were so few fans at the game. That era of Oregon football wasn't like it is today, and I'd like to think I played a part in the growth over the years.

In the years just prior to my joining the team, the Ducks were running the wishbone with guys like Kevin Lusk and Mike Jorgensen. Then Rich Brooks hired Bob Toledo as offensive coordinator, and that's a big reason why I became a Duck. For one thing, I knew Brooks' daughter, who was a year younger than me at Sheldon High School. That was a really enticing deal, my loyalties to Rich. I was a hometown kid, so I loved Eugene, I loved being here. And then when they brought in Bob Toledo, I knew we were going to spread it out, and I'd have a chance to play early on.

Toledo was the quarterbacks coach and offensive coordinator. He was a great guy, really energetic, an Italian-type dude, fun to be around. We called him Banquet Bob because he had that belly on him, and I know he took advantage of the banquet circuit when he was out there recruiting. I think his ingenuity on offense, kind of bringing in a new scheme, that's what Oregon needed, big-time. Bob came in and brought some excitement to it. We got some pro sets, three receivers and four receivers, stuff we hadn't seen around here as Oregon fans in quite a long time. We lost some games, but we were a lot of fun to watch on offense. He taught me a lot of football.

My freshman year they were trying to redshirt me, although I think I was number three on the depth chart. The second game of the season, we went into the Big House at Ohio State and lost 31–6. Jorgy lost 12 or 14 pounds in the first half because it was about 120 degrees on the field. We went into those places in my career to make money. We weren't going to be competitive. We were just a bunch of scrappy Oregon, southern Oregon, a few California kids, a local bunch just trying to go and scrap.

The toughest part of the whole four years was probably staying eligible my freshman year. I was a hometown, local kid. We stayed at the University Inn down there on campus. All my buddies would come into town, and if it was raining and stuff in the morning, we'd just close the blinds back up and go back to sleep. I didn't handle the responsibility deal really well, and that caught up with me quickly. Probably my one regret is that I didn't put more time into the academic part of it. I wish I had taken it more seriously, which I didn't. But I at least kept it together well enough that, when my chance came, I could take advantage of it.

136

This was still 1983, my first year in the program, and Jorgy broke his leg against UCLA with three games left in that season. Mike Owens went in, and he struggled, and they decided to take the redshirt off of me and throw me in there with three games left in the season. I think I went in for the second half, I believe. I was nervous. I still remember to this day the goose bumps running throughout my entire body, and I probably weighed all of about 180 pounds. We were down about 21–0 and came back to make it 21–13, ended up losing 24–13. That's where it all started for me.

Of course, the game everybody remembers from that season is the Toilet Bowl, the scoreless tie in the 1983 Civil War. That was my third game. I really don't worry about it. It's comical to me, when I think back on it. It was ugly. I remember throwing a flat route at Ladaria Johnson's feet, probably a 10-yard throw that would have been a touchdown had I been able to get it to him. I remember Paul Schwabe, our senior field-goal kicker, missed a 19- and a 20-yard field goal, and I think Oregon State missed some, too. That game was just destined for infamy.

My sophomore year started out with four straight wins, but then we turned around and lost the next four. That streak ended when we beat UCLA

Two decades of outstanding quarterback play at Oregon began when Eugene native Chris Miller starred for his hometown team.

down there, knocking them out of the Rose Bowl in 1984. We won 20–18. That was a good feeling.

Junior year, we played another one of those payday games, at Nebraska. Usually in those situations, we'd at least show up and compete. There was only one game where I felt like we really showed up and laid an egg, and there was some intimidation factor and awe factor, which is when we went and played Nebraska and got our asses beat 63–0. That was like, what the hell just happened here? That was when steroids were just starting to become pretty prevalent. I can remember looking across the line at the nose tackle, and he looked like his neck was going to explode.

My senior year started off with a win over San Jose State, and then Colorado came to town. It was a really close game, and Derek Loville got us within one at 30–29 with 44 seconds left. We went for two, of course, trying for the win, but the receiver ran out of the back of the end zone. I smashed my helmet on the ground because I was so pissed, because I knew we were going to lose, and all the little pads popped out. But then we recovered an onside kick, I hit a long pass to J.J. Birden to get us into field-goal range, and Matt MacLeod hit the kick. We won 32–30. After the two-point play, I was walking on the sideline, and the pieces of my helmet padding were scattered everywhere. There were tears in my eyes, and the next thing I know, Tim Cooper recovered that onside kick, and I was scrambling to get my stuff back on. And Birden got flattened after that catch, and the ball came loose, but they called it a completion to set up the field goal. That was one of the best wins of my career, for sure.

We went down and played pretty well at USC later that same year. I hadn't practiced all week because my elbow was hurting, but I completed 33 balls, and threw for nearly 380 yards. We almost had a chance to beat them. I remember hitting Latin Berry on a swing route late in the game, and he got tackled just short of a first down. We got that play and got a chance, but we ended up losing 35–21. I had all those yards, and after the game Ted Tollner, who was USC's coach at the time, came up to me and said, "Son, you just made yourself a whole lot of money."

The game against Oregon State my senior year was a great memory because that was the year they were supposed to beat us. They hadn't beaten us in so long. My freshman year was the 0–0 tie game, and we won the next two, but 1986 was supposed to be different. Instead, we went up there to Corvallis and beat them 49–28, just lit it up. Derek Loville made some great runs, Bobby DeBisschop had a great game. Afterwards we were all smoking cigars, hanging out in the locker room with some of the alumni and coaches. That was a pretty good way to end it. It was special.

I wish I could have been one of the guys on the team who got us to our first bowl game. We went 6–5 my sophomore year, and a couple years after I was done Oregon basically bought themselves to the Independence Bowl at 6–5 again, by basically guaranteeing a certain number of fans. I would have liked to have my name tied to that legacy, but I take a lot of pride in what we did here. When you think about where we came from—the gear we wore, the equipment, the facilities over at Autzen, 110 or 120 dudes lifting weights in an un-air-conditioned weight room in the east end zone, having to roll up a big metal door just to get air circulating through there—to where they are now, it's amazing. I take a lot of pride that we were a part of building that.

Sometimes back then we had to settle for playing the spoiler role. But we went into every game trying to win. Did we doubt that we could win some of them? Probably. But we worked our asses off. We always played the Huskies tough. We played teams tough, but sometimes they just had a few more guns, a few more bullets in the gun than we did. But it wasn't for the lack of effort or time that we put in. We had fun. We didn't get to any Rose Bowls or Holiday Bowls or anything like that, but we laid the groundwork.

Chris Miller set 13 school records during his Oregon career and was named first-team All-Pac-10 twice. He was the 13th overall selection in the 1987 NFL Draft by the Atlanta Falcons, played 10 seasons in the league, and was named to the Pro Bowl in 1991. Miller returned to Eugene to coach high school football at South Eugene High from 2001 to 2006 and then ran a youth recreational sports organization. In 2009 he was named quarterbacks coach for the NFL's Arizona Cardinals.

ANTHONY NEWMAN

DEFENSIVE BACK

1984–1987

MY SOPHOMORE YEAR, I REMEMBER we were playing at Nebraska, and we were getting whooped up on. But we were playing hard. The Cornhuskers ran a play up the middle that caused a pile-up, and afterward our defense—guys like Jerry Mikels, Don Pellum, Tom Talbot—were yelling at each other, keeping ourselves hyped up, having fun. We were getting beat about 50–0, but that was our pack. And no matter what was going on, we were in it together. We created a tightness that still lives on today.

Besides getting an education, which was the most important thing, the best thing about playing at Oregon was the friendships. I'm a family person, and family also includes friends. The friendships I formed, it was unbelievable. Ron Gould was in my wedding. Don Pellum was in my wedding. There was Doug Judge, who took care of me when I was a young pup, took me under his wings. I didn't have brothers and sisters growing up, so those guys ended up being like my big brothers. So that was important to me. Those were people I looked up to and counted on. They were there for me, especially when things got hard.

I don't know what it's like at other schools, but the Ducks, we had a tight group of guys. We believed in each other. We were 6–5 half the time, but it was always a battle. When we were on the field, it was a battle every weekend. We weren't a USC or a UCLA. We went through the same things—the training camp, the offseason. We could look in each other's eyes and know we were a pack, a pack that was important and unique. Other schools were different. They had different records, different battles. We all knew what we were going through.

Joe Schaffeld recruited me, and to this day he's like a grandfather. Coming out of high school in Beaverton, I was this running back who didn't play defense a whole lot. Being the state player of the year, I was mostly recruited as a running back, took trips to Nebraska and Washington. Arizona State and Oregon were the only schools that liked me as a defensive back. I had attended a football camp in Eugene before my senior year, and I was getting pick after pick. They were like, "Wow, we're going to get you as a DB." So they came at me on defense right from the beginning.

I made my decision while watching an Oregon game. I was standing on the sideline when the Ducks played USC, and the Trojans had these huge defensive players. Jack Del Rio was just tearing up our running backs, running faster than them. At that point I was going, "There's no way I can play running back at this level. I'm going to play defense and have these guys on my side." Add in the better odds of reaching the NFL and having a longer career on defense, and that sealed it. So it came down to Arizona State and Oregon. And I actually committed to the Sun Devils on a trip there. The sun was still shining in December, much different than winter weather in Portland. But I reconsidered. I wanted my parents to be able to see me play, and a lot of other Oregon kids were leaving the state that year. I was thinking, *I'm staying in-state, and when I'm done playing people here will hopefully appreciate that.*

Doug Judge and Don Pellum immediately took me under their wings. Doug was a strong safety, and I was a free safety. I have no idea why he decided to watch over me, but everywhere he went, he asked me to come along. I was just a little puppy, following the guy around. Don Pellum was always there, too. One night my freshman year, they were shaving the heads of all the freshmen. I had a Jheri curl and was like, "Heck no, I'm not cutting my hair!" They were dragging the freshmen out of their rooms and shaving them, but Don let me stay in his room all night, and when they came knocking at the door, he didn't let them in.

I loved playing for Rich Brooks, but I was scared to death of that man. He put the fear into you. You didn't see it during recruiting, but he was an intimidating force. I didn't really get comfortable with him until my senior year, when I felt like I could really talk to him. For three years, whenever I walked

After a standout career at Oregon and 12 years in the NFL, Anthony Newman returned to Oregon as a television analyst.

by his office, I turned my head so we wouldn't make eye contact, and he wouldn't notice me and call me in. My senior year was totally different. He warmed up to me that season. But not in the early going, that's for sure.

My first year, three of us played as true freshmen: Elliott Dunning, Rollin Putzier, and myself. We went 6–5 and beat the Beavers to end the season. Probably the middle of my sophomore year, things started to change for me a little bit. I was the backup at free safety behind a guy from Eugene, Dan Wilken. He hurt his foot and couldn't play again, and my role changed. The second game of that season we played at Colorado, which was a wishbone team. I was scared. I probably lined up 20 yards deep. They'd run the option, and I'd be late getting to the play, not making tackles, not getting it done. Rich Brooks called me into his office after that game and said, "If you want to play here, you want to be on the football field, you'd better get 100 percent better." Right there I said I better shape up. Not be so scared to get after it. From that point on, things changed.

Two of my most memorable days came when I was a junior. Arizona State came to Autzen Stadium in the middle of the year, and I was playing strong safety. They had this fullback, I don't even remember his name, but he was a load. We were banging shoulders, getting after it, all day. About the third quarter, he came around the corner on a pitch play. I knew I couldn't take him on straight up, so I thought, *I'm going to jump over him. I'm going to make it happen.* I jumped completely over him, landed on the running back and made the tackle in the backfield. We ended up that year 5–6, but we beat the Beavers again, and I had three interceptions that day.

143

I owe a lot of my development as a junior and senior to Jim Radcliffe, the strength and conditioning coach. I was a weight fanatic, had lifted my whole life. But Jimmy had some new stuff for us, and I took it to heart, and got bigger, stronger, faster, quicker. And then Denny Schuler, the assistant coach, helped me develop as a football player. He got me to start using my brain rather than just relying on my athletic ability. That was really my forte in my 12 years in the NFL—using my head, knowing what the other team was trying to do. Denny taught me how to watch film, what to look for in terms of alignments, all those different things. Going into my senior year, everything really started to come easy because of all that hard work.

We opened up that season at Colorado as big underdogs. They had their option quarterback and a good running back. On one play I had to take the quarterback but also watch for a pitch. I was coming up on him in the option, getting ready to hit him. I stopped, knowing he was going to pitch, knocked it down, and recovered the fumble. We ended up winning 10–7. We lost the next week at Ohio State 24–14. It got out of hand late, but we battled, played a great game. Then we won three in a row and were feeling pretty good heading to UCLA. But then Bill Musgrave broke his collarbone, and things went off-track.

That senior year was a good year. We got in *Sports Illustrated*, ranked 17th or 18th. That's when things started to change for the Ducks. We were 6–5 and in the running for a bowl game, but Stanford was picked for the Liberty Bowl. But we were a good football team until we lost our starting quarterback. A lot of guys on that team were young—Musgrave, Derek Loville, Terry Obee, Latin Berry. They went to a bowl game a couple years later.

We knew things were evolving. Oregon started getting more California kids. Things were taking a turn. I didn't feel that freshman and sophomore year. We were just trying to survive. But my junior and senior year it changed, especially senior year. We beat Washington at home, and then USC at home. We were saying we've got a team here. That changed everything. And our fans made a huge difference.

We beat the Beavers 44–0 in the last game of 1987. Derek just went off, and their offense couldn't do anything. That was the way to end a career. It was fun. It was a blast. I bleed our colors.

Anthony Newman was a first-team All-Pac-10 selection in 1987, and was invited to the Hula Bowl and the Japan Bowl following that season. He shared Oregon's MVP award as a senior. Newman was a second-round pick by the Los Angeles Rams in the 1988 NFL Draft and played professionally for 12 years. He began serving as an analyst for Oregon football telecasts beginning in 2003.

J.J. BIRDEN

RECEIVER

1984–1987

I GREW UP IN PORTLAND, WAS BORN AND RAISED in Northeast Portland. I was actually involved in the bussing program. I used to bus out to Lake Oswego schools, and that's how I ended up at Lakeridge High School.

At that point, football was pretty much the farthest thing from my mind because I was more of a track athlete. I played junior varsity my first couple years. By my senior year I got to play varsity, and I was all-state and all that, but I couldn't get any offers. Everybody wanted me to go to these little schools, but I wanted to play in the Pac-10. I got a bit of a chip on my shoulder. I thought I would wait and see if I could get a track scholarship, and see if I could work my way on to a Pac-10 football team that way.

I watched Oregon growing up, when they were running the option. They were bad most of the time. They had Reggie Ogburn and those guys, and I just remember thinking how boring the offense was. That's coming from a receiver, of course. But I had always thought that if I was able to play Division I football, why not stay in state? Why not stay in Oregon and be one of the guys who stayed home and helped a local team get better?

Track went great my senior year at Lakeridge. I did really well at state, placed second in four events, won two, so I had a lot of Division I schools that were recruiting me for track. But I had an ulterior motive: I wanted to see who was going to let me play football too. I kind of bounced around the Pac-10, and all the schools said no to football except for Idaho, Boise State, and Oregon. Even the Ducks said I'd have to run track the first year, and then if I wanted to walk on to the football team the second year, they'd see what they would do. It wasn't even really definite.

So I got to Eugene in 1983 and didn't play football that fall. I just kind of watched and paid attention, but there was no playing football for me that year. I used to go and sneak in and watch the practices because I was pretty angry that they didn't really recruit me in football and I wanted to see how they were doing.

Rich Brooks, I guess he knew I was watching practices, because I was hiding behind the goal post one day the following spring and he walked all the way down the field over to me. I was like, "Uh oh. I'm not supposed to be here." And he said, "I know you've been watching practice. Do you want to play?" I said, "Yeah." And he said, "Come see me tomorrow." So I went to his office the next day and he said he'd give me a shot, he'd give me one year. He told me they were transferring my scholarship from track to football, and if it didn't work, they would just transfer it back. All I was thinking was, *This is the door I wanted to have opened for me.*

I didn't really feel pressure early on because I know they really didn't think I was going to be good enough. I was the sixth-string guy when I came in, but I wasn't worried because I knew I was pretty good. I knew I just needed a shot. I wasn't the typical track/football player. I could catch, and I understood the game, too, and worked hard and everything. I went in at 153 pounds, standing about 5'10", and they were definitely concerned about my size, but it took them about a week, and then Bob Toledo came up to me and said, "Man, we didn't know you were this good." I said, "You guys never gave me a chance!" After that point I started climbing that depth chart pretty fast.

Playing in Toledo's offense was exciting, high-flying, because he was coming at you so many different ways. He was running it and throwing it. It was a dream offense for me, because, although I know ball control and securing the ball is important, this was a coach who liked to throw it, too. This is before all those offenses you see today that spread you out and throw it so much. It was rarer then. He always liked the double moves, the hitch 'n' go, the stutters, out and ups—you always knew you were getting some exciting plays from Toledo.

The quarterback at that point was Chris Miller, and he was just an athlete. He was such a very good, athletic quarterback. I didn't realize how good he was until the next couple years when I started paying attention, and I thought, *Wow. This guy is unbelievable.* He threw great deep balls and had great awareness on the field. And he was an athlete. He could run, do everything that you would like a quarterback to do.

My first two years were very much the same. I was second-string, behind Lew Barnes, who was very good. I backed him up for two years, and I hardly got in the game. He never came out. I caught about three balls one year, six balls the next year. The other guy was Scott Holman, and those guys stayed healthy, so I didn't get many chances to play. They never got hurt, and they didn't use a lot of three-receiver sets back then.

Lew was very good. He was shorter than me, but he was strong and quick. The funny thing about it is that because of Lew's success, that's when I started to realize I might be able to play in the NFL. My junior year, Bob Toledo said, "You're the guy now." He said if I continued to improve, I'd get a shot, and I said, "A shot where?" And he told me the NFL, and I said, "You gotta be crazy," because I wasn't thinking about the NFL at all at that point in time. But then the draft came, and Lew Barnes got drafted, and I was like, "What? He got drafted in the NFL?" So then I was thinking maybe I could do that too. I patiently waited my time and just tried to get bigger and understand the game better, and then I got my shot my junior year.

I was one of the rarities in football because I only went through one spring ball—usually I was competing in track during that season. But in 1986, after Lew and Scott graduated, I redshirted in track and participated in spring football to get ready for my big chance at playing. That was the year that I was "the guy," and I had a really good spring. I remember this article from the local paper, the *Register-Guard*, which said, "The rapidly improving receiver, J.J. Birden, is latching on to the number one spot." I felt that this was my shot and I needed to make a statement.

At that point in the development of the program, we were kind of like that little kid hanging out in the neighborhood wanting to get their shot at the big boys. We felt we were good enough, but we just weren't there yet. We would go 6–5 or 5–6 every year. By my junior year we got some really good blue-chippers, like Derek Loville and Chris Oldham, some really good players. I remember thinking that we were getting the players, so even though we weren't quite there yet, we were almost getting there. Our biggest weakness was that we lacked depth. We started the 1984 season 4–0, and when our guys started getting hurt, we didn't have the studs to back them up like we do today. We had no depth, and we couldn't keep it up.

My first two years as a backup, the biggest highlight was playing UCLA freshman year. The game was on national television, and it was the rare time that Lew Barnes was injured, and I got to play because I was the third receiver. And I was so terrified. I was involved in a big third-down play, running an in route over the middle. This was back when I didn't understand the difference between man and zone defenses. So I didn't understand what kind of coverage I would be up against, and I just got lit up by this safety, James Washington. I caught the ball, but I broke a finger on the play. I went to the sideline, but I didn't tell the trainers I was hurt because I didn't want to come out of the game. I just told Chris to not throw me the ball anymore. I told him to not tell the coaches because this was my only chance to play, but to not throw the ball to me unless he had to. So I played the rest of the game, and I remember Scott Holman made a great catch between his legs, and we ended up winning that game. For me, that was a real big achievement because I got to play on national television and I took a real hard hit, and even though they all said I was too small, I caught the ball.

To be honest, my last two years as a Duck were not all that impressive. My junior year, I started out playing really well through the first four games. The first game I had about 10 catches, but then I broke my arm the fourth game, against Nebraska, and missed nearly the rest of the season. I came back against the Beavers, but the injury cost me half the season. That was horrible because I started out as one of the leading receivers in the Pac-10, and then when I broke my arm, everybody was like, "See, told you. The guy's too small, he can't stay healthy." So that was really frustrating.

Entering 1987, I had a lot to prove. I took the offseason very seriously and put on a couple more pounds, and worked really hard with Bill Musgrave and all the other guys. Musgrave was entering his redshirt freshman year, and it was really hard to believe that he was so young, even then. He was so poised and smart as a quarterback that I just couldn't believe he was 18. When you were in the huddle with him, it was like being in the huddle with a veteran. He just seemed so ahead of the game to be so young.

When the season came around, I had a good start again, but then I twisted my ankle against UCLA and missed five games. It's just funny how my college career worked out, because I played nine seasons in the NFL and yet I had the most unimpressive college career. I broke my arm my junior year, then twisted my ankle my senior year. But I had a couple touchdowns in

J.J. Birden was a fleet-footed receiver who also starred in track and field for Oregon. *Photo courtesy Getty Images.*

149

there and a couple memorable catches. I didn't catch a lot of balls over the course of the four years I played at Oregon.

I was just happy to have had the chance. I was worried that Oregon wouldn't give me my shot initially, but they did in the end because Brooks was willing to give me an opportunity. And that's all I wanted. I just wanted a chance, and it was very flattering. It made me feel good that first week when Bob Toledo said, "We didn't know you were that good."

Being able to maintain my track career the entire time was important to me, especially because I was one of the rarities who did two sports and also graduated. One thing college taught me was the ability to stay focused on a goal. When I was in track, the goal was to do what I needed to do there but stay focused academically, and then on the football field it was the same thing. By the time I got to the NFL, I knew what it was like to practice for hours and stay focused for hours, because in the NFL it's physical, but it's the mental part that separates the real athletes.

Bob Toledo one time had sat me down and told me that I needed to learn defenses. I didn't know defenses at all, I just wanted them to throw me the ball. He told me I had to learn that stuff, and by my senior year I started to really learn the defenses and understand what was going on with the other side of the ball. And that's what you have to do in the NFL. Another tip he gave me was to learn all the receiver positions, because if I did that, I would be more valuable. The more you know, the more opportunities you get. I took that to the NFL. I was always the guy who they could move around, who was willing to do what it took to play.

John Ramsdell, the receivers coach, was another guy who had a big impact while I was at Oregon. Over the course of my entire football career I had about three really good coaches who impacted me, and he was one of them. Because John was more than just a coach. He really spent a lot of time teaching me the game, and teaching me to be a receiver, and teaching me to be a good student. He kind of set a foundation for me there, and then when I got to the NFL with the Chiefs, Al Saunders continued that training.

During my time in Eugene, we didn't have the big weight room or any of the other fancy amenities the Ducks have now. We just had this and that, but we had a group of guys who believed that we should be in the upper echelon. We knew were missing a couple things, but with the core guys we had, we were willing to do what it takes so that we could start getting those types of athletes who could help us get over the top. When I reflect on the Oregon program, what I always tell people is that during my years we set the foundation of the run that has continued to this day. I thought our years were when we started turning the corner. My senior year, we were 6–5 and we almost went to a bowl game. A couple years later Oregon finally made a bowl game, and now it happens year in, year out.

Anthony Newman, the safety, and I were tight in those days. We're still really tight today, very good friends. We were from the same area, had played each other in high school. Newman, Latin Berry, and myself were close. Latin Berry and I were really tight because Lat and I used to compete against each other in track. What I loved about us three—and I really mean this because this is one of the things that really disappoints me about the Oregon high school athletes today—is that they don't really make a concerted effort to stay at one of the Oregon schools, whether it's Oregon or Oregon State. I wish that they would stay local. When we got together, we stayed here and helped our school get on the map, to be one of the top schools in the country. We became Ducks, and we're still Ducks to this day.

J.J. Birden was a four-year letterman in both football and track for the Ducks. He was the 1987 Pac-10 champion in the long jump. Birden was selected in the eighth round of the 1988 NFL Draft by the Cleveland Browns and spent nine seasons in the NFL with Kansas City and Atlanta, retiring from football after the 1996 season. He currently lives in Lake Oswego and is a health food distributor.

BILL MUSGRAVE

QUARTERBACK

1987–1990

GROWING UP IN COLORADO, I WAS ALWAYS interested in playing in the Pac-10. I had some interest in Oregon, and Neal Zoumboukos was recruiting me for the Ducks, sending me a ton of literature. He had the whole state of Colorado, although I think there were only two guys from Colorado at Oregon when I got there, Rob Marshall and Gary Robertson. I didn't know either of them before I got to Eugene, but I got to know them once I got there. It wasn't many guys from my home state, but Zoumboukos tried hard to get at least one guy out of Colorado a year. I went to a basketball game at Mac Court while on my official visit to Oregon, and that was very impressive, to see how electric that environment was. The next day Bob Toledo took me up the river to a trout farm and told me if I became a Duck I would have the chance to catch all the big fish we saw there. That was really all I needed to hear. I was a big fisherman, coming from Colorado, so that sealed the deal for me and Oregon.

I just had a good feel for the entire program. When I arrived on my flight for the official visit, Zoumboukos took me up to the top of Skinner Butte overlooking downtown Eugene, so that I would have my bearings of the town. He showed me some other landmarks around Eugene, which helped me while I was on my visit. Coach Zoomer knew I was the kind of guy who liked to have my bearings and not just be floating around someplace where I didn't really know which way was up. I felt comfortable on campus at that point. I could picture myself playing and going to school there.

My host was Gary Robertson. Of course they put me with a Colorado guy. Gary was a fantastic guy. He has a heart of gold, even to this day. I still stay in touch with him. He's just a fantastic gentleman, so he made a good impression, and I could see myself being a teammate of his. Also on that visit, Rich Brooks was really promoting the fact that they were going to build a dome over Autzen Stadium. I joke about this to this day, with guys like Derek Loville. When we were on our visit, they had a model built up in the Stadium Club at Autzen, just an incredible model of a domed Autzen by some architectural firm. Of course, it was going to have a wooden look, that being forest country, and a dome was a real novelty at that time. It still hasn't come to pass, which is probably a good thing in retrospect.

I felt confident about the direction of the program when I signed on. They seemed ready to turn that perpetual corner. Reggie Ogburn had won six games a couple times, early in Brook's tenure, and then Chris Miller won five or six games a few times. I think the foundation was being laid, that a bowl game was definitely on the horizon. That was the goal at that point, because there hadn't been a bowl game since the 1963 Sun Bowl. So when we went in '89, it was the first postseason appearance for Oregon in 26 years.

That recruiting class of 1986 was a fantastic class. There were a bunch of super young men, not just football players. Derek Loville, the late Russell Lawson, Rory Dairy at safety, and then Todd Kaanapu and Andy Sunia, who both still live in Eugene. And then there were some super upperclassmen who were already there, tough guys. None of us were necessarily blue chip recruits, but I think we all knew that the essence of playing football and succeeding is toughness and being resilient, and it happened that a lot of us had those traits.

Redshirting in 1986 was no big deal to me. It was fun to watch Chris Miller play and practice. I got to learn the system and learned a lot of football from Coach Toledo. Coach Toledo knew so much about Xs and Os, it was amazing. I think it helped that he was not only an offensive coach; he coached the defensive backs at USC for years, Ronnie Lott and Jeff Fisher and all those guys. I learned a lot of lessons in that first year playing for him that I tried to apply later on in my career as a quarterbacks coach. I alternated traveling on road trips as the third quarterback that season, but I never got close to playing. Pete Nelson was the backup, and Kevin Smith, from Salem, was the other number-three guy.

The next offseason, with Miller gone, I was just trying to compete for a spot with those guys, Kevin Smith and Pete Nelson. I don't know if I really outplayed them, but the chips fell where they did. Kevin Smith was injured in the spring, as I recall, and Pete Nelson hurt an ankle in the final scrimmage, before we opened up in Boulder against Colorado. So I got the call to start my first game, as a redshirt freshman, and in my home state, of all places.

It was fun to go back to Colorado, because I'd been in that stadium a number of times cheering for the Buffaloes, and that was the first time I'd ever been in that stadium not wanting them to come out victorious. It worked out. We competed hard at Ohio State the next week, beat San Diego State at home, and then came back and got back-to-back wins against Washington and USC. To start 4–1 against some pretty quality opponents felt significant to us. We ended up being ranked in the polls for the first time since 1970.

But then I got hurt, which ended up becoming kind of a theme during my career. We had already lost a couple games, and then came back home to play California. I got hurt on my first play of the game. Ken Harvey, who was an 11-year NFL player, came around my buddy Gary Robertson, who was playing left tackle, and injured my leg. I missed the next couple of games, but luckily I was able to come back and play against the Beavers. That was fun for me, to participate in my first Civil War game as a redshirt freshman. I knew about the Beavers already, having been kind of immersed in the rivalry from my redshirt year. I knew that Erik Wilhelm was a heck of a quarterback, so I kind of enjoyed that matchup. I enjoyed it even more when we won 44–0, I suppose.

Because we started off so fast in '87 before experiencing some injuries, I think we wanted to start off fast again in 1988, but this time close it out. As it turned out, we started off even faster, going 6–1, and we had a tremendous lead against Arizona State until I tried to emulate a Derek Loville move, which led to another injury. It was a pass play, and I didn't like the coverage so I decided to scramble. I always liked handing it off to Derek Loville and watching him do his thing, and you know how people always like to emulate the great ones. I remember trying to emulate Dr. J's dunks when I was little, for instance. Well, I remember trying to shake this middle linebacker from Arizona State who had come up to tackle me once I crossed the line of scrimmage, and as I was focused on shaking him out of his boots, the weak

Bill Musgrave's leadership and poise under pressure helped spark the recent renaissance of Oregon football.

side linebacker came flying in from my left-hand side. Seeing as how I lacked the peripheral vision and instincts of Derek Loville, I got clocked—broken collarbone, out for the season.

I got to play three years with Derek, who was a heck of a runner. He was one of those running backs that didn't have the best top end speed, but he had quickness. Derek had great vision. He may not have run the fastest, but he had quickness, and that's almost just as important an attribute, because guys who aren't just speed demons, they allow the hole to develop and evolve and them jump through it when the time is right. Derek was one of those guys.

He was a senior in 1989, and I was coming off my injury. I wasn't quite ready to go for spring practices. Dr. Ken Singer did the surgery on my collarbone, and it was still touch and go. In fact, I sat out the first one or two weeks, and then finally Coach Brooks, I think he had enough of me being on the shelf. He just kind of shoved me out there, whether it was with a red jersey or not, just to get us going, because it was a frustrating time for the program after starting the season 6–1 and then losing that chance to get over the hump the year before. So the last nine or 10 days of spring ball, I jumped back in there and we tried to get our rapport back amongst our passing game and our offense, and got ready to open up the season with Troy Taylor and Cal.

There were a lot of good games that year. We played well against BYU, who was really good at that time, but they scored at the end to beat us. The Arizona State game a couple weeks earlier was a big one. We were 3–3 entering that one, which was going to be played on the road in a driving rainstorm, and we knew it was a big moment. Right before the game, we got together as players and said, "Hey, this game is crucial if we want to be bowl-eligible." We talked about how the program was headed in the right direction, and one of these days the program was going to break the bowl drought, and we would be more proud of ourselves if we were the ones that did it, rather than proud of future generations who accomplished that task. So that was our mindset, and we ended up winning four of the next five.

I know there was a lot made of Bill Byrne having to purchase a bunch of tickets to secure our spot in the Independence Bowl, and the athletic department losing money on the game, but it didn't affect the players. We were just focused on playing the game, trying to beat Tulsa. At that age, I don't think we realized the financial implications and that there were certain costs to doing business, and that was one of them. We were really proud of our year, to go 7–4 and have a chance to keep playing. Jeez, if you're 7–4 these days, you get to be in a New Year's Day bowl.

It was freezing that day in Shreveport, Louisiana, probably the coldest game I ever played in. We ran into a real storm down there. I know the fans froze. I think I was especially nervous in the first half, and that led to a couple turnovers. But in the second half, Joe Reitzug ran a great post-corner route for a touchdown, and then Derek Loville carried the mail for us to get back down and win it in the fourth quarter on a field goal. Winning that game, we felt like we really accomplished something we could take pride in.

And then of course we wanted to build on it. We were excited to break the drought. We kept hearing about 24, 25, 26 years without a bowl game, and I think with the way there are so many things that were right about Oregon—a fantastic coaching staff, a great place to go to school, a wonderful part of the country—that it was just a matter of time before the program became a perennial bowl-contender. We had really wanted to be a part of that rather than on the outside looking in and admiring from afar, after we were done playing.

We started 2–1 in 1990, and then BYU came to Autzen for a rematch of the shootout we lost the year before. Ty Detmer was still playing, so the game got a lot of attention. We felt like we were on national TV or something, whether we were or not, but at least we were on a network. This time the defense came up big, with all kinds of interceptions against Detmer, and we won 32–16. It was just a fun day to be at Autzen Stadium. Probably the most fun game of my entire career at Oregon, when I look back.

My last appearance at Autzen Stadium, about a month later against UCLA, was pretty memorable. That set up as a tough game because they had a heck of an offense. Tommy Maddox was the quarterback, and he had some good receivers to throw to. We were trying to keep pace with them, scoringwise, and were just struggling to keep our heads above water. We scored to get within a field goal late, and then got the ball back again. We called a time-out, and then Rich Brooks and Mike Bellotti dialed up a play that I still see the Ducks run to this day. It looked like we were kind of running a jailbreak or a quick screen to the right, and the guy that looked like he was supposed to be the blocker ran up the sideline. That day, that blocker was Vince Ferry, our second-string tight end, who had come in when our all-conference tight end, Jeff Thomason, had blown his Achilles earlier in the day. I don't know if we practiced that play much—in fact, it was kind of a new concept we developed midseason—but sure enough we got a good coverage where the corner filled and the safety didn't get off the hash, and we just happened to hit them right there in the honey-hole.

157

There was bad news during that game, though. One of their safeties, I think it was Matt Darby, after a pass on which I was trying to hit A.J. Jones on a corner route, he picked me up and planted me like a tree, like defenders do. That sprung something again in my collarbone, which I had hurt a couple years before. I tried to play the next week against Cal, and got hit again late by Rhett Hall down there, and did not play again in the regular season. Bob Brothers played against the Beavers and won the game for us in a driving rainstorm in Corvallis.

We finished the regular season 8–3, better than the year before, and got a little upgrade in the postseason. Instead of going to Louisiana, we got to go to Anaheim for the Freedom Bowl, so that was fun. We felt like we were hitting on all cylinders that day against Colorado State. We were throwing the ball down the field, hitting some long seam routes. Joe Reitzug got dinged up a little bit, but he gutted it out. We had a great young running back that year in Sean Burwell, and he really carried us, too. Of course, our line blocked up and down the field. It was an exciting game, a real shootout, and we just fell short on a two-point conversion at the end. We completed a pass to Michael McClellan after our last touchdown and thought he was in the end zone, but the officials said he didn't cross the goal line.

After my last game as a Duck, I didn't want it to end. It was a fantastic experience. I got a lot of breaks along the way, and was certainly in the right place at the right time in numerous instances. I just felt very fortunate to accumulate all those memories.

Bill Musgrave was a four-year starter, a three-year team captain and Oregon's MVP in 1990. He graduated as the Ducks' career leader in total offense, passing yards, passing touchdowns, and completion percentage, and a 25–10 record in games he started and finished. Along with being a first-team all-conference pick, Musgrave was the GTE Academic All-American of the Year in 1990. Musgrave was invited to the Hula Bowl, the East-West Shrine Game, and the Japan Bowl after his senior season and was a fourth-round NFL Draft pick by the Dallas Cowboys in 1991. Following a six-year playing career, Musgrave entered the coaching ranks. Most recently, he became the quarterbacks coach for the Atlanta Falcons in 2006.

The
NINETIES

DANNY O'NEIL

QUARTERBACK

1991–1994

Ｉ CAME UP TO OREGON, AND AT THE TIME it seemed like I went to a whole different world. I moved away from Southern California and all the things that were comfortable down there—family, the beach, and all the different fun things to do. What it meant to be a Duck was to come up here with a full commitment to play Oregon Duck football. At the time, there were a lot of other California players. In the '80s and '90s, a lot of California guys felt the same as I did. We came up here to play football—and sacrificed some of the comfortable things to play football, so what it meant to be a Duck was being around a bunch of guys who made a similar commitment: "I'm here to play football." We worked out. We wanted to watch film. We made sure we showed up to all the workouts, and we'd do it. In the summertime, we stayed here to work.

I came to Oregon basically because Oregon seemed to want me more than the other schools wanted me. Now, with the Internet, it's a whole different deal, but when I was being recruited, you felt like it was just you and the coaches. I could have gone to USC or Alabama, but for both of them I was like their second guy, and they wanted their first guy. And I sensed that in their recruiting, that they were afraid to offer me a scholarship. And, I could be wrong with this, you'd have to ask the coaches, but I think I was Oregon's number-one guy, and that was apparent in the way they recruited me.

Nick Aliotti, now the defensive coordinator, was my recruiter. I have and always will have a great affinity towards Coach Aliotti. Maybe he's one of those guys that makes a lot of guys feel this way, I wouldn't be surprised, but he made me feel like I was his guy. He made me feel that he would look after me away from home, even after I got here. I felt like he really had an interest in me, not only as a person and making the right decisions, but also in my football career. He was interested in me on and off the field. He was always there for me, looking after me, even after I signed and was on offense, on the opposite side of the field from him.

Back then, you couldn't weigh and you couldn't measure during recruiting, which was beneficial to me, because I'm 6′, 165 pounds, and I didn't gain much weight. As I understand, had Mike Bellotti, who was offensive coordinator then, known that I was that height and weight, he wouldn't have even recruited me, but Coach Aliotti kind of hedged and told him I was 6′2″ and 185. On my recruiting trip I wore my basketball shoes with thick heels and always had a jacket on, so they couldn't tell I was a little small.

Besides Coach Aliotti, what sold me was that with Bill Musgrave they had just gone to a bowl game, and to me that solidified that the program was headed in the right direction to be competitive. I didn't know much about Oregon, but I, like everyone else, like to be treated well, and Oregon treated me well. They recruited me very hard, so that's what pushed me over the edge to come to Oregon. I wanted to go where someone really wanted me, and I wanted to play for four years. I liked the idea that I was told by the coaches that I would be competing for the job my freshman year.

161

Once I got up there with my family, we were driving from the airport to Eugene, and we drove in and there was a sign that said, "Welcome to Eugene," and there's nothing around but the sign. So we got out and took a picture by the "Welcome to Eugene" sign because it was like, welcome to what? What am I looking at? This is where I'm going to be living, in the open country? Which I like; I now live on a farm. I like the open country, I love the open land. But that was my first impression, that I was moving to nowhere. But I was so committed to wanting to be a great football player that it was all good. I was here to play football.

The first year, thankfully, I was committed to playing because I think for a lot of California guys it is difficult to get over the weather, the rain, no sun. It didn't bother me too much. I remember thinking, *Man, it rains a lot.* I was just here to play football. It was just part of the process. I think a lot of guys have trouble with that. A lot of guys who live in Eugene have trouble with that. You end up just really enjoying the seasons; the problem is, our rainy

Danny O'Neil blossomed as a senior quarterback, leading a late comeback against Washington and setting a Rose Bowl record for passing yards.

season is a little bit too long. I love the seasons, in contrast to Southern California. In Southern California we have one and a half seasons, a perfect day, and then a little bit of a cool day, and then you come up here and it's totally varied. I like the different seasons. I still do.

My redshirt year, they brought in two other quarterbacks, Doug Musgrave and Brett Salisbury. Musgrave could have gone anywhere, and Salisbury was, like, 23, and I was 19 at the time. And that was a blow, because I was looking to play, and now we have these two other guys that they brought in. So what happened was that I had to beat them out, and I did.

My first home opener against Washington State in 1991 was a good memory. I played pretty well, and we won. And then a week later at Texas Tech I played really well and helped the team get a win down in Lubbock, Texas.

Then we went to Utah, and I was horrible. I played really poorly. It was a real wake-up call. They were a good team that year, but they made me look like I was 15. I went from playing really good as a redshirt freshman, to playing really bad, and then I got hurt. I broke my thumb and only played five games. I couldn't redeem myself, and I had to just sit.

My sophomore year was a good season. We went to a bowl game. I played like a sophomore. I don't think I played spectacular, but solid. My junior year, I broke a lot of Oregon records but didn't win. So my sophomore year I didn't play as well, but we won. My junior year, our offense was really good, but we didn't win, so I was still miserable. For me and certainly my class, it was great we were able to at least end on a great year. I think that kind of makes your affinity for everything well worth it. I think, even though I've always loved Oregon and would always love Oregon football, something tells me my affinity toward Oregon football changed greatly after our senior season. I remember my feelings not being quite that strong my first four years. It had nothing to do with Oregon or Oregon football. It's just that losing is miserable. And there were a lot of losses; half the time I played my first three years, I lost. Football is a blast, and competition is exhilarating, but losing doesn't make anything okay. And there were a lot of losses those first three years.

Prior to my senior year, I would get hate mail. I would be yelled at. I think Bellotti always believed in me, and that I was always going to be the guy. I don't know if that was true for the other coaches, nor do I know if that was true for Rich Brooks. One good thing I had going, one of my better qualities, was that I liked to compete. So unless they just yanked me and put some other guy in—which they could have, and I think they probably thought about it a couple time—I wasn't going anywhere. If it came down to a competition, I was going to win it every time. I think Bellotti understood that—whatever you say, he's going to be our starter.

My senior year, we didn't start off very good. We started off 1–2, with our one win against Portland State. Then we played Iowa. It was a big program, Hayden Fry was a big-time coach, so there was a lot of pressure in the game. They ended up not being very good, and we won and that was an important game for us. Then I got this weird thing with my finger that turned out to be an infection, and it looked like I might be out indefinitely. Tony Graziani took the team down to USC and they won in the Coliseum. When I went into Coach Bellotti's office, I said, "So, the doctor said I might be ready next week. What's going to happen?" But I knew the answer. He said they had to go with what's working. That was a big blow to me, because the year before I had broken the school record in yardage and I was feeling like I could do this thing, even though we weren't doing very well as a team that year.

I went in as a backup in the Washington State game because Graziani got hurt, and we still lost the game. But we rebounded against Cal, and were 4–3. Washington came into town, and, to me, that was the big game. Every game was critical, but for me, and I think the team, that Washington game was the big one. Back then Washington was the team we really wanted to beat, even though they were so good in those days. I think particularly our senior class was unique in the sense that we did believe we could be good. We had put in a lot of years, and we could go back to all our losses, and we thought we could have won those games. You really began to get that sense by your senior year—if you make plays you can win. You don't have to be more talented than the other team to win, you just have to beat them. I think our senior class had that idea, that Washington is Washington but we could beat them.

164

The Huskies were up 20–17 in the fourth quarter when we went 98 yards on offense to take the lead back. People thought it was a bigger thing for me than it actually was—there was some media talk about me not being able to lead the team with a game on the line. It bothered me because I hadn't done it, but it's not like I ever doubted whether I could if I needed to. It's just that, right at that moment, we had to do it, and here you had to do it against Washington—the stage was so perfect. A 98-yard touchdown drive against Washington. I mean, Washington is good today, but back then they were "Washington." It was a bigger deal than today. I think when you beat Washington at home and come from behind, it solidifies what you always believed, that you could beat them.

Of course, that wasn't the end of the game, because Washington put together a drive the other way, which was lame because our defense had been playing so well all day. All we had to do was stop them once and we would win, and we did, right at the end, 31–20. And, of course, that interception by Kenny Wheaton has gone down in history as one of the greatest plays for a reason. It was a spectacular play. I think it deserves its place very much because it was amazing. Some people always say well, yeah, it overshadowed the 98-yard drive, and I think, well, it sure did. That was an amazing drive. But what a play by Kenny, too.

That year ended in the Rose Bowl, which I remember more for the over-all experience than just the game. We played pretty well, but we lost 38–20.

When you lose, it's hard, especially now you think, *Gosh we should have won.* Everybody wants to win. The game itself, you felt like it was a big game. There were 100,000 fans, a blimp up above, it was on national television. We played Penn State, who was ranked No. 2 in the country. You knew it was a big game, and that was a great memory, just being able to perform in such a great game. Obviously, the outcome is not as exciting, but it still represents a championship season. To get to the game, you had to do something special, and we did, and so the Rose Bowl represents our year, the championship year, more than just the outcome of that one game.

When I think back to my Oregon experience, more now than even then, I identify and appreciate and miss a lot of those guys that I battled with. I've always looked at it like we were like warriors. You put on the pads and you fight on Saturdays. For our senior class, in particular, we went through extremely difficult times as football players, and then it culminated in the Rose Bowl. For our senior class, it's hard to really match that. When they do great now, it's just as exciting, but I think in particular for us to come out of nowhere after having so many difficult years, it made it really special.

Danny O'Neil was a first-team All-Pac-10 selection as a senior, having completed 182-of-341 passes for 2,212 yards and 22 touchdowns. He passed up the chance to play professionally in order to enter the ministry, and is presently a pastor in Eugene.

CHAD COTA
SAFETY
1991–1994

I HAD A COUSIN, JULIE WHITE, WHO RAN TRACK at Oregon. She was a 400-meter hurdler. So we kind of had a Duck family, growing up in Ashland. I definitely recall coming up to watch Duck games when I was a kid. I wasn't always sure I'd get to play football there. And then in the 1989 state championships I had an interception against Roseburg. That pretty much sealed my scholarship offer from Oregon. I had been looking at Oregon State and Utah, too, but I wanted to be a Duck.

Denny Schuler was our defensive coordinator at the time, and he became the biggest influence on me after I first got to Eugene. As far as the players, Rory Dairy and Eric Castle were the guys I looked up to early on. I didn't mind redshirting in 1990. That was pretty much my plan. Almost everybody redshirted back in those days. The jump from high school to college was definitely an adjustment, but I felt like I was comfortable playing at that level and I knew that I was fine. The speed and the size of everybody was an adjustment. That redshirt year got me plenty of time to get acclimated and ready to play next season.

Oregon had a pretty good tradition at defensive back before I got there. Not only Castle and Dairy, but Anthony Newman, who was a guy I really looked up to and loved to watch play. I tried to emulate him the best I could. Once you get a tradition like that going at a position, kids want to come in and keep it going. Herman O'Berry was another good defensive back who

Chad Cota was one of the most respected members of the "Gang Green" defense that was crucial to the 1994 Rose Bowl season.

came on the same year I did. I think Coach Schuler kind of got that movement going, and once Nick Aliotti took over the secondary, he kept it going strong, too.

From the 1990 season I mostly remember that BYU game. That was a huge moment for our program. Daryle Smith had three interceptions against Ty Detmer. That was huge, great for our secondary.

I went into my freshman season in 1991 thinking I'd get to play mainly special teams and maybe the dime situations when we needed an extra defensive back. It worked out that, during fall camp, that's what happened. But I guess we just didn't really have a strong safety that really stood out. Paul Rodriguez was starting, but he was struggling a little bit.

Then Eric Castle got hurt against USC, which was a night game on ESPN. I suppose that's when I made a name for myself, because I went in and had a good game. I had a huge hit on Mazio Royster that night. I came from free safety and just blasted him, knocked him out of the game. After that hit, I never left the field. I ended up starting from there on out. But that was definitely a great moment. I just came full speed and had one of the better hits I've ever had.

Our offense had a down year that year, and our defense was okay. Castle and I were playing together, and we played well together. That was fun to play under him, to have him coach and kind of mentor me.

Based on that experience, I felt pretty established coming into 1992. I don't know if you'd have called me a leader in those days. I'm more of a guy that wasn't a big presence in the locker room. I just liked leading on the field.

We took a lot of pride in our defense. Coach Schuler really talked about how we were one of the best defenses in the Pac-10. And then once we got the quarterback established, once Danny O'Neil got established, we knew some positive things were going to happen for the team.

Sophomore year, we went to the Independence Bowl. That was when Alex Molden came in and we had a really young secondary, all sophomores or freshmen. We knew we had a good, young team coming up.

But then 1993 was a step back. That was a frustrating year. The most frustrating loss of my career was that season. We were 3–0 and we went down to Cal. We were up 30–7 at halftime, and they came back and ran all these reverses and fake plays, and we ended up losing. I lost three nights of sleep after that game. That was one of the hardest losses of my life. We could have been 4–0, ranked in the top 20, and on top of the world with that win. It just devastated us. That was a year that really could have been positive. We still could have gone to a bowl game, and then we lost to Oregon State. It was awful.

The following offseason wasn't hugely positive. It's not like you could tell a Rose Bowl season was coming. But we felt good, and we knew we had a good team. We knew we didn't have a weakness on defense, and then Danny O'Neil came into his own on offense. Cristin McLemore stepped up at receiver. The year started really slow with early losses to Hawaii and Utah. The Iowa game was a make-or-break game, and we came out at home and really played great. We really felt positive after that week. After those two losses, everybody wanted Rich Brooks' head, but after that Iowa game, we just got in a groove. Our defense played really aggressively. With our corners, O'Berry and Molden, we could put those guys out on an island in coverage and just bring the house against the run.

More than individual memories, the 1994 season at this point seems just like one big run. We just had that snowball effect and kept going and going, starting with that 'SC win. We went down to USC and we hadn't beaten an L.A. school in years. That was a huge boost for us, and we kept going from there. Starting with the Arizona State game, there was a lot of pressure at that point, because we knew that if we kept winning we were going to the Rose Bowl. You knew it, but you just rolled with it. We were a pressure team. We knew it was all on us. We controlled our own destiny. Those last three games were all big games. It definitely helped to have a senior-dominated team.

The whole Rose Bowl experience was a great week, being down there amid all the excitement. I remember all the fans and having some of my family there, and then on game day going into a stadium with 100,000 people and half of them were Duck fans. It was pretty unbelievable. U of O going to the Rose Bowl was just not even heard of prior to that. Years before that, talk of a Rose Bowl might come up and everybody would almost laugh about it. It seemed that out of reach. That's what was so amazing. We knew the whole state would go nuts. There was no way the Ducks were going to the Rose Bowl, but it happened.

My NFL career was pretty much a mirror image of how we were that Rose Bowl year. I was kind of an overachiever, and I carried that throughout my career. People told me I was too slow or too small. I didn't believe it. I thought I had great speed and I could hit with anybody, and that's kind of how our team was. We didn't believe any of the naysayers, and that's how I went about my NFL career. We knew we were the underdogs, and we went out there and did it anyway.

Chad Cota led Oregon in both tackles and interceptions as a junior in 1993 and was a first-team All-Pac-10 selection in 1994. His teammates voted him Oregon's most outstanding player as a senior. He was invited to both the East-West Shrine Game and the Hula Bowl after his senior season, and he was taken in the seventh round of the 1995 NFL Draft by Carolina. Following an eight-year pro career, Cota returned to Ashland, Oregon, where he works and runs a charitable foundation to support youth athletic programs.

RICH RUHL

LINEBACKER

1992–1995

M Y DAD, DICK, WAS A LINEBACKER AT OREGON STATE and went to the Rose Bowl with the Beavers back in 1965. I'm sure he never thought then that 30 years later I'd be doing the same thing, but with the Ducks.

My dad didn't really pressure me either way. He didn't really care where I went, just wanted me to make a good decision. I considered Oregon State, for sure. I had quite a lot of offers my junior year of high school down in Roseburg, but then I broke my leg and I missed about five games. Then it came down to pretty much Arizona State, Oregon State, and Oregon.

I wanted to stay somewhat close to home, and Oregon at that time was kind of on the rise. And, just like it is for a lot of guys today, a huge factor in recruiting is the facilities. At that time they were just building the administrative building, what's now the Casanova Center. I climbed a ladder to the second level of the building, and that was pretty cool in my eyes. And of course Autzen Stadium itself was pretty neat. That was a big decision. A tough decision. My mom's an Oregon State alum, too. But when I chose Oregon, my parents were both really supportive of the decision.

Recently I was talking to Don Pellum, who has been linebackers coach at Oregon for a while, and I don't even know if I would have been recruited at this point. The guys they have now all look so good on paper: they can all fly and are massive, whereas the guys we had at that time were just hard-nosed, well-disciplined, good athletes—not exceptional athletes, but good athletes. We had the few exceptions that were great athletes, guys like Alex Molden, Kenny Wheaton, Chad Cota. For the most part, though, we were just a bunch of hard-nosed guys who played hard.

Pellum was one of those guys who you appreciate more and more only after you're done playing for him. He wasn't particularly hard on me, but I know there were guys who thought he was tough to play for, at the time. And now they see him as the great person he is. He has great compassion for his players, including me.

Rich Brooks was tough. I can't say a lot for Mike Bellotti just because he didn't become head coach until my last year and he was just kind of learning things, but Brooks was tough. He and my dad went to school together, and I thought I might have a better relationship with him during those years because of that, but that wasn't the case. Since then, I've golfed with him and hung out with him, and he's super fun and nice, a great guy to hang out with. But he had this thing about him, where he was stone cold to his players. I think he wanted that intimidation factor.

I redshirted my first fall, and that was difficult. It was a lot to learn. It's amazing for me to think about some of those freshmen who are able to come right in and start playing immediately because there is so much to learn. Just the hand signals alone coming in from the sideline, there's, like, a hundred different signals. And then you have to learn all the plays on top of that. It's difficult. But it's doable, too, if you put in the time.

That's when I started getting to know a bunch of the guys I'm still good friends with today, particularly people like Troy Bailey and Jeremy Asher. I realize Asher and I are kind of grouped together in people's memories, the two inside linebackers on the Rose Bowl team. I don't talk to Jeremy that much these days, but when we get together it's like we're back living together again. We were actually big rivals in high school. He went to Tigard, and we played the state championship against each other our senior year, and then we met in track in the shot put. I was the victor. I won state. We have a lot of the same interests, mannerisms, everything, so we got to know each other pretty well after our first year, and then we moved into a house with a couple other guys and lived there for our next four years. We were probably destined to be linked—you spend so much time with the person, with defensive meetings, and then individual meetings with linebackers, and then you're talking about the same plays, and we were probably going to play together just because we were the same age.

And Troy, he lived with us, too. He was kind of an ass, sort of the class-clown type of guy. He's a super good friend of mine now, always has been. We came on our recruiting trip together. We weren't meaning to, we just ran into each other. He was a big, clumsy, skinny kid with a size 16 shoe. Everybody was all friends. There weren't cliques here and there. One thing that was difficult for me, coming from Roseburg, was how racially diverse it was. Simply put, I wasn't used to seeing a lot of guys who were black, and a lot of those guys are my real good friends now. It's cool. There was nothing like that in Roseburg. I mean nothing. So it was a growing experience. It was really odd to come in here initially. I mean, I didn't have any racial tensions by any means, but it was just different. Kenny Wheaton and I lockered right next to each other. He was a quiet guy, but funny, super funny. Isaac Walker, there's another guy I got along with really well.

My first two seasons were interesting. I hate to say this, but I think we had a lot of bad apples my first couple years, and then they kind of went away, and our group stepped up at that point. When they were gone, it just seemed like everything started to click with the teammates that were left. Everybody was pretty close. I didn't feel like the coaches really believed in me at first, and they recognized that after a while. I guess I was what you would call a "gamer," much better with the lights on than in practice, and it took a while for them to see that in me. Jeremy was always the favorite. He was a great athlete, with much better speed than I had, and it showed in practice every day. Things were different with me. Things just change when you get on the actual game field. It's a drag to walk out there on the practice field every day, play against the same guys every day. It's more intense on the game field, and that's where I felt like I really turned it on.

173

I cracked the starting lineup in '93, my sophomore year. Another guy, Dave Massey, got a couple injuries, and I got to step in and play. I think I played about four games, and did pretty well. I felt like I could play at that point, definitely. Although at that point, I was scared. Those were some big guys out there. There's a lot of development going from a sophomore to a senior. There's a lot of growing and development, and it's a little terrifying at first. You don't want to screw up, especially early on, but after you play a couple times you get the confidence that 'I'm worthy of being out here.'

By my junior year, I think it was a tighter group at that point. The veterans had a couple of years under our belts, and a lot of those guys had played their sophomore years and had now become upperclassmen, so we had better leadership. On our defensive squad, Chad Cota was a big leader. We were counting on making it to another bowl game. We had a lot of juniors and seniors on our squad at that point, so those guys had been together for four years now.

That's the group that became known as "Gang Green," because it was really a good defensive team. All those guys on defense, we were really close. Everybody had a responsibility on every play. I guess we just kind of relied on each other. We were a very disciplined unit. The average person watches a football game and thinks the defensive team just runs to the ball, but everybody had a gap responsibility, everybody had a segment of the field they have to defend if it was a pass play, and everybody shared that responsibility. We just worked really well as a group.

That 1994 season started rough, with losses to Hawaii and Utah after we opened by beating Portland State. The Hawaii game was a real low point. About 90 percent of the team had never been to Hawaii, and we didn't respond to that very well. The upshot was Chad Cota and a couple of the other veterans called a team meeting afterward for players only, no coaches. I'd been in on those earlier in my career, but they didn't mean as much because I wasn't playing as much then. This time, it really changed the team, and we got on a roll shortly after that. We saw what our potential could be, I guess. Guys played harder and were more disciplined, game in and game out.

The Washington game was just monumental, thanks to Kenny Wheaton's interception. That was probably the highlight of a lot of guys' careers at the university. We were on a high after the offense had put us ahead, and then we got in this stupid prevent defense, which I call the "prevent you from winning defense." It was definitely scary. They were getting down to the 10 or the 15, and I was thinking, *God, it's coming down to this.* So when Kenny picked it off, it was just such a big relief. It was definitely nerve-wracking up to that point. I hate to say it, but I didn't think it was going to be a positive ending for us. It didn't look good at that point. They had driven the length of the field. But one guy stepped up and made a big play.

One of the images everybody remembers now is me running up and screaming in the face of Washington's quarterback, Damon Huard. I was just so excited and jacked up at that point. I was just talking trash. He was running after Kenny, and I was running to try and block him, but I didn't get there before he kind of gave up on tackling Kenny. So I just came around the corner and gave him an earful, and it was cool because it was on all these dif-

An intense middle linebacker, Rich Ruhl (48) paired with Jeremy Asher at inside linebacker on two of the most successful Oregon teams ever. *Photo courtesy Getty Images.*

ferent TV channels after the game. I was hanging out at the bar after the game with my dad, and all these highlights came on, and they were just constantly showing that play. Coincidentally, I actually ran into the referee from that game about five years later, and he asked me, "Who's that guy who got in Huard's face?" I told him it was me, and he said, "Oh, we should have flagged you for that." Glad he didn't. Huard and I are friends now, ironically enough.

My senior year, I think we had the potential to be a little bit better than we were. The thing about the Rose Bowl year compared to the Cotton Bowl year was that we caught the breaks when we needed them. And maybe we created those breaks, too, but there's a fine line between being 5–5 and 8–3.

Had a couple plays gone our way, we could have been even better. But it was fun. We had a great time at the Cotton Bowl. I got my first and only interception that day. I was just reading the quarterback, kind of dropped back in my zone, and the guy came across the middle, and I got it. I was an all-state tight end, so I had the hands to make the play; I just never seemed to be in the right place at the right time. So that was pretty neat. The only other thing that stands out more about that game was that it was colder than hell. The day before, it was about 85 degrees. We had a tough time keeping our eyes open for the picture because it was so bright and we had to squint. The next day, it was hailing and sleeting—not great conditions for your last game.

Besides the interception, one of my other favorite highlights was a play I made on Washington's running back, Napoleon Kaufman, during that 1994 game. He caught a swing pass out in space, and I made a lucky guess and got him. But when I think about memories during that era, I don't necessarily think about the plays or the wins or the losses. It's the camaraderie of the relationships, hanging out in the locker room, forging the relationships we still have now. It's just great when we all get together again. It's just so much fun getting together with those guys.

Rich Ruhl had 106 tackles for the 1994 Rose Bowl team and was named Pac-10 defensive player of the week after making 17 stops in the Civil War win that clinched the Rose Bowl berth. He was an honorable mention all-conference pick as a senior, and was invited to play in the Hula Bowl. Ruhl has since returned to Eugene and works in the insurance industry.

ALEX MOLDEN

CORNERBACK

1992–1995

WHEN I GOT TO OREGON, I DIDN'T KNOW how to cover. Coming out of high school, I was a strong safety. Most everything I did at that level involved hitting. I'd never covered anybody in my life. Well, maybe a tight end or something. But in high school, I was coming up to the line every play, banging into running backs. Coverage wasn't something I focused on much.

I was pretty heavily recruited coming out of Colorado Springs. I really had my heart set on going to Tennessee, to tell you the truth. I was almost there, and I was really excited about them because I knew more about them. Colorado had just won the national championship, but I had wanted to get out of the state. And then USC, I grew up watching them, so I had some interest in the Trojans.

But I had never really seen the Ducks play until the Freedom Bowl in 1990. When I finally got my visits lined up, I went to Colorado State, Colorado, Tennessee, and Oregon. After the Oregon visit, I canceled my trip to USC. I was burnt out and, anyway, I kind of had my mind made up between Tennessee and Colorado. But then they started throwing dirt at each other and it really turned me off to both of them.

And I had a bad experience meeting Johnny Majors at Tennessee. I got out there, and he invited me into his office and said, "We like you, and we're thinking of offering you a scholarship." I was like, "What? What do you

mean 'thinking'? I know I'm from a little town, but I'm an All-American."
As soon as he said that, I knew that wasn't the place for me.

Then my next trip was to Oregon, and there was just something about it.
The coaches told me there was a possibility that, if I redshirted, I would be
a four-year starter. One of my goals was to start as a freshman and be a part
of something big, something I can be a part of to help launch a program into
the national spotlight. But I had two senior corners in front of me with
Muhammad Oliver and Daryle Smith. I had to be patient.

Actually, there was also a point when I thought that I was going to be a
Sooner. Oklahoma was one of the first schools to call me. I was so excited to
be a Sooner. But I was playing safety in high school, and I just knew that I
was going to be a safety in college. Well, not only were the Sooners one of
the first teams to call me, they were also one of the first teams to tell me that
they wanted me to play corner. I wanted to be a big-time safety like Ronnie
Lott, so that turned me off to Oklahoma. I kind of blew them off after that.
And then every school after that called and told me that I was going to be a
corner! So I finally had to get my head wrapped around that, the idea that I
was going to be playing cornerback in college no matter where I went. If
Oklahoma would have said I could play safety, I would have been a Sooner.

A huge key to my development was learning to play bump and run, and
my first position coach, Denny Schuler, deserves a lot of credit for that. Corner is a much more physical position than some people think. That part's hard
to coach—not just the basics of playing off the line and learning terminology and zones and such, but learning the footwork you need to be physical
with a guy off the line and get out into the pass route with him. I learned so
much from Coach Schuler. He was a fantastic coach. He also helped me with
playing zones and where your responsibilities are. In terms of bump-and-run
coverage, I watched Herman O'Berry, Daryle Smith, and Muhammad
Oliver, and all of them had different techniques. Herman O'Berry was more
physical, Muhammad used his feet to get in front of his receiver, and Daryle
was more of a combination, but he didn't quite have the athleticism and speed
the other guys had. I watched them on film, and I would go out to practice
and match up with a receiver and try to do everything I'd seen them do.

In my first year, I had failures and I had successes. In my first one-on-one
practice, I got out there and played off about eight yards, and Coach Schuler
called a timeout and asked me what I was doing. I told him I was playing off,
and he told me that I should play bump-and-run. From that point on, I had

Schuler's coaching ingrained in me—that because of my speed and athleticism, I was bred to be a bump-and-run corner. Later on, Nick Aliotti was a pure bump-and-run guy. The Rose Bowl year of 1994, we blitzed about 85 percent of the time, so I would play bump-and-run unless we didn't have a safety in the middle. I learned to play more zones and zone dogs with Charlie Waters. Those three different coaches, I learned different things from all of them. I think I was scared to death of Schuler for years, but he really put it in my mind that I was a bump-and-run corner. With Aliotti, he really cultivated that and believed in me, and he was a pillar of strength for me. So now I had better technique and my confidence was building. Then Charlie Waters came in and in our first one-on-one meeting he told me, "Hey, you can play right now in the NFL. What I need you to do is be a leader and help me coach. We'll be able to do other things because of you." Giving me that responsibility helped him get even more out of me.

I think if you had switched the coaches around, I would totally be in a different place mentally, given what they tried to teach me. It was important to get the technical base from Schuler, and then the mental stuff from Aliotti and Waters.

It was a great combination, and then you put that together with a team where there were no superstars. Everybody knew their role, and nobody was out there trying to make anybody else look bad. There was no bickering or arguing. That was always very important in college, having guys with one common goal. If you're looking for keys to the Rose Bowl season, you can start with quality coaches and then players who were coachable.

Of course, it isn't all coaching and attitude. You need to have talent. You look at my freshman class, with guys like Ricky Whittle, Cristin McLemore, and Troy Bailey. The biggest thing was that we knew we had talent. I don't really want to say anything negative about the previous years, but the caliber of athletes and commitment wasn't quite there yet those first two years, 1992 and 1993. As a whole, we didn't have that level of commitment, and I think we really took it on our shoulders, that we had started something brand new and we had everything we could possible need in terms of speed and strength.

Some of that owes to Jim Radcliffe, who was one of the best coaches on the planet for strength and conditioning. I didn't find out until later on that this guy was a guru in the field. Some of the stuff I ended up doing as a pro, I recognized was stuff from my old coach. We thought we had all the pieces

Alex Molden's skills as a cover corner were an asset both to Oregon football and during his long NFL career.

in place, and we wanted to make sure we took advantage of that. We would try and see who could stay in the weight room the longest, stuff like that.

My goal was that by my senior year, we could win the Pac-10 and go to the Rose Bowl, and we actually topped that by doing it my junior year. I ended up doing more than what I ever thought I could, by being an All-American junior and senior year. That was just above and beyond what I thought I could do, and part of that was in the offseason, guys coming together and doing what was inconvenient, not just doing stuff because the coaches said we should. That's where I think that leadership kind of manifested itself. I wasn't one of those loud locker room guys. I was more the quiet leader, but you knew that the 1994 team had great leadership up and down, just from the way we rallied after the 1–2 start.

We also had some great coaches, and they came and told us that we were better than that. We didn't allow ourselves any excuses for the slow start. We couldn't blame anybody but ourselves, and after that we had a new level of commitment, a new sense of urgency. We really stepped it up defensively. You definitely have to play together as a defense, nobody can try and do somebody else's job. I stay in touch with Patrick Chung, and before the first game in 2008 we traded some text messages. I said, "Do your job, don't do anybody else's, and be that leader." He texted me back that it was the best advice he could get because he wants to do everything. But you've got to trust in your teammates.

We had so many good receivers in the Pac-10 when I was playing, from Curtis Conway and Johnnie Morton at USC, to J.J. Stokes at UCLA. I lost more battles than I won against guys at that level. My junior year when we went down to USC, Keyshawn Johnson was a big-time receiver and a big factor, and I really relished going against him one-on-one. I think I gave up one or two catches to him for 30-something yards combined. Between me, Herman O'Berry, and Kenny Wheaton, we knew if we didn't give up big gains then we would have success. I knew all we had to do was stop the big play because we had the offense. We just had to shut people down and let our pressure get to them.

I can't really say I have any regrets about picking Oregon. Even with getting hurt at the end of my freshman year and basically having to play on one leg my sophomore year. I learned so much because I took my lumps. I became a better football player. The only thing was, there were two plays that stick out in my mind from my senior year, where if I had made them we would have been in the Rose Bowl. There was a big play against ASU at home, where a receiver caught a fade right over the top of my head, and then one big play from Brian Manning of Stanford. He caught a big pass that set them up for the go-ahead touchdown. Those two plays from my senior year bug me because the team that we had my senior year, I knew we could have repeated as Pac-10 champs.

Overall, though, being a Duck went above and beyond what I could have expected because I wanted to be a start of something that was bigger than me, something more on the national platform. And now I'm looking at the Ducks today, and we're consistently in the top 20. People know who we are. I would like to think that what we did, we were able to build a part of that. I always wanted to be a part of a great secondary and a great team, and we had some special guys who made some special plays at special moments.

Alex Molden was a four-year starter who earned first-team All-Pac-10 recognition as both a junior and a senior, and was a first-team All-American in 1995. He finished his career with a school record for passes broken up with 60. Molden was the 11th overall pick in the 1996 NFL Draft by New Orleans and went on to play nine professional seasons.

JOSH WILCOX

TIGHT END

1993–1996

THE FIRST GAME I PLAYED IN WAS AT COLORADO STATE, the opener of '93. And the very first play I got in, Willy Tate got hurt, so I had to play 80 snaps. It was a two–tight end set, and he fell on his shoulder. He got hurt, and they were like, "All right, you're up." My second catch, I fumbled. I didn't get through it perfectly, but I kept going. That was my time. Where else would I have wanted to have been?

I started the next game, our home opener against Montana. Then I started a few more games that year when guys were hurt. I was the number-two guy. But getting to play for the Ducks, how awesome was that? That glow never wore off on me—getting to play for the Ducks was the most important thing in the world for me. It never wore off on me until I left.

I was a ball boy for the Ducks as a kid. I was on the field for some memorable stuff—when Chris Miller was hurt, and when Terry Obee ran that reverse against the Huskies. I was right there. For me to be there and be a part of that, and then have a better career than I ever could have imagined, to be part of the history, to catch 100-something footballs at Oregon, I never thought I'd do that. It sounds cocky, but nobody's done it since, and I'm a slow white guy. That's what I was there to do, to play football.

Oregon was always where I wanted to go. I wasn't as highly recruited as a lot of others. Oregon and Oregon State pursued me, and Oregon State wanted me to play defense. But I always wanted to be a Duck. I grew up watching tight ends like Jeff Thomason and Bobby DeBisschop. If you look at it top to bottom, one of the most underrated tight ends ever at Oregon is Thomason, by far. He had so much talent, could catch, could block, played as a true freshman. Justin Peelle was probably the culmination of everything, and Jed Weaver. And I guess that tradition of being a tight end drew me to Oregon, too.

Tate and Vince Ferry showed me how to adapt to college, adapt to the Pac-10. My eyes were wide open just learning how to practice. I couldn't tell the difference between a Cover 3 defense and a Cover 2 defense for a year and a half. I'd go down and run a button hook or something with Junction City High School, or run to the corner. That was the extent of what I knew about football before becoming a Duck.

I played under Willy for a year, and then he decided to not return his senior year, so then it was my turn, and you either go with it or you falter. At that time I had Neal Zoumboukos as my coach, trying to teach me to work. Even though I still probably screwed up, he got me to perform the best I could as a sophomore. Coach grew faith in me, and having those guys showing faith in you does a lot, gives you confidence.

At that time it was just us against the world, and we thought we could do it. Rich Ruhl, for example, wasn't highly recruited. Most of the *SuperPrep* guys I was around were lazy and not very tough. That's why I don't put a whole lot of credence into a lot of that stuff. Granted, it's good to have some of these five-star guys. But some of these five-star guys have already peaked.

My sophomore year was the 1994 season, which started 1–2. That next week was a tough week of practice. Rich Brooks realized that he had a young team, and if he put us through hell week, there were enough guys who would step up and say something. That's what we're supposed to do. We're supposed to work hard and win, not just get a scholarship and show up. But college sophomores and juniors think they can do anything in the world, and that was maybe good. If we lost, we thought we could get them next time. It wasn't like, "Oh, we're scared." We didn't have time to think about it.

As an Oregon fan, seeing Tony Graziani, our backup quarterback, lead the win at USC two weeks later was special. Everyone thought he was the man, and he had confidence in himself, but that day he just stepped up and showed he's the man. And then Kenny Wheaton's pick against Washington, that was unreal.

A member of one of Oregon football's grand families, Josh Wilcox was a hard-nosed tight end and also one of the team's true characters.

The next game was back at home against Arizona. We knew it was going to be a dog fight. That was a physical game. Our defense did a lot for us all year. I think our offense was more a big one or two plays. But, you know, the Arizona game we were both highly ranked. That was their Desert Swarm defense, and we hung in there. I caught a touchdown pass in the corner of the end zone, and we held them, 10–9.

I remember that I cut that play off early because a guy blitzed, and I was probably too slow to get to the end zone. That was a play that we had game-planned all week, and Mike Bellotti, the offensive coordinator back then, made the right call. Danny O'Neil threw it perfectly, and I guess that's when practice paid off. It was something that we were aware of all week. I remember that. If this situation comes up, and this guy goes there, make sure you cut it off. It was just one of those football things where after you practice it a million times, it just happens.

I was disappointed with the Rose Bowl loss to Penn State even though I had a decent game—11 catches, 135 yards. I still am. We should have played much better. There were probably some guys who were a little wide-eyed. But that's the competitor in me, wanting Oregon to be the best. It's a hard standard to hold. I honestly thought we could have beaten them. We should have beaten them, if we played the smart game we could have played. At the same time, we haven't been back since.

I'm still embarrassed about the Cotton Bowl the next year, too. We had seniors who didn't show up and want to play because it was cold that day. There were a lot of guys who wanted to play hard, and there were more guys worried about being by the heater. We were 9–2 in the regular season, and we should have beaten Stanford. We were one game away from going back to the Rose Bowl. We did have a better record than '94, good numbers, had a good offense, but we tried to get too cute with it. You can only shift so many times in the Pac-10 before the guys know what's going on. It was a change, too. That was Bellotti's first year as head coach. I think the '95 team, we wanted it bad, but the '94 team was just a magical year.

In 1996 we were young and had some unfortunate injuries. We didn't have a firm running back until Saladin McCullough got in shape. He wasn't pre-pared for that. I remember his first two days of practice, he was hurt. We had just signed him. We were young, and some of the guys didn't know how to practice. I remember some ones and twos had to do scout team, and I thought that was ridiculous. Graziani was hurt, and Ryan Perry-Smith was the quarterback. He was a heck of a pocket passer.

We only won six games that year, but I would do anything to win. At one point in my senior year we weren't doing so hot, and I went in on the kickoff team. I wasn't worried about my stats or anything like that. I just wanted to win. I was there to win. If I had to block, I blocked. I had confidence that if we needed a play, we would throw the ball to me. I don't want to be cocky, but you have to have that confidence in yourself. I wanted to help them because I wanted to help the team win.

Finishing my career with a win at Oregon State was great. I was probably one of the last ones out of the locker room after that. There's no better feeling than pummeling those guys up there, especially at that old crappy stadium. They don't like coming down here to play, we don't like going up there. I respect those guys, I like those guys, good people, but it's the backyard, man.

Since then, I've kept a reputation as kind of a wild man. I'm a smartass. It's always been part of my personality. I have fun. I'm outgoing. It's football, so I have fun with it. The coaches would never have questioned how hard I worked on the field. But you need a guy who will be the smartass guy. Media will ask me questions, and I'll come up with something funny. I'm not going to give you a popcorn answer because I wouldn't want to hear it. My team came first, I mean, yeah, I want to catch the ball and all that, but I want to win. I had fun with it. I wore it on my sleeve. Sometimes good, sometimes bad, but why fake people out with who I am? I'm a Duck, and that's important to me.

I'm still close with a lot of guys from when I played. Of the coaches that I had there, the best coach I've ever had in my life was Jim Radcliffe, the strength coach. He showed me how to prepare, how to work, how to be a teammate. All my position coaches—Steve Greatwood, Coach Zoumboukos, Tom Osborne—all three different personalities, but I still talk to all three of them. I still talk to my academic advisor. I've been to Reggie Jordan's wedding, I've been to Ryan Perry-Smith's wedding. Hearing about my dad's stories, what college means to him, and then going through that same thing was amazing. I grew up doing Christmas with guys he played with at Oregon. They're like my second family. Eric Winn played with me, and his dad played at Oregon, just stuff like that.

And I'm proud I was part of one of the biggest turning points for Oregon, that Rose Bowl year. Just a doofus from Junction City who wanted to be there, and having fun with it. Nobody in the world thought we were going to do that. You always dream of that. I don't know if it was our goal, but we just went out and played.

Josh Wilcox finished his career as Oregon's all-time leading receiver among tight ends, with 103 receptions. He played in the Hula Bowl after his senior season, then played two seasons in the NFL with the New Orleans Saints after signing as an undrafted free agent. His father, Dave, and younger brother, Justin, also played for the Ducks.

KENNY WHEATON

CORNERBACK

1994–1996

OREGON WAS ONE OF THE FIRST SCHOOLS to contact me during the recruiting process, and that meant a lot to me. I ended up being recruited early on by a lot of different colleges, but I didn't have my SAT scores at the time, so a lot of schools dropped off. But Oregon stayed with me throughout, and specifically, Rich Brooks stayed with me throughout. Denny Schuler was the one that recruited me, but Coach Brooks came to my home a couple of times, so it just showed me and my family that they were really interested in me.

Then, Coach Schuler left before I arrived for my freshman year. That was hard, because other than Coach Brooks I had no communication with anyone at the university. I felt lost. I actually seriously considered transferring when I heard the news. What kept me was that the university did stay with me throughout. And so in the end I stuck with my allegiance to Oregon rather than just my allegiance to a single coach on the staff.

The transition from where I grew up, Arizona, to Eugene was tough at first because when I went on my trip there was snow on the ground. I remember coming back home and my mom asking me how I liked it. I told her I didn't think I was going to go there because it was too cold. I told her I thought I was just going to stay home and go to the University of Arizona. I can't lie and say I fell in love on my trip because I really didn't. It was a long way from home, and I'm a real momma's boy, always have been. But when I got there in the fall, starting with camp and when school started, the people were great. Everyone—from the students to the people I'd run into at stores—just seemed to be happy. After that first year, I wouldn't have wanted to be at any other place.

The secondary at Oregon was very impressive when I joined the team. That was actually one of the things working against Oregon during recruiting, because I was looking at what they had there already. There was Alex Molden and Herman O'Berry, and then you had Chad Cota, who I still say is the most underrated safety in college history. You're sitting there in the meetings with these guys, and even though our record wasn't great at the time, you've seen them playing good football. It was an impressive group, and all it did was just elevate me. It made me work even harder. And I had a lot of confidence in myself at the time.

I didn't want to redshirt my first season, but I did it. When you're being recruited, everybody pretty much tells you what you want to hear. Not that they promised me a position right away; some people did, but they didn't. It was just that I was under the impression I was going to be able to come in and fight for playing time, and it didn't happen. I was upset with that. But a couple of older guys, like Dino Philyaw and Chad Cota, helped me get through that. Basically they just saw talent in me and they were there with encouragement, telling me to just take my time to get better.

Redshirting ended up being for the best, I came to see. I realized that I had talent, but my talent wasn't really what I thought it was. I could have gone out that first year and competed, but I probably wouldn't have really made a mark. There was a lot for me to learn. The game was more difficult than I thought.

In 1994 we had a lot of guys who had been there longer than me, so coming in I didn't really know what to expect. I hadn't moved up the depth chart. I had a good spring camp, but I still didn't know. Coming into fall camp, I wasn't a starter, not even the starting nickel back, but a couple injuries happened, and I got my chance. Up to that point I had started to like Eugene, but I was still ready to transfer because I didn't feel like I was getting a shot.

With Coach Schuler gone, the secondary coach was Nick Aliotti. He's very intense. Coach Aliotti can have you rattled if you don't have a lot of confidence only because he's really into it and really intense. As a veteran, you like that, but in your first year, I don't know if that was a great thing at the time for me. It was cool because he brought fire from a coach's point of view. He and I are very close now, but it wasn't always that way from the beginning. I just think at the beginning he didn't have a lot of confidence in the redshirt freshmen. Guys went down, and I busted my butt, but he wasn't too quick to put me in. But he finally did in that USC game and there was no looking back from there.

I want to say my first play in that 'SC game was an interception. I ended up Pac-10 player of the week, I know that. My first Pac-10 game at the Coliseum was amazing. I had an interception, six or seven tackles, a pass breakup. I had a really good game, and if anyone asks me, I'll say that was the best game I played in my life. The best play I ever made was that interception against USC. The quarterback was Rob Johnson. I was in the nickel, covering the receiver in the slot, and he ran about a 10- or 12-yard in across the middle. I was playing bump-and-run on him, and the quarterback threw the ball, and I still don't know how I got it. To this day, you can watch the tape over and over, and I don't know how the ball got in my hands. I had great coverage and I ended up getting my hand in there and it popped right to me. It was a big game because it was USC, and they were highly ranked. Nobody gave us a chance to win, and the interception was early in the game, so the momentum changed. And just for personal reasons, that was my first time playing in a Pac-10 game, and I proved to everyone else that I belonged. I felt like I already knew I could play, but after that play, it was like, "Okay, now Coach Aliotti sees that I can play."

In that USC game, our defense really had confidence, the way we moved, everything. We went out there and played with a team that people considered the best in the nation, and we beat them. We can play football, we realized. That's when we really started becoming Gang Green, as they called us.

Three weeks later was the Washington game, and the play everyone remembers me by. It was the fourth quarter, and they were driving down to win. If they scored, the game was pretty much over. They drove all the way down, deep into the red zone. Then they came out in a three-receiver set. From watching them all week on film, which I always did, I knew that when they got in this area in this set, there was a certain guy that they loved to throw to. On top of that, I was thinking to myself that if I were the quarterback, I would throw at me because I'm the freshman. I'm not going to throw to the corners on the outside. I'm going to throw at this young guy. It was like slow motion. I was fighting with myself, because when I see the play had started, and they broke the huddle, I was thinking to myself, *Okay, do you jump it, or do you just play it honest?* Then, as the ball was snapped, I just figured I'd jump it, take my chances, and I did. I pretty much knew he was running the out, so I jumped the out, caught it, and just went from there. Catching the ball was slow motion. Running wasn't. Catching the ball, from doing my film study, it was almost like I knew that was where he was going. My number-one thing was to not drop it. It was slow motion when the ball was coming to me, but once I caught it, everything sped up again.

It is a little weird being identified so closely by just one play. I love it, but at the same time it took me years to understand that the true Oregon fans understand that Kenny Wheaton has done more than make that one play. At first, I do have to say that it would bother me, because I thought people thought that was the only thing I'd ever done. When I really thought about it over the years, I realized the true people know I came to play week in and week out.

The Rose Bowl was a great experience, but more than anything it was great to look at the coaches and the older players who were seniors, and the fans, to see how Eugene just went crazy. To some extent, just being there was a win. Before the game even started, I felt like we won. It's not like I was going into the game thinking we didn't have to work, it's just that the fans were great throughout and we hadn't been in so many years. To me, it was more like, *Okay, here Danny O'Neil, here Chad Cota, the guys who paved the way and all the other guys who paved the way before them. This experience is for you.*

192

Coming into 1995, right off the bat you could tell that the attitude for the entire team was different. We went in expecting to win. We went in expecting to dominate on defense. It wasn't that we were hoping to win, it was that we were supposed to win. That was a good season. It could have been better. We expected to have the same, if not better, success from the year before, but all in all it was a good year.

I started every game that year at corner. I had some good games that year also. I had an interception return against Pacific that was kind of crazy. It was a short-yardage play that was fourth and inches, and they had everyone close in except one wide receiver wide, and Alex Molden was covering him. Instincts just told me there was no way they were trying to run the ball. They were going to try and get a big play. I was on the opposite side of the field, and sure enough the quarterback dropped back to throw, and my instincts just took me back to the middle of the field. He was trying to throw it to the guy Alex was guarding, and I stepped in front of it. From there, my entire defense got in front of me and blocked like crazy, and I took it back.

No one in Oregon history is more defined by one play than Kenny Wheaton, but he was a productive defensive back throughout his career.

You had to pick your poison as a quarterback going against us back then. That's the way we looked at it. Alex was the guy everyone looked at as the prototype corner. He covers, and he was a very good man-to-man cover guy. I was the guy who pretty much did it all other than covering. I would come up and tackle, get in and blitz. It was tough for quarterbacks because they had to decide if you wanted to go to Alex or Kenny, and you lose either way.

Of course, we got beat pretty bad in the Cotton Bowl. I wasn't happy with that. Of all the games I played in college, that's probably the one I'm still really sour about, because that game we didn't show up. If somebody would have seen us the first time that game, they would have thought we didn't deserve to be there. We had worked hard all season, and then we got in the bowl game and we just didn't transform into the Oregon team we had been.

At the end of the day, I've always been the type of player who says you don't make excuses, you just put them pads on, but we did not show up as a team.

Personally, I thought we would be good in 1996, too. We had a lot of young guys who wanted to step in and play. We had some guys who weren't proven, but they were talented. It was pretty much a crapshoot. Would we be as dominant as the last two years? Probably not. The only thing I was waiting on was to just see guys get out there and kick, scratch, and fight. We had a different defensive coordinator. It was my third defensive coordinator in three years of playing. It was tough. Everyone had to learn a new system. I can't honestly say I was heading into the season thinking we were going to win the Pac-10. That's what you shoot for, but being realistic, we had some guys who hadn't really played. It was disappointing because we didn't go to a bowl, and having those two seasons before, we had gotten used to it. Our defense wasn't very good, so that was upsetting. It was tough, and for me personally, along with all that, I was getting a lot of phone calls about getting into the NFL.

After the interception against Washington, the decision to go pro early is probably the number-two question everybody asks me. Being totally honest, when I sat down with my mom and dad and my two brothers, everyone agreed it was my decision, just don't look back with whatever you do and don't second-guess yourself. That's what I did. Do I regret it? No. Did my professional career turn out the way I would have liked it to be? No, by no means, but I have no regrets. It just came down to a point where, that 1996 season, I would get the ball thrown at me once a game maybe, and we weren't doing that good as a defense. I was looking ahead at coming back with the same guys, even younger. Do I come back and risk getting an injury? Or do I go ahead and try and live my dream while my stock is at its highest? So I made the decision to leave. I would tell anyone at that point, you do what you have to do. You've got X amount of dollars sitting in front of you, and your dream is sitting in front of you, and you've got a chance. I had two parents at that time who worked six or seven days a week. That was my number-one thing, was being able to provide for them.

But those four years at Oregon were probably the most crucial years of my life, because being in Eugene continued to teach me how to be a young man. My mom and dad instilled a lot of great values in me, but going off on my own and being there, it taught me a lot about the world. I learned that from Eugene, and it's not just the football aspect. It's a wonderful place to go to school, and I enjoyed every second of that. Everywhere I go since I left, I let everyone know that I'm a Duck and I'm proud of it. My wife is a Longhorn, and we go back and forth. I always go back to the 2000 Holiday Bowl, because that's all we can talk about, the last matchup between Oregon and Texas. And we know how that turned out.

Kenny Wheaton was a two-time second-team All-American who led the Pac-10 in interceptions as a sophomore and was voted Oregon's team MVP in 1996. He was an All-Pac-10 pick each of his three seasons, and was the first player in Oregon history to declare himself eligible for the NFL Draft prior to completing his eligibility. Wheaton was a third-round pick of the Dallas Cowboys in the 1997 draft, playing three seasons in the NFL before going on to a distinguished career in the Canadian Football League.

DIETRICH MOORE
SAFETY/LINEBACKER
1996–1999

GOING FROM ALASKA TO OREGON, which had a lot of California kids who all seemed very tight-knit, was a wild experience for me. Nobody really thought of Alaskans being football players, so I guess I sort of felt like the outcast as first. People would ask, "People play football in Alaska?" Or it would be, "There's black people in Alaska?" Questions like that. One of the funniest questions anyone ever asked me came from Dameron Ricketts. He was giving me a ride home from practice, and he was asking me about Alaska, what it's like, common questions people would ask. Then there was a bit of a pause and he said, "What language do you all speak? Do you all speak English?" I'm pretty sure he thought I knew how to speak Inuit or something.

The only places I had taken recruiting trips to were Oregon and Washington State, because I wanted to play Pac-10 ball. I had been injured my senior year of high school, and some schools dropped out of the process. Oregon State was one that I didn't have any interest in. My first trip was to Washington State, and then I came to Eugene a couple weeks after that. I went to Mike Price's house in Pullman, Washington, and nobody was really talking to anybody else. It was just a weird vibe. Then I came to Oregon, and it was the complete opposite. I got off the plane, and the coaches were there to welcome me, and they took me to my host, Damon Griffin, and I ended up hanging out with him and his roommate, Eric Edwards. They took me to a party. We went over to Kenny Wheaton's house, and he and his friends were very welcoming.

The funniest part of the recruiting trip was when I got picked up from the airport by Joe Schaffeld and his wife. We were riding back to the hotel, with me in the back seat on the passenger side, and he was driving. All of a sudden he puts his hand on the head rest of the seat next to his, right in front of me, and I find myself staring at the Rose Bowl ring that was on his finger. I stared at that thing the whole ride, and I thought, "I might have to try to get one of those." I didn't think anything of it at the time, but as I learned more about recruiting and recruiting tactics, I realized he probably did that on purpose.

My first few weeks here were just rough, making the transition. I thought I wanted to go back home, but I knew my mom wouldn't let me and I was in it for the long haul. And it didn't take long for that feeling of being an outsider to change. I got a sense of the family atmosphere at Oregon during recruiting, and it really turned out to be true when I arrived on campus. That was one of the main reasons I became a Duck. During fall camp my first year, I was doing the freshman initiation thing of carrying a guy's shoulder pads and helmet back to the locker room after practice. Mark Schmidt, one of the seniors, told me, "Make sure that once you carry someone's pads, you know you've done your duty. If anyone else asks you to carry their stuff, you let me know." It was like, all right, cool, I've done what's expected, and they accepted me. I would have carried as many pads as I needed to, to fulfill that duty.

I was fortunate enough to play as a true freshman, and that kind of created more acceptance and respect. I felt like I earned respect earlier than a lot of freshmen do, guys that don't have the opportunity to play their freshman year. It was an interesting situation because, going through fall camp my freshman year, I was fourth on the depth chart and I wasn't getting a lot of reps, so I thought I was going to redshirt. A few weeks before the first game, I had a meeting with one of the defensive coaches, Rich Stubler, and he told me that they wanted me to play. I got all excited. Every freshman wants to come play, whether you feel like you're ready or not. But then the next week in practice, I was not getting any reps and I was still fourth on the depth chart, and I didn't see how it was possible to play if I wasn't getting any reps. I got the courage up to go speak with Mike Bellotti, and told him I wanted to redshirt because I didn't want to waste a year playing on special teams and not actually playing defense. So I got my redshirt. I actually redshirted the first full week of playing.

After the third week, Rich Stubler brought me back into his office and asked me if I wanted to play, and I said yes. There were a couple guys at my position who had gotten banged up, so I was up to number two on the depth chart when I came out of my redshirt, and I played on three of the special teams, plus certain defensive packages. The very first snap I ever went out on defense was a goal-line play against Arizona State my freshman year, down in Tempe. I was sitting on the sideline when the coaches said, "Goal line, get ready." So I get up and get ready to go in, but I was standing there with my mouth piece out and my chin strap unbuckled. I had no idea my chin strap was unbuckled. Michael Fletcher was standing right next to me, and he was like, "You better get ready to go in! Put your mouth piece in! Buckle up your chin strap!" They ended up scoring, but I don't think it was entirely my fault.

A few weeks later we were playing California, and Chris Young was nursing a bad shoulder coming in. Cal had Tony Gonzalez, a super tight end. First play of the game, they threw a little five-yard dump pass to Tony Gonzalez, and Chris went to make the tackle, but Gonzalez ended up going for about 40 yards. The coaches were pretty upset, so I went in and played pretty much every snap after that. I had about nine tackles, played a really good game. Tony Gonzalez only had a few more catches after that. It was a solid performance.

The thing I truly appreciate about my experience was my coaches. I had the opportunity to be coached by three different coaches, so there were a lot of different teaching styles and a lot of different attitudes towards the game, and you pick up on that. You always shape yourself based on experiences you have, and I know that a lot of interactions and the way that I was coached has shaped me into the person that I am today, with the kind of attitude and outlook I have. Don Pellum, my linebacker coach, is a guy who is truly invested in not only developing athletes, but people, and he was real big on academics. He was real big on being a good person, and that was something that stuck with me. He's a tough love kind of guy, kind of one of those guys that when you're being coached by him, you're like, *Damn, he kind of trips out sometimes.* But then once you graduate and you actually get out into the world, you find yourself reflecting on the experience you have and what it all meant, and it puts it into perspective and you appreciate it more.

Michael Fletcher ended up being one of my best friends on the team. He and I roomed together our last three years when we went out on the road, and we were some of the very few in the offseason who decided that we wanted to do our workouts in the morning. Both his parents passed away

Dietrich Moore's intelligence and athleticism were valuable assets to the Oregon defense.

during his career, and they both happened during the season. I respected him a lot for going through what he went through. He would go to the funeral on Friday and show up and play a heck of a game on Saturday. It was something that really made me respect him, and having conversations with him in the hotels during those times I think created a pretty unique bond between us.

Another impressive guy during my career was Reuben Droughns. I loved watching that kid carry the ball, because it seemed like as the game went on he just got stronger and stronger. Akili Smith was a pleasure to watch. He did some great things. It was a joy being able to work a little bit with Kenny Wheaton, just seeing how smart of a player he was.

The individual play I'm most fond of was my first interception, which I ran back for a touchdown against Arizona State in 1998. The night before I had been talking to my mom on the phone, and some of her friends were at the house. One of them yelled from the background that I needed to get an interception and run it back for a touchdown, and I did it. We were playing a zone, and the quarterback rolled out, so I slid across the field with him. He was running right and tried to throw back to the left, and he must not have seen me. I was running down our sideline, and he tried to make a play on me, and he took a bad angle and missed. But this offensive lineman nearly got me!

He had a pretty good angle of pursuit, and I remember this big old hog reaching out and me just barely avoiding him. The next thing I knew, I was in the clear, and fans were screaming everywhere. It ended up being the play of the game. I tell you, I was out of breath, but it was a good tired. It was a televised game, and some friends of mine got the clip and made a recording and gave it to my mom, which was special.

There was another memorable game against the Sun Devils back in Autzen the next year. They scored really late in the game to take the lead, and people in the stands started walking out to their cars. The next thing you know, we were driving, and the fans who stayed started going nuts, so there were people who had left who started to come back in the stadium. Joey Harrington threw a touchdown pass to Marshuan Tucker to win the game. That was memorable because you had a chance to see some fair-weather fans, and a chance to see some fans who were really committed to what we were doing. We won a bunch of close games that year. It was the first true experience I had where it's really not over until it's over. Some people say, "I'm a realist, and we're not going to win." It just goes to show that anything can happen.

I had always known Joey was going to be a good football player. How great he was going to be, that I didn't know. He was a sophomore that year, in 1999. Two years earlier, my sophomore year, was his redshirt year. He was the type who was always trying to get better, even if he was the scout-team quarterback. He would really take things seriously, really try to run the offense, instill the leadership qualities that a quarterback has to have. He started it his freshman year. He didn't look at scout team as trying to get his year in and move on. He would come out to practice and break the huddles, and try and read our defense and try to pick us apart. It was a competitive thing for him, which you don't find on many scout teams, because guys have different attitudes about it. His attitude about it was: it's an opportunity for me to get better, get noticed by the coaches. Just to see how he carried himself on the scout team his freshman year was something that was impressive. That was why I knew he was going to be great player. That's what kind of took him to the next level, was his approach starting from the early years.

My last game was the Sun Bowl in 1999. Late in the game they were driving on us. There was a third down, and we needed a stop, and I was thinking, *Come on, let's blitz*. They brought me and Matt Smith off the edge against a single blocker, who picked up Matt. I came free and forced a fumble, which Saul Patu recovered for us. The offense took over, and Keenan

Howry caught a touchdown pass to give us a four-point lead. So our defense had to take the field again with less than a minute left in the game, had to go back for one last stand. My very last play, we were just in a prevent package, one of those where they had a long ways to go and not enough time. It was just, let's get through the next couple plays and we'll be Sun Bowl champions.

Being a football player meant a lot of people might not know your face, but they knew your name, so when I would get introduced to people they would ask, "Do you play for the Ducks?" Playing for the Ducks gave you a minor league version of the celebrity status in Eugene. Even today people will hear my name, and they will recognize it as familiar. I was a business major, and there aren't too many football players as business majors, so I remember getting some looks when I walked into some of my classes. There were instructors I had who were fans. And then I always enjoyed having conversations with people who thought all athletes were spoiled, telling them about what my experience was really like, that it's a year-round duty. But I had no complaints. I love Eugene. The environment and community was a lot like Anchorage: very recreational, a lot of sense of community, a place where people will come and retire, but still a college town. I loved the campus life. It was great, especially the rain. Okay, maybe not the rain. But everything else was great.

201

Dietrich Moore was a three-year starter at linebacker who was named the football team's top special teams player in 1999. As a sophomore, he won the Higdon Trophy as the athletic department's top sophomore student-athlete. Moore spent three years as a graduate assistant coach with the Ducks before moving into student development with the University of Oregon.

PETER SIRMON

LINEBACKER

1996–1999

WHEN I MET THE GUYS I WAS GOING to be playing with at Oregon, there was never a doubt in my mind I'd be a Duck. There were guys like Chad Cota, Jeremy Asher, Alex Molden, Kenny Wheaton, Rich Ruhl, Troy Bailey. I just remember thinking, *I can hang out with these guys*. I can be a part of this team. As a recruit, you see the schools that are recruiting you and you start seeing guys that you say, "When it's all said and done, and I'm a junior or senior, I would like to play like that or be respected like that or be able to help build a program to that point." And I think that when I decided to be a Duck, it was based on who I was following and what guys I thought I could be part of a team with, and part of a continuing legacy.

For those guys, I think attitude and effort trumped talent. Not to say they weren't talented; some of those guys were incredibly talented. But the core guys were hard-working players who got everything out of their talent. I hate to say those guys were the foundation of where Oregon is today, because there were a lot of guys before that who got them to that point. But I think those guys, their final years was the new era of Oregon football. You look back at how after Jeremy left I took his jersey number, 44. It's not that I wanted to be exactly like him, but it's a number I wanted and a number I liked watching when I got recruited. I felt some sort of allegiance to it and I wanted to promote linebacker play at Oregon like he did.

Steve Greatwood recruited me for Oregon, and I believe Joe Schaffeld came and watched me play when my high school played Pendleton. I ended up knocking myself out that game, oddly enough. The recruiting process for me came down to who was going to prove to me they thought I was worthy of a scholarship offer. Who wanted me bad enough to show that commitment? Oregon offered me my first visit. That first attention means a lot, and Oregon was the first Pac-10 team that came on strong. And I became a Duck.

Some guys didn't like redshirting, but I thought it was a great experience. I can remember every Saturday at the old University Inn, we'd sit around at one of the lounges and we'd just hang out and talk about what we did the night before while we gathered around the TV and watched Oregon football. Sometimes we knew what plays were coming and kind of knew what the game plan was. That redshirt year might have been the most special year in terms of getting to know guys and knowing your spot and where you are with everybody else, and I think that was the strongest year of forming those friendships that last until today. Nathan Naggi, Justin Wilcox, Deke Moen, Derek Krug—those were the four guys I was tightest with from our class. Our first game we played in '95 was against Utah, and we all went out to Justin's folks' house to watch. You look back now, and it didn't seem like much, but those were good times.

Out on the practice field, I was getting moved from free safety to linebacker. Bill Tarrow was coaching me, and I just kind of fell in line. I tried to stay close to the back of the line, to see if the guys in front of me knew what they were doing, and then just emulated them. I never had the deer-in-the-headlights thing. I always respected all the guys, but it was always still football. It was always interesting the first couple of weeks to see guys who you'd read about as recruits. You'd read stories about a guy who was just supposed to be "the man," and then he'd get there and you'd think, *This cannot be the same guy I was reading about.* So you learn pretty fast that what they say about you and about other people isn't always accurate, and that you've got to make your own judgments when you hear about the next best thing or the greatest recruits. That was throughout the whole time at Oregon, where you'd read about how some kid's going to come in and Oregon's just going to be a pit stop for him until he goes on to bigger and better things, and those people never really pan out. I don't know if that's some cultural thing with Oregon or not. But one position where Oregon has always seemed to have things

203

Playing beside stout middle linebacker Matt Smith, Peter Sirmon ranged all over the field to make plays for the Ducks.

work out well is at quarterback. Mike Bellotti has obviously been the constant to that, and they've done a great job of evaluating young quarterback talent, figuring out what they want and then developing it. I don't think anyone on the West Coast has a track record as smooth as Oregon's or Bellotti's. They've had some players in the NFL that maybe haven't gone on to what some folks thought they could, but that's not the players' fault, that's the fault of the NFL's evaluation system.

That first year I redshirted, Charlie Waters was such a big influence on me. I never really got to play in the games for him before he left, but the way he carried himself, and the way handled himself through some tough times in his personal life, he was someone you looked at and said, "That's a man." He's seen a lot of things, been a lot of places, but he's still really personable. He was just someone who all the players, not just me, really gravitated towards. He's been a guy who I think about a lot as to the way he carried himself as a man, as a coach.

My first snap was in 1996. We were playing Fresno State, and I was the right wing position on a punt. Tom Osborne, the special teams coach, had been harping on this one point, that he didn't want us to let our guys get inside of us. So what happens? I don't think my feet moved at the snap, and the guy across from me went inside me. Luckily he whiffed on the punt, and I just remember thinking, Thank goodness, because I don't think I touched my guy. I was just petrified in that first game. That would have been a pretty inauspicious start.

After that, my transition onto the field was pretty smooth. I had 17 tackles in that Fresno State game, but they rushed for almost 250 yards, so it was kind of a wash. That was an overtime game, on our way to a 3–0 start. But then we had some hiccups and got bumped out of the Aloha Bowl by Cal. It was great though, because we finished strong and we had momentum going into the offseason.

The way we started the '97 season, with the kickoff return at home against Arizona, that was a pretty special way to start the season. I just remember the energy in the stadium when Saladin McCullough ran it back. That was incredible. And another vivid memory from '97 was the final play of the Washington game up in Seattle, which we won 31–28. Marques Tuiasosopo ran a little keeper, and I tackled him to end the game. That was a huge game, one of those you always remember. It was just a little read-option play, and he kept it and got around the outside. To this day, when I seem him, I make

205

sure I tell him about that. I saw his dad up at a football camp last year and I talked about it then as well. I can't help it. The Washington game was always an emotional game for me, being from Washington.

On the field the most frustrating aspect of my career was my chest injury, when I got hurt my junior year. I think I was better my junior year than my senior year, actually, in terms of how I felt and how I moved around and kind of the focus that I was taking into the season. I was really excited about that season, and the whole team had prepared really well. All the pieces were there, and Akili Smith was there in his second year ready to have a better year. That's a season that got away. I think that could be the most talented team that's ever played here. Unfortunately there were some injuries, like Reuben Droughns' broken leg at UCLA. That was a group of guys that might not have had the obvious results like the Fiesta Bowl team a couple years later, but talentwise I think you could put that team against anyone else in Oregon's history. It would have given anybody else a hell of a game.

Senior year was great, finishing with the Sun Bowl win. It continued this progression that had started with six wins in 1996, and then the Las Vegas Bowl in 1997, and then the Aloha Bowl in 1998, and finally the Sun Bowl. I think our class was the first class in my opinion that was the beginning of the new era in recruiting. I don't think we surpassed those guys that were ahead of us, but I think we helped grow the program. It was also a matter of pride for us that when some of the newer recruits came in, we didn't want to feel threatened by them, but we wanted these guys to come in and be better than us, because when we're done we want to look back and enjoy these games and these players. In the last 10 years Oregon has been talked about 100 times more than it has been in the past. The first week of practice when Joey Harrington was there, I told Jeff Tedford, "He's not like the other freshmen that have come in." He handled himself well, and I knew he was a leader that guys really gravitated towards, and the fans liked him, an all-around good guy.

That final time in an Oregon uniform, at the Sun Bowl, I remember enjoying the game and leaving the field thinking I had done the best I could. You know going in that there's a finish line, and I think when you know that it makes it a lot easier. I think we had accomplished a lot of things as a team, and I had achieved some of the personal goals I had for myself. Those were all kind of put to bed when that season finished. But leaving with the kind of guys that you could be best friends with, that's the first memory that comes to mind for me at Oregon before the football.

Peter Sirmon was Oregon's leading tackler in both 1997 and 1999, and was a first-team All-Pac-10 selection as a senior. Sirmon was invited to the 1999 Senior Bowl, and was a fourth-round pick of the Tennessee Titans in the 2000 NFL Draft. Following a seven-year professional career, Sirmon retired from playing. In 2008 he became the linebacker coach at Central Washington, and he returned to Oregon as a graduate assistant coach in 2009.

MICHAEL FLETCHER

SAFETY

1996–1999

I KNEW ABOUT OREGON BECAUSE OTHER GUYS from my high school had become Ducks, and they started recruiting me my sophomore year. My first love was Colorado, and I actually committed there before visiting Oregon. But then Rick Neuheisel took over at Colorado, so I decided to take my trip to Eugene. It was the best time of my life, as far as recruiting trips go. This was right after the Rose Bowl season of 1994. Once I started getting a little more information about Oregon—seeing Kenny Wheaton with "The Pick," watching the Rose Bowl—you could just see the team was building toward big things.

I went to the game at USC in '94, and Oregon was just flying around making plays, and that's what got me excited about the idea of becoming a Duck. My official visit was the weekend we beat UCLA in basketball. It was right after the Rose Bowl, and everyone was getting back to class, just was a crazy weekend. My recruiting trip ended up being, like, five days long. After sitting in Mac Court watching those games, watching the students storm the court, I went home and two days later committed to Oregon. They recruited me as an "athlete." I played quarterback in high school, and I had never even played defense. Everybody just recruited me as an athlete.

Initially I was a cornerback. When I was redshirting, I knew I was going to have an opportunity to eventually play there because Oregon had a lot of older guys. Chad Cota, Herman O'Berry, Alex Molden, Kenny Wheaton, all of them were great players. Charlie Waters was the defensive coordinator, and initially I didn't think he liked me very much. He would always have me just stand off to the side and watch other guys do drills. I was the only one who had to do that, and being young, I figured he thought I must not know what I'm doing, but what he really wanted was for me to watch Kenny and Alex practice and learn their habits.

Technique-wise, I watched everything Alex did, but when we watched film, I studied all of those guys. Kenny Wheaton was the best player on the football team. His football knowledge was special. Everything that came his way, he made a play on it. Then I started gearing my game after Kenny, because I was a cerebral guy and liked studying the game. With practice and footwork drills, I'd always go with Alex. When we were watching film, I was sitting there with Kenny. For me, it felt like I was getting the best of both worlds.

We ended up having a scrimmage with just the freshmen, and I ended up doing pretty well, and that's when Charlie Waters seemed to come around and start thinking I could play. I redshirted with the rest of the class, even though they thought about using me as a punt returner. Charlie Waters told Mike Bellotti not to use me for a whole year just to return kicks, because he thought I had a pretty good future on defense and wanted to let me play the full four years there.

I had fun in 1995 even though I was a redshirt. We had a lot of great veterans on that team, and watching them was good experience. The first home game was against Illinois, and we all dressed for that. I remember thinking, "I'm actually here." We came from behind to win that game, and the crowd just went crazy. That was one of the loudest crowds I ever heard at Autzen Stadium. It felt like it was shaking. A few weeks later, a bunch of us redshirts got together and drove to Seattle for the Washington game. It was me, Justin Wilcox, Deke Moen, Buddy Smith, Richie Thomas, Chris Young, Derien Latimer—a big group of us carpooled up there. The year before had been "The Pick" in Eugene, and that's when Oregon-Washington was really turning into a competitive rivalry in the Pac-10. I didn't really know how serious the rivalry was until going up and watching it played in that stadium. Patrick Johnson ran a kick all the way back, and we won. We got our ass kicked in the Cotton Bowl, so that year was just a rollercoaster for me, from the beginning of April to New Years Day. To experience so much in such a small window of time, I grew up quite a bit.

Coming into 1996 we had a new defensive coordinator, Rich Stubler. Before that I was solely a corner, and he started moving me all over the secondary. We opened up in Fresno, which is a crazy, intense place to play. The crowd really gets into the game. They had a running back named Michael Pittman, and trying to tackle him made me realize real quick just what playing college football was all about. Kenny Wheaton returned another interception for a touchdown, and we won. But it took overtime, in the first year they used overtime in college football, which is something I will always remember.

We were putting up a ton of points on offense, but we had about five freshmen starting on defense, and it started catching up with us in the middle of the season. That year got cut short for me out at Arizona State, when I tore some ligaments in my ankle on a punt return. It was bad timing because the Sun Devils had a great team that year, went on to the Rose Bowl, and I was playing well. At that time, Pat Johnson and I were splitting duty on punt returns, and that was my first game really having some success on the punt return team. Rich Brooks had moved on to coach in the NFL with the Rams by that time, and they were playing the Arizona Cardinals the next day, so they were all at the game on the sideline. It was great to see those guys, and at one point Coach Brooks came up to me and told me I was a hell of a player and he was glad I came to Oregon. I ended up coming back for the last two games, but a bunch of losses in the middle of the year really hurt. The good news was, we were starting to get some rhythm on defense late in the year. We needed to find a quarterback, but we knew we had Akili Smith coming in the next spring.

We had some other weapons, so I knew if we could just find a quarterback we'd be pretty dynamic on offense. Saladin McCullough was a great running back. He was a guy whom you'd watch in practice, and he was terrible. In the game, I've never seen anybody else run like him. He just glides, just kind of walks. It looks so easy for him. I remembered him from high school too, and he was just ridiculous then as well. The opening kickoff of the 1997 season, he took it all the way back for a touchdown, and Autzen went nuts. Pat Johnson was the other returner, and he made a key block early in the return, fell on the ground, got back up, and blocked somebody at the end of the return, too. It was just amazing. I still remember that film, just watching Pat run by everybody. A lot of fans don't really get to see that stuff because they obviously don't watch the film like we watch the film, but that was a key aspect of that play, Pat's hustle. That was also the first game for Rashad Bauman at cornerback, and the way he played really impressed me, because he was probably only 160 pounds at the time but wouldn't hesitate to come up and hit guys. He was more naturally gifted than most any of those other guys, with his ability to close on the ball. And then the fact that he was never afraid to hit anybody, that made me like him more. Obviously, he came in with a lot of confidence. He talked a lot and did his thing, but he was one of those kids who backed it up. He was one of those people I could go to war with.

The '97 season was up and down for us, but we ended on a high note when we beat Air Force in the Vegas Bowl. Our first two offensive plays were touchdowns, 69 yards and 76 yards. That was a crazy year for me personally, though, because I was in and out of the lineup. Coach Stubler was rotating people, and we'd have whole different lineups at different points. The momentum we had on defense in 1996 hadn't really carried over. We gave up 58 points to Stanford, and in that game I was on track to start but then didn't play one snap on defense. I guess I was in Stubler's dog house or something. We had two weeks to prepare for Washington State, and I started out fifth on the depth chart, but then it seemed like every day somebody got hurt, and I ended up starting. We only lost 24–13 to a really good WSU team, and Stubler moved me to safety that day. That's where I really started to excel, because people got to see me in the box a lot, being around the ball, and I think I kind of found my home in that game. I think I kind of found my niche.

211

Akili Smith had a great spring in 1998, and then we replaced Saladin McCullough with Reuben Droughns, so I was really excited going into the fall. The way that Akili just kind of took off in that spring, it was amazing. It didn't seem like he was the same guy. I couldn't believe it. And Reuben just wanted to run over everybody. I've watched a lot of college football over the years, and I really feel like, if Reuben had stayed healthy, we could have won a national championship that year. I think that's the best offensive team Oregon has had. We just blasted Michigan State to start the year. But then in that huge game at UCLA, we lost a lot of people to injury, and things got off track.

Every game felt like it was a classic that year—just watching Reuben shred everybody, and Akili throwing the ball all over the field. I kind of took off as a returner that year, too. The only problem was that our defense was on the field so much because we scored so quickly. The last two games, the Civil

A fiery leader and the heart of the defense, Michael Fletcher's versatility was valuable both on defense and special teams.

War and the Aloha Bowl against Colorado, were both track meets, and we got outscored. My muffed punt in Corvallis doesn't really haunt me personally, but I know for a lot of people it's the play of mine they remember the most. I wish I could get that changed. It was the only turnover in the game. It was a line drive punt in a game that was really windy and rainy, and I thought I could catch it. But then it just died right in front of me, so I tried to jump over it, and it hit my leg. They got the ball and had the momentum, and Oregon State won the game. I've never dwelled on negative things in my life, though. Mike Bellotti threw me right back out there, telling me that I was still their guy. I had to go right back out there on defense, so I didn't even have time to think about it.

It was weird playing Colorado in the bowl game after my recruiting experience with them. I wanted to beat those guys so bad since I had committed there, but we lost again, just like in the Cotton Bowl after the '95 season. That was a neat experience going to Hawaii and watching Akili have such a great year. That '98 team, I just wished we had stayed healthy that year.

By my senior year, we finally felt pretty good about the defense. We grew up a lot and had a lot of veterans returning. We started 3–3, the last loss coming at UCLA when we got tackled inside the 1-yard line with no time left. That was the last college game I lost. We had a players-only meeting after that game, and some of the veterans made sure everybody knew we were determined to finish 9–3 and do whatever that took. We knew we had talent and had not been playing as well as we could. We made a pact that we weren't going to lose again, and we finished it off with six wins.

213

I lost my mom right before the California game in November. I had lost my father just prior to the Civil War in 1997, and honestly, I think it was helpful for me to endure that during the season. Your teammates and your coaches are your family, and they helped me through it. I really enjoyed those guys. Walking off the field after winning the Sun Bowl was a real sense of accomplishment. You felt like a champion. Winning your last game, that's what people are going to remember you by. We had a group of guys who had been putting it on the line for four or five years, staying together to get it done on the field, and even though we had a lot of trying times during my tenure, it was more fun than anything. It was great to go through it with guys like Justin Wilcox, Peter Sirmon, and Brandon McLemore.

The only thing that disappointed me more than anything with my Oregon experience was all the coaching changes on defense. I look at players who followed me like Patrick Chung, with all the success he had, and I feel like I could have been a guy like that, with all the accolades, if I just had some continuity. But I had a different coach and system every year. After a while it was valuable to have all that different knowledge of various defenses, but at the time it was tough to keep all of it straight. I did pretty well, but I felt that as a unit we could have been a lot better if we had had the same system all four years.

Playing at Oregon was the best time of my life, the best five years I've ever had. When we left, we had won six games in a row, and 14 in a row at home. We helped usher in a new era of Duck football, with the new uniforms and everything. It feels good to know your blood and sweat was a part of that. I still live and die with every snap those guys take, even if I'm thousands of miles away. I bleed green and gold.

Michael Fletcher finished his career second all-time in punt return yardage at Oregon. He was a first-team All-Pac-10 selection in 1999 as a defensive back when he led the Ducks with four interceptions, and he was named Oregon's MVP in a vote of his teammates. Fletcher went on to a distinguished professional career in the Canadian Football League.

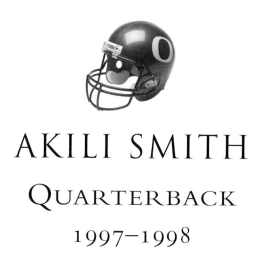

AKILI SMITH

QUARTERBACK

1997–1998

My dad, Ray Smith, was one of my early influences. He was a coach. He coached me all the way through little league, Pop Warner, all the way up. All I knew where I grew up, in San Diego, was sports. And that's all I did, was play. I played football when it was football season, basketball when it was basketball season, and baseball when it was baseball season. His biggest thing was, my dad wanted me to be a baseball player because he got drafted by the California Angels but didn't have the opportunity to play in the big leagues.

My first year of football, I played defensive line and ended up getting cut because I was too young to play Mighty Mite football. Then the following year my dad put me at quarterback, and I never looked back after that. I got cut at seven years old, and then the next year I played at eight. I was a big Randall Cunningham fan, and John Elway as well. Those were my favorite two quarterbacks. Obviously, I was a fan of Randall Cunningham because he was such a good scrambler and runner, and he just made plays. And then John Elway's leadership, and what he was able to do out there on the football field, his release and everything, I just loved it. I kind of wanted to put myself together with both of them, like a John Elway/Randall Cunningham type of deal. That's what I was going after.

In high school I got drafted to play baseball by the Pittsburgh Pirates, and it just didn't work out. I couldn't hit the curveball, and I had a quarterback arm. You've got to have a different type of arm in baseball. My arm wasn't that strong from the outfield, so they moved me to the infield to play first base.

I first became aware of Oregon football when the Ducks played in the Rose Bowl, with Danny O'Neil at quarterback. That's when I started to recognize the Ducks—it was in that Rose Bowl. I got a letter from Oregon when I was still in high school, and they were recruiting me to play defensive back or safety. But I really didn't talk to them much my senior year in high school.

After I went to junior college, Chris Petersen started recruiting me. One day I was at practice at Grossmont College, and I looked over to the right, and here came Mike Bellotti and Chris Petersen. And that pretty much sealed the deal as far as me becoming a Duck. When they both came down to recruit me, and showed that kind of interest, that was pretty much a wrap.

I got there for spring in 1997. It was a big adjustment, obviously. Dirk Koetter was the offensive coordinator at the time. There was a different speed to the game and a different terminology in terms of the playbook and stuff like that—it was a huge adjustment my first year. Patrick Johnson had been in charge of my visit when I first came up there, so I hung out with him and guys like Damon Griffin and Saladin McCullough. I got to know all the playmakers on offense, the guys I'd be playing with.

I loved it in Eugene when I got up there. It was the first time I had seen it. It was a small college town on the West Coast. It was real green. As far as football, Coach Bellotti and Coach Petersen sold me on the fact that, over the few years prior to that, Oregon had the most wins in the Pac-10. Like a lot of people, I hadn't been aware of that. Obviously, USC has taken over these days, but at that time, when I came to Oregon, they were pretty much the best in the Pac-10, and that pretty much sealed the deal for me.

Playing for Coach Koetter that first season was okay, I guess. Jeff Tedford came in the next season, and for some reason he was just able to simplify it better for me. He just split the field in half and taught me that if the coverage was two deep, read this side, and if it's a single safety, read that side. I didn't get as much of that from Coach Koetter. He was more of a progression-based type of coach, where Coach Tedford split the field down in half, and that paid off for me.

Saladin's big kickoff return against Arizona was the first play of my career at Oregon. I played okay in that game, didn't play as well as I wanted to. Our other quarterback was Jason Maas, and he worked tremendously hard. He was a good guy and he deserved the opportunity to play, and the coaches knew that. That's why we split time that season. It wasn't hard for me, because I knew deep down inside that I wasn't 100 percent ready to lead the team my junior year. Maas had been in the program and in the system working hard. They gave us both opportunities, and we just didn't finish as strong as we wanted to in a few games.

Definitely the high point was probably the Las Vegas Bowl, hitting Pat Johnson on that touchdown bomb on the first play of the game, and then prior to that going to the University of Washington, when they were No. 3 or No. 4 in the country, going in to their place and pulling off that unbelievable upset. Again, I hit Pat Johnson for a touchdown at the end of the game, which probably was the biggest highlight of my junior year. Both plays were "22 zone pass, double-go." It was the same play. My mind was just so free at the time, late in the Washington game, and all I knew was we were facing the No. 3 team in the nation. We had a good week of practice, nobody was intimidated, and everybody came out there and played well. That is the loudest stadium that I've probably played in. Autzen Stadium in Eugene is loud, but that Husky Stadium is so loud. When they started coming back, with the fans roaring, the field was shaking. It holds more people than Autzen. At that time Autzen was about 45,000 or something. Husky Stadium was 75,000 or 80,000, and the whole field was moving. I couldn't believe it.

By the time the bowl game came around, I had started getting a little more comfortable with the system. But to be honest, it wasn't until Coach Tedford got there in the offseason, and we started playing checkers and he started splitting the field down in half and really teaching me how to read the defense, that I really got comfortable. I hadn't heard of Coach Tedford or anything like that, but when he got there, he sat me down and we started talking. He started teaching me how to read things, and I was just like, "Wow. I'm glad he's here."

He would just put 11 checkers on offense and 11 on defense, and we'd sit there and he'd put the defense in Cover 2 or Cover 3 or blitz situations and ask me what I was thinking. We were sitting there, and he was moving them around and telling me what formations to put the offense in, and it just seemed as simple as us sitting there playing checkers. He was blitzing guys and putting them into different coverages and then I figured out where to go with the ball. When I started off, I wasn't playing checkers too well, but

218

The best offense in Oregon history may have been the 1998 unit quarterbacked by Akili Smith.

by the time the season started, I had mastered that game of checkers. It definitely worked. We did the checkers exercise, and then he had me on the board mapping things out. It was my first time actually getting on the dry erase board and drawing Xs and Os. He had us doing all that stuff, watching film, and then when you got out there on the field, you just had to go out there and execute. By that spring, I felt comfortable.

Jason Maas was back again that year. But to be honest, I was comfortable with the offense and with the work I put in with Jim Radcliffe in the strength and conditioning program. I ran my fastest time ever in the 40 that offseason. Nothing against Jason, but I told myself going into that Michigan State game to open the season, "I'm not coming off this field." It was fun. We went out there against Michigan State, and Reuben Doughns played well, I played well, the defense played well, and we jumped on them so quick, I believe the starters were finished midway through the third quarter.

I was so happy when we got Reuben, after Saladin was finished. Coach Bellotti knew we had to get him the football. And Reuben and I had the same birthday, so we would laugh about that. That UCLA game when he stayed in bounds and broke his ankle, that was just a horrific loss for the rest of the season.

We were 5–0 going into that UCLA game, with ESPN *College Gameday* and everything in there, all the hype. We pretty much knew we would have an opportunity at the national championship if we could get a win. That's what was on our mind the whole time, to go out there and take care of UCLA on national television, and catapult this team to national prominence. Going into that game, I think we were No. 11, and they were about No. 3 or No. 4, and we knew if we beat UCLA at UCLA, we would jump up to about seventh or eighth. We were ready to go. We were looking to play in the national championship.

The first drive of the game, we were driving, and there was a fumble. The next time we were driving down the field, there was another fumble, but we were still in the game. We stayed in it. Late in the game, we were going down there to kick a field goal to win the game. We were going to send Reuben on a run to the outside, and I told him in the huddle to stay in bounds in order to keep the clock running. He ran over there and, while he was fighting to stay in bounds, he got hit and broke his ankle. And the next thing we knew we were heading to overtime. In overtime they kicked a field goal, and we couldn't do anything in our offensive possession. I had all my family there, and I went in the locker room and cried like a little baby. All my family was up from San Diego, and I cried and cried and cried. I came back out and had to regroup, but with the loss of Reuben it ended up being tough for the remainder of the year.

We knew we had to practice hard and get ready, though, because 'SC was coming to town. They weren't as talented as they are now, but they still had a tremendous amount of talent on that football team, and it took my long touchdown run to win it. That was a "Speed Option Left" out of an ace formation, and it was third and one or something like that, and I saw a crease and just took it. I was thinking just to do whatever I needed to do to get the first down, and then I saw the crease and went in for the score. Then we lost to Arizona, but we came back to beat Washington in what was a really big game. They came in to Autzen and, even though they weren't as good as the year before, Marques Tuiasosopo was playing pretty well that year. I knew it would be a big game, and we were able to hold at home.

We lost the Civil War in double overtime, and more than anything I remember us not being able to stop Ken Simonton. He scorched us that game. Then came the Aloha Bowl against Colorado, which was kind of a similar game. We didn't play very well, but it was high-scoring, and we had a chance late. We just started off so bad. I threw an interception to the house on a little play we had worked up, and they came out steamrolling. We went into the halftime, and I remember taking my shoulder pads and helmet off and just throwing that stuff into the wall at halftime. Everybody just seemed to wake up, and we came back out there, battled back, and almost pulled it off.

We had a pretty special offense that year, that held a bunch of records for points and yards. There was Damon Griffin at receiver along with Tony Hartley, and we had Jed Weaver at tight end. Once Reuben went down at running back, Herman Ho-Ching actually came through for us at UTEP. That was a battle right there. Damon Griffin and I had a pretty good connection. I would just read the coverage, look at Damon, and signal whatever I saw, change the play if we needed to. Tedford gave me the freedom to do that, and it paid off. He let me check to whatever I wanted to, as long as it was the correct check. Damon came through all year.

Being named Pac-10 offensive player of the year was a big thrill. I just wish we had beaten UCLA so I could have had it all to myself and not have had to share it with Cade McNown. That would have been cool.

Overall, playing at Oregon was so much fun. I wish I had had more than two years at Oregon, but coming out of junior college I only had the opportunity to play two years. It was just fun. There's something about playing in Eugene for the Ducks. Once I got to Cincinnati in the NFL, I went from a fun experience to a terrible experience, and it was just a big time culture shock. And to be honest, I just didn't handle things well in Cincinnati at all. I started to miss Oregon and the experience of playing for the Ducks more and more.

I talked to Mike Bellotti and some of the other coaches, Neal Zoumboukos and Gary Campbell, guys who were still there after I left, and they would tell me that I needed to come back more often. But the reason I didn't come back more was I just felt like a failure when I left Oregon. I was just so embarrassed by how I struggled in the NFL that I didn't want to come back and see the people that had supported me my senior year at Oregon, because I felt like I let them and the university down. It took me some time to get back to Eugene. I was just so upset that I let the coaches and the trainers down, and everybody who looked out for me when I was in Eugene. But I've started to come back around again, attend some games, and it's so great seeing people who helped me get to where I'm at today.

Akili Smith threw for school records of 3,763 yards and 32 touchdowns to share Pac-10 offensive player of the year honors in 1998. He was invited to play in the East-West Shrine Game and was ultimately taken with the third overall pick of the 1999 NFL Draft by Cincinnati. Following his pro career, he returned home to San Diego to raise his family. Smith works in real estate and coaches quarterbacks at Grossmont College.

SAUL PATU

DEFENSIVE END

1997–2000

I DIDN'T EVEN PLAN ON GOING TO COLLEGE. Didn't even think about it. It wasn't talked about much in my household. For the most part, with the things that I was into at the time, I didn't have what I would call good guidance. My parents were from the islands. They ended up getting into education, so they stressed getting an education, but there was no real direction on what kind of education. It was just "get your education." It was real general, no real direction on that aspect.

But then I came down to Oregon, and it just felt right. I was a Seattle kid, and I knew that we played Washington, so that was exciting. When I got qualified and came down here, it was just exciting to be here. I was in a place where everyone wanted to get a degree and wanted to play football at the highest level. It just felt like, "Man, this is what I've been searching for," you know? I had always worked really hard at what I did—even the bad things I did! But everything I did, I did pretty hard. So it was just nice to be around that kind of atmosphere.

Pulou Malepeai was the guy who watched over me at first. It was almost like he had a hidden camera in my dorm room. He would call me up and tell me to come over, wouldn't tell me for what. But I respected that; in our culture, in the Polynesian culture, you respect your elders, no matter if they're right or wrong. So, I'd be like, "All right, I'll be over." I would be thinking he might need help moving his furniture or something. But no, he'd have dinner there waiting for me. He did that all the time. He knew how it was to be in the dorms and not have your parents around, not to have a support system. It almost brings tears to my eyes thinking about it now, because those were the things that I appreciate, things that I remember. So at any point in time when I'm in a position to help somebody who could need it, I want to be there for them, because it has been done for me. Even if it was ramen noodles, he'd share with me what he had. That's really being like the heart and soul of the team, that family spirit on the team, being there for each other on and off the field. If I know I can depend on you off the field, I know I can depend on you on the field.

If there's one thing I remember best from practices, it's the two-minute drill, what we called FUJI. And I still hear about it from the guys now who play, because I have the opportunity to have a relationship with some of the players on the team now, and they're like, "Man, FUJI sucks!" I mean, I always loved it. FUJI is the time where it's just, like, 100 percent all out; you get warmed up, and then right off the bat you're into the fire, full contact. I loved it. Some guys don't like it, partly because it was always one of the first drills of practice. FUJI was always the time where, no matter how you feel, you have to be at the highest intensity level, because the drill is created for a high-intensity level. It's like the best and the worst drill. It's fun because you've got some guys that are having fun, like myself, but then there's some guys that still needed to warm up a little bit. Coaches would start yelling immediately, that's for sure.

223

On the field, one of my moments that sticks out is probably the Michigan State game in '98. That was a game where we'd been talking about this all offseason as the first step toward bigger goals. We'd been saying, forget about the Rose Bowl, let's talk national championship, and this was our chance to do it. We'd been there all summer long, working out together and hanging out together. In years past most people would go home for the summer, but we stayed down here and sacrificed, got ahead on our credits in school so there could be no excuses in the fall. We worked out every single day together. Every single thing was waiting for that game, and then we finally got to go out there and show everybody what we'd been doing, show them the fruit of our labor, and, man, we just blew those guys out, 48–14. It was exciting.

The 2000 Holiday Bowl against Texas was a blast. The last game I played here, we won. It wasn't just any game. We were playing Texas, who has a good tradition, and everyone was predicting that we'd get beat. They've had some great players that came out of Texas, and it was good because we'd seen those guys walking around—guys like Shaun Rodgers, Casey Hampton, Leonard Davis—and they had this walk to them, like, "Man, this is going to be a walk in the park." They had that receiver, Roy Williams, and Chris Simms at quarterback. Still to this day, in my mind I feel like Major Applewhite should have been playing for them. That might have made things different. But for us, for the most part the feeling, the spirit that we felt in practice was that we had our own swagger. We felt like we had something to prove to the world, that we were here in Eugene, Oregon. We're the Ducks. We're not a slouch! We trained hard and we were trying to get after it just like the Florida States and the Miamis. We were out here working hard. We wanted people to understand that. Hopefully they did after that game.

I don't have any regrets about my career. Early on I thought I might, but I don't have any. I feel like things happen for a reason. When I was going to have my daughter my freshman year, I was in a relationship, and I was going to leave school. And Joe Schaffeld pulled me aside and spoke life into me. I was pretty much packed and ready to go when I came in to talk to him. And I just told him, "Coach, I don't know, I've got to support my daughter." I wasn't raised to pass that by and carry on with my everyday life. And he put things in perspective, basically telling me that I could be a better dad by having a better education and then having a better job than I would get if I left right then. Then he also told me to look at what I could do, instead of what I couldn't do. It also helped having my parents' support in helping take care of my daughter, and also my daughter's mom's family supported the fact that I was trying to better my life here at Oregon. I stayed and I ended up graduating with my degree and moving on to bigger and better things.

I left and played professionally for eight years, bounced around the NFL for my first two years, and then really found a home in the Arena Football League in Colorado, so it was a blessing. There were just great people I met and got to be around—to see their mannerisms, how they do business, how they interact with each other. It was great to be around great leaders like John Elway. Without that conversation with Schaffeld, none of it would have happened—meeting my wife, meeting a good mentor of mine that I met soon after that, Pastor Keith Jenkins here in Eugene. So all these relationships and different experiences wouldn't have happened if Coach Schaffeld hadn't taken the time out of his busy schedule to speak life into his freshman who hadn't

Saul Patu commanded the respect of his teammates through his work ethic and passion for football.

even busted a grape out on the field yet. That's just the type of guy that he is, who does the right things whether it's within his job description or not.

To this day I've kept in contact with Don Pellum. Really, all the coaches were great leaders here. And that's what I think it starts with, the coaches being great leaders and sowing those seeds for the players to be great leaders. To be honest, on a team if you've got five or maybe six great leaders, the rest of the guys will follow. We just had a great chemistry, a great camaraderie.

In '98 we decided as a team we needed to do things more, and Mike Bellotti orchestrated an environment where these things could happen. He created an environment in which leaders could step up. I always tried to lead by example, but wasn't as vocal at the time. Akili Smith stepped up, Saladin McCullough stepped up, Michael Fletcher did, even young guys who weren't seniors. But the main thing was that, as a player, you're one of the best at your position, maybe not even in the conference but in the nation, and therefore you want to be leading by example on and off the field. And then you have permission to lead the guys now, because guys respect that. Guys respect that you lead the team in sacks, interceptions, etc., and then they give you permission to tell them what to do.

There was one time, and I won't mention any names, a guy was saying something at halftime, just barking and getting on guys, and he was a guy who didn't really lead by example. I give him credit for having the courage to say something to try and motivate the team. But there were guys who did not give him permission, someone who did lead by example went off on him, like, "Don't tell me anything unless you do it," and they almost got into it in the locker room. We ended up winning the game, but it's things like that, you've got to make sure that, as a leader, you're leading by example.

For the most part, if I were to say there is something within football that I'm most proud of, it would be two things. One that I respected everyone, so I listened to everything that the coaches told me and even people out in the community. I filtered what I felt worked, because I practiced and figured out what was good or what was bad. I was proud of myself in that aspect, that I was a student of people who were older than me, who had knowledge or experience. And on the other side, I tried to make myself available, because guys, outside of football, for the most part people just see them as athletes. Nobody knows that maybe an athlete is starving at home because he's in the dorms and doesn't get a salary check and his parents don't have any money to send him. They don't see the times that maybe one of the athletes got a girl pregnant and is ready to drop out of school to support his child, and there's nobody there to put it in perspective that he could actually be a better dad if he finished his degree. But athletes are just kids, too, and sometimes they need help. Because I've been mentored that way, I tried to mentor guys as well.

Everything that I tried to be for other people, it has been done for me, and it is something that I appreciate and know it has blessed my life. Why hold on to it? It's not mine to hold on to. People did it for me, so at some point I might be able to do it for someone else, or at the very least do it for my kids. Even after football, I look back, and it's just the relationships. Yeah, you have great times, won a championship out at Colorado, won some bowl games here at Oregon. There's been some great plays I've been a part of. Those are all good things. But the things I can hold on to and pass down are the times, the experiences, the relationships, coaches pouring into me, me pouring into other people, them pouring into me. Those are the good things, man. Those are the things that really stick out, and really bless the people that you are a part of, my kids and my family. I try to pour into my kids what I feel, like everything that has been poured into me—especially the things I learned as a Duck.

After finishing his career in 2000, Saul Patu received the Joe Schaffeld Award as Oregon's top defensive lineman and shared the Gonyea Award as the Ducks' most inspirational player. He played professionally with the Colorado Crush until returning to Eugene in 2008 as a youth pastor. He also mentors youth through the Patu Foundation.

227

The
NEW
MILLENNIUM

RASHAD BAUMAN

CORNERBACK

1997–2001

MY REDSHIRT FRESHMAN YEAR, Joey Harrington, Justin Peelle, Chris Tetterton, and I used to sit in the dorms talking. One time they asked me what my goal was at Oregon, and I said to win a national title. Flat out. And Joey was like, "Well, let's get it done." That was always our mindset. Always. I think that's the first time I had ever heard, and the only time I had ever heard, true national championship talk. We were freshmen and we were thinking national championship. I know where Joey was ranked coming out of high school. I know where I was ranked coming out. We had a great class coming in, so it was kind of like, "Why not?"

When I got to Oregon, there was this swagger to the program. I felt like it started when Mike Bellotti took over the reins of the team. You could see the Ducks were on their way up, and that was something I wanted to be a part of. When my class got there in 1997, they were coming off a rough season, but before that they had gone to the Cotton Bowl and the Rose Bowl. I didn't want to go too far from home, and didn't want to stay at home, either. I had never been up to Eugene. Also, I had never played on turf. I know it sounds crazy but that's really what made me come to Oregon.

This seems crazy, I know, but one of the reasons I ended up a Duck was artificial turf. Seriously. I had never played on turf. In Arizona, where I grew up, it's all grass. I just had never played on an artificial surface and thought it would be cool. So when I found out Oregon had turf, and figured out I didn't want to go to Oregon State, Washington State, or Washington, I picked the Ducks. It's crazy that little stuff like that does matter, you know? But it's something that I had never done. I went to Arizona State and Arizona, and they had grass. I had played on grass my whole life, and it was just one of those little factors that helped in picking the Ducks.

I'll never forget my very first rep in practice the first fall. I went against Pat Johnson, and I heard about his speed, and he ran right by my ass. I was like, Goddamn! Rich Stubler was our coordinator, and he used to call me "Sweet Feet," and he said, "Yeah, Sweet Feet, welcome to the college level." After that Michael Fletcher kind of took me under his wing, became a tutor to me. He had been tutored by Alex Molden, Kenny Wheaton, and Herman O'Berry when he was a freshman, so what they gave him, he was trying to give me. He taught me the position.

The first game of my career, we played Arizona in Autzen Stadium, and Saladin McCullough returned the opening kick for a touchdown. That was probably the best introduction I could have had for my career. It couldn't have gotten any better. Sali told me he was going to run the kickoff back, and then he did it. It was like, "What the…?" And you know how that stadium gets. It was a night game, so it was really loud. My senior year, it got so loud that Arizona State had three straight false starts, back to back to back. That was probably the loudest I've ever heard it in that stadium. That game was unbelievable. Brandon McLemore started the game in the secondary, and on the second series I went in, and we never looked back. Of course I was nervous. I was a young buck with no experience. But once you get out there, it's football. That's something I do. I do football. Once you get out there, everyone is playing football.

That season ended with us beating Air Force in the Las Vegas Bowl. After the game, we were really up because we knew that a lot of us were coming back. I mean, we lost a lot, but Akili Smith was going to be more advanced. He was going to understand the whole playbook. Saladin would be healthy. Pat Johnson was gone, but Tony Hartley, it was his time. We had a young team, but we knew we had a good group coming back, and big things could be coming. That was the first year that we really hit summer hard. Everybody stayed. Nobody went off to California or Washington. Everybody stayed for the summer, and that was the first time that our team really got a chance to gel.

I think of '98 as a disappointing year because of what we could have accomplished. It could have been a big year. We went to UCLA with both

232

Few defensive backs in Oregon history have been able to match the coverage skills of Rashad Bauman.

teams ranked really high, and if we had got that game, it would have been over. We had four beatable teams after that. But that loss took a lot out of our team. Reuben Droughns got hurt, Akili threw a couple picks. We had never been on a stage like that, and it took a lot out of us.

The bad news is, we recovered mentally just in time for the Civil War. Our confidence was sky high again by that point. It was like, let's get this out of the way and go to a great bowl game. I don't want to say we were looking past it, but our confidence, which was our biggest asset, was our biggest defeat in that game.

A lot of folks wonder how our 1998 team would have done against the 2001 team. Akili Smith's team against Joey Harrington's team. Personally, I think the 2001 team would smash them. We had more depth at wideout, more depth at running back. For the corners, I was on both of those teams, so I had more experience then. In 1998 the team was probably a little stronger at linebacker, though.

233

It was the following spring, early 1999, when I blew out my knee. I remember that like it was yesterday. I was going against Cy Aleman, and we were both having a pretty good day. He ran a slant route, and I told him, "I'm gonna pick this off." He went to run the route, I jumped it, and I beat him to the point. But my foot gave, and the grass didn't give with it. My foot just stayed planted, and it popped, and I felt it instantly. And I remember lying on that ground just screaming. Ironically, I also felt a little pride in that moment. Usually when a guy goes down in practice, they just move the drill up a few yards and keep practicing while the guy gets worked on by trainers. I would see it happen every day, and I know that's just football, but it used to piss me off. Well, when it happened to me, practice stopped completely. That was a great feeling. It was almost like, something's not right. So it was a good feeling that they stopped practice, and to see them come up and see how serious that was. I cried the first game that next season, at Michigan State, cried at that game because we lost. I cried at the beginning, and then during the game I was happy because we were winning, and then everything started going wrong. If I had been in there, we would have won that game.

After that, I went through the rehab and everything. I remember the preseason rankings came out for the 2000 season, and I just wanted to see if I was going to get any buzz, and I was preseason first-team All-Pac-10. That fed my ego. That was what I needed to see. By that time Joey Harrington had gotten his feet wet. We knew that this was going to be special.

When we got off the bus at Wisconsin for our second game, I think that was the most confident I had ever seen our team. And it did nothing for us. We lost. I couldn't believe we gave that game away. That was the whole state of mind of everybody. It wasn't just me or the offense or the defense or the coaches. Nobody was upset or crying, it was just like, "I can't believe we just gave that game away." But after that we kept on rolling, got right back on it, and we ran into Oregon State. We were playing that game for the Rose Bowl. I loved it. It was a great week. I remember everything about that week. It was just building. They were good. We were good. That was the first time that had happened since I'd been here. It was like, "Yeah, they're finally doing something since I've been here. We've got a rivalry."

Once again, we dropped the ball. Oregon State didn't beat us, we beat ourselves. We had six turnovers, and they ended up winning by 10 measly points. We were still confident going into the Holiday Bowl. Texas is Texas. They were huge. Everyone was talking about how they were going to dominate Saul Patu, our defensive end, because he was only 248 pounds or something. They didn't give us a chance. And you know how we are, we loved that. That's what we thrived on. Jeff Tedford, our offensive coordinator, put together a game plan that was unreal. He messed them up. That offensive game plan was genius, really. That right there, that evened that game up. Once the defense went out there, and the offense had put up seven points, it was almost like giving David a sword. That's what they did, they gave David a sword, and once our confidence was up, we weren't going to be beat.

Coming back for my senior year in 2001, we had been there, know what I mean? Now it was our last year. We had been in these situations, so it wasn't really a big deal. We understood what to do if we got down, we knew how to get out of it. It was easy for us. It felt like we were a professional college team. A lot of people look at USC like that now, and that's how we felt. We just felt really professional, wanted to take care of our business. We always showed up on time for practice. We worked hard. It was almost easy for us on Saturday, because we'd put in the work. It was cake, it was easy. Then we hit the Stanford game. We were kicking their butt the first two quarters, up 21–3 or something. Let's get these fools off our field, that was our mindset. But, once again, just like Texas did for us in the Holiday Bowl, we gave David a sword against Stanford. I allowed a touchdown catch by Teyo Johnson on a fade route. I knew it was coming, even called the play out to one of our safeties, Rasuli Webster, before they ran it. I said, "He's running the fade. I got it." He ran the fade, and we both came down with the ball in the end zone. I was thinking it would go to the defense. I stood up, and the ref threw up a touchdown signal. I was like, "What do you mean? We've both got this ball." It was like I said, we gave David a sword. Their confidence built up. Once they thought we could be beat, and once they got their confidence rolling, it was too late. I remember looking at that clock at the end of the game, and thinking, "What just happened?"

Even though that was our only loss, the BCS bypassed us for the national championship game and sent us to the Fiesta Bowl. All I could think about was that we were supposed to be playing for the title the next day. Don't get me wrong, I respected Colorado. I loved the Fiesta Bowl. It was great, but it was all I thought: I was supposed to play tomorrow. I was supposed to be in California, at the Rose Bowl, playing for a championship. That was my biggest disappointment as a team.

My best memory? Probably the fans. Even if we lost, I tried to shake every fan's hand when we walked off the field. They loved us. And I loved them back. I loved everything about Oregon football.

235

Rashad Bauman was a first-team All-Pac-10 selection in 2000 and a second-team all-conference pick in 2001. After his final season, Bauman was invited to the Senior Bowl along with his fellow starting cornerback, Steve Smith. Bauman was picked in the third round of the 2002 NFL Draft and has played professionally with the Washington Redskins and Cincinnati Bengals.

JOEY HARRINGTON

QUARTERBACK

1998–2001

I GUESS YOU COULD SAY I WAS LITERALLY A DUCK from birth. My dad was in one of Len Casanova's final recruiting classes, and then played for Oregon under Jerry Frei. When I was born, Cas sent my father a letter of congratulations, as they had become pretty good friends by that time. The theme of the letter was along the lines of, "We hear you have a talented player we should be looking for in the next 17 years." Basically, I had a scholarship offer to play for Oregon right then and there. It was signed, "Sincerely yours, Len Casanova."

Growing up in Portland, I always watched the Ducks. In this state you didn't root for both Oregon and Oregon State, and we were definitely a Duck family. But to be honest, I was open to going to other schools—to play quarterback, of course; I was always a quarterback. I asked one time in high school if I could play some free safety, and the coach just kind of looked at me and laughed and kept walking. I was just always a quarterback.

I didn't actually attend an Oregon game until my junior year of high school, when they started recruiting me. The fact of the matter was, I had always wanted to go to Notre Dame. Having been raised Irish Catholic, that seemed like the place for me. Growing up, I had a picture over my bed of the 1992 Snow Bowl between Notre Dame and Penn State, when Rick Mirer, Jerome Bettis, and Reggie Brooks were in the backfield for the Irish. Actually, I ended up playing with Rick Mirer in Detroit years later, and my mom actually got him to autograph that photo.

My first scholarship offer was from Oregon State my junior year. Jerry Pettibone was the coach then, and he said they were going to be changing the offense, that they were going to throw the ball and not run the option. I listened to him, just because he and Dad were friends. Denny Schuler was at Oregon State when they recruited me, and he had played with my dad at Oregon, so that's how it got started between me and the Beavers. I went down there on a visit just to listen to them, even though I knew I wasn't going to go there.

I really only had two other offers at that point, from Oregon and Stanford. After the first playoff game of my senior year, in which I played pretty well, Washington State called and said, "Hey, we heard about your game, and we want you to talk to Mike Price. We're not sure if you're good enough for a scholarship, but you're back on our radar." Arizona State had a quarterback get hurt, and they called about possibly bringing me in for a visit, but neither one of them offered me a scholarship. The only real offers were from Oregon and Stanford.

The Stanford offer came due to me going to camp there, and they were really the ones that recruited me the hardest. It's funny, I remember talking later with Mike Bellotti, and I think he said I was about the fifth guy down Oregon's list as far as quarterbacks went that year. My official offer came around when the other guys went to other places.

237

Since I really was not that highly recruited, I made the decision that I would commit early, in December. I gave both schools a deadline, and said I would have a decision by a certain day. Then I stood in front of a mirror with an Oregon hat and a Stanford hat, and put them on and took them off, and I remember sitting in the living room with my parents, just going 'round and 'round about the pros and cons of each place. It really came down to the fact that I had a hard time turning down a Stanford degree. That's what was hanging me up. But if I had a decent career at Oregon, Oregon grads take care of each other. I knew I was going to stay in the state of Oregon to live, and a degree from the University of Oregon, here in the state, will do you just fine. And then it also came down to the fact that if I stayed at Oregon, my grandfather could watch me play. That was it, that was really the deciding factor, to be able to have my family and my grandpa come down and watch me play. And he ended up being able to watch me in every single game at Autzen Stadium. He bought season tickets behind our bench, in the left corner of the end zone, in the northeast corner, because it was closest to the porta-potties.

Coming to Eugene was kind of a whirlwind, honestly. I remember getting violently sick during my first fall camp at Oregon. I had a couple days there just throwing up from some sort of a bug. Despite that, I had a very good camp, as it turned out good enough that I almost played that first year, in 1997. Coach Bellotti doesn't remember this, but I remember it like it was yesterday: he asked me to come and see him after camp that fall. I missed him when I went to his office, he was gone for the night, so I went home and woke up the next day to talk with him after his morning meetings. He said, "Had you caught me last night, I probably would have told you that you were going to play some in this first game against Arizona." We had a Thursday night game against Arizona to open the season. "But, now that I've had a night to sleep on it," he said, "we're going to redshirt you." I had no clue he was even considering that. I was the most naïve freshman ever. But I was absolutely fine with it.

Looking back on those first couple years, there was just a very strong core group of guys from that class who were very focused and driven, and really grew together. Justin Peelle, Rashad Bauman, Garrett Sabol, Steve Smith, Chris Tetterton, Jim Adams, Ryan Schmid—guys from all walks of life who found a common purpose. There was Wesly Mallard, who was a walk-on wide receiver and ended up playing linebacker. It was scholarship guys, star recruits, walk-on guys—just a great mix of people and personalities. And we had a really great group to learn from, veterans like Peter Sirmon, Justin Wilcox, Deke Moen, Blake Spence, Jed Weaver—a group of guys who really knew how to work and had a commitment to Oregon, the state, and the program. We had a great group of teachers, and then, to be honest, we started to get a little better and get a little more talent. By 2001 it was just the perfect combination of talent and will and leadership.

But back to that first year. I remember specifically sitting in the University Inn, our dormitory, with Justin Peelle, Rashad Bauman, and Garrett Sabol, and Rashad and I were talking about winning a national championship. He said, "I didn't come here to finish third in the Pac-10. I came here to win a national championship." He and I were leading the charge on that, and it was a different tone that we were setting for the Ducks. There were people who, I won't say they doubted it, but it had never been done before, and so we definitely made an effort to start cultivating that idea as soon as we got in there.

I didn't start playing regularly until my redshirt sophomore season, in 1999. A.J. Feeley and I were competing to replace Akili Smith, and although A.J. was named the starter for the opener, in those first couple games I was completely prepared to play because they told me I was going to. They told me I would get in there. Bellotti has a history of playing a couple quarterbacks, so I figured that would be the case. The opener against Michigan State, he told me I was going to play, but A.J. just played so well that there was never a time to take him out. Those first couple games, A.J. just played too well to do anything, and he basically was winning the job. It was tough, because they told me coming out of camp that we would both play. It became really hard after about three or four games of not getting in there. And like any immature kid, I started thinking that this wasn't the place for me. Honestly, I did think about leaving Oregon.

We were 3–2 going into a game against UCLA, and by then A.J. was starting to have some elbow problems. He didn't play all that well, and when I didn't get into that one, I figured I'd never play. We were 3–3 facing a game against Arizona, and again the offense had some struggles in the first half. That's when I got my chance. They came to me as we were going out there for the second half and told me I was up. My first pass was a deep comeback on our sideline, and then I threw a fade up the left sideline. I hit them both. I was a pretty excitable player, and I was a little amped up, let's put it that way.

I came off the bench the next week against Arizona State, as well. That was the beginning of everything, the spark to our run over the next two years, as far as I'm concerned. We had 54 seconds to drive down and win the game. On the winning touchdown, we called a play called 757 throwback, and Marshaun Tucker ran a post corner on the left side. We had won two in a row, on our way to going 27–3 over two-plus years. From then on, we believed we could win every game we played, no matter the circumstances.

Now, in order to believe that you are going to win those close games, you have to have it happen a couple times. And for it to happen a couple times, sometimes the ball has to bounce your way. Honestly, sometimes you've got to get a little lucky. With the Arizona and Arizona State games, and then the Sun Bowl that year, we caught some breaks. On the winning touchdown against Minnesota in the bowl game, I didn't throw a great ball to Keenan Howry, but he made a play. We had to convert a fourth down earlier in the drive, and sometimes it just seemed like we got those breaks, and then we used those breaks to win and build confidence. That was the biggest thing: after that season we became the most confident team that I've ever been a part of. That was the difference between us and everyone else those years— we believed we were going to win the game no matter what happened.

A Duck from birth, Joey Harrington was a clutch performer who directed the only 11-win season in Oregon history, in 2001.

We opened 2000 with a win, and by that time the talk of a national championship for Oregon really seemed legitimate, at least among the players. But then we went and lost at Wisconsin. I remember standing in their weight room giving a press conference after that game, and I was just a wreck because of all the talk we'd had about a national title, and then to lose right out of the gates, that was a tough one. But the confidence of that team just dug us out of too many holes that season. None bigger than at Arizona State the last week of October.

That ASU game was a once-in-a-lifetime deal, it really was. Of course, that game wouldn't have carried the weight that it does today had we not pulled the one out at Washington State the next week. We went to Washington State, and Jed Boice blocked a field goal at the end of the game to clinch a win for the Ducks. It was those types of breaks that we created. We were just such a confident team that we created those breaks.

The Arizona State game was back and forth the whole way, and I remember walking up and down the sideline just screaming, "We are not going to lose this game!" Once we got into a little bit of a rhythm, I honestly had the feeling that there was nothing that Arizona State could do to stop us. It was just one of those days for the offense that was truly once-in-a-lifetime. It felt like everything that left my hand was going to be a touchdown. Late in the game, one of our cornerbacks, Steve Smith, made a good play and broke up a pass to get the ball back so we could make what could have been a game-winning drive. I threw a ball down the middle to Justin Peelle, and one of the safeties tried to make a play on the ball instead of tackling Justin and missed them both, so he took off for about a 30- or 40-yard gain on a seam route which got us down the field quickly. Then on fourth and goal from about the 5- or 6-yard line we threw him a little stick route, and at that moment we found out just what it means to say football is a game of inches. One of the defenders just tapped the back of Justin's heel enough to prevent him from pushing off, and when he met the safety at the goal line, the safety had more momentum and just dropped him literally an inch short of the goal line.

Arizona State got the ball back just needing to run out the clock for the win. In all my time trying to rally guys on the sideline, that was probably the most I had to wing it a little bit. There were a lot of times I was on the sideline thinking, *God, we may lose this game*, but I never told anybody or let on to anybody else that was what I was thinking. But that day at Arizona State was probably the toughest time to fake it. And then they fumbled, and we recovered. The confidence came right back: we had the ball and we were going to score. It took one play, another pass to Justin, for us to score and force overtime, and at that point there was nothing they could do to stop us. Coincidentally, the corner Peelle beat on that play was the same guy Marshaun Tucker beat on the winning touchdown the year before.

Hands down, that was one of the most satisfying wins of my career. And then the Civil War in Corvallis that same season was hands down the worst moment of my college career. Not just because losing cost us an outright Pac-10 title and the Rose Bowl, but because I felt so helpless. For as confident as I felt at Arizona State, I felt just as helpless at Oregon State because I threw five interceptions and fumbled once. Four of the interceptions came on tipped balls. The fumble came as we were going in on the 5-yard line and I got blindsided by somebody. It was an absolutely helpless feeling, and to have that feeling with a Rose Bowl on the line was tough.

I was sitting in the Portland airport after that season, and I had someone come up to me and introduce himself, said he was the back judge at the Oregon State game that year. It turned out that I had really let him have it during the game. There was a ball I threw to Justin Peelle while he was going up the seam, and Justin got held and it ended up getting tipped and intercepted, but only because Justin got tackled coming out of his route. I made a bee-line for this guy and just laid into him. Well, he came up to me in the airport and told me he was the guy, and he told me I was right, that he had been graded down by the coordinator of officials for that play, and that it should have been a penalty. First thing I thought was, well, that's great, but it doesn't give me the ball back!

I still don't think I'm completely over that game. I have four bowl rings, and we played in five bowl games during my career. I have my Vegas Bowl, Aloha Bowl, Sun Bowl, and Fiesta Bowl rings, but the year of the Holiday Bowl in 2000 I didn't want a ring. I got a DVD player. I didn't want it because it wasn't a Rose Bowl ring.

Understand where I'm coming from here. Growing up in Portland, there was no NFL team, so the Super Bowl wasn't that big a deal. The Rose Bowl was the pinnacle of football, as far as I was concerned. I remember going to the Rose Bowl with my dad when I was younger, maybe 11 or 12 years old. There was a wall listing all the Rose Bowl MVPs from throughout the years. I counted it out, and the last two spaces on that board were going to be my junior year and senior year of college. I had been through three years of college football going into the Civil War in 2000, and only once did I have a chance to play in the Rose Bowl, so I knew it wasn't something that came around every year. My thought was that was my chance to be in the Rose Bowl, the one chance to achieve my dream. And to lose that in Corvallis on a day where I felt so completely helpless was tough.

Ironically, we ended up in the Holiday Bowl, where I created some high-lights that I hope will live on in Oregon history for a long time. It probably starts with the touchdown pass I caught before stumbling into the end zone. That was a heck of a catch, let's be honest. Slow that thing down on video, you'll see that it was fingertips. There was some hand-eye coordination there, but in terms of foot-eye coordination, I needed to work on that. But overall that was the perfect way to remedy as much as you could what had happened against Oregon State. Texas was Texas, and to go out and beat them like that, that was a huge confidence booster. And I got a great DVD player, which I probably gave away two years later, anyway.

After the disappointment of the Civil War, and with only one more year left in college, I have never been more focused my entire life than I was in that offseason. There was a single, solitary reason for waking up in the morn-ing, and that was winning a national championship. Because that year the Rose Bowl was the national championship game, and the only way we were getting to the Rose Bowl was if we played for the national championship. I woke up every single day with that as my first thought. I ate Rose Bowl, I drank Rose Bowl, I lifted Rose Bowl. There was nothing else on my mind for the next 12 months.

The Wisconsin game was an incredible way to start the season, after los-ing there the year before, and then we just got on a run. There were about three or four games there where we were just phenomenal, and even against Stanford we put up 42 and only lost on a couple fluke plays. The thing about that season was, it wasn't so much about those big comebacks anymore. The groundwork had been laid the other couple years, and we were making our own breaks that year, not hoping to get lucky now and then. Getting slapped by Stanford was one of those games where it just kicks you in the gut, and you had to refocus and really get yourself back on track, because we were going up to play at Washington State, where it seemed like we played seven years in a row. That's one of the weeks that really sticks out in my mind, hav-ing to get rid of the feeling that we just messed up, and really focus on beat-ing a very good Washington State team. Because if we let that next one go, we were done for sure. There was no coming out of a two-loss season if we wanted to contend for a national title. And we pulled it out, and still only had the one loss entering the Civil War.

That game was awful, and not just because the weather was rainy and windy. I never had a good Civil War game, ever. You know how many touchdown passes I had in my career against the Beavers? Zero. I never threw a touchdown in my career against Oregon State. That Civil War in 2001 was miserable, and it got to the point where I just wanted to get out of there with a win. It was miserable all over, partly because they had moved the game back to December. We had never played a game in Autzen in December. It was about 38 degrees and raining sideways, and both defenses that day were playing tremendously. It was a low-scoring game—we were down 6–3 at the half—and I remember just wanting to get one or two good drives and get out of there with a win. We ended up taking the lead, and then we got the ball back just needing a first down to get the win. We called a bootleg coming out of a timeout, and Coach Bellotti told me, "Call 24 Load and keep it. Don't tell anybody else. Let everyone else just run the play. Just don't hand it off. Just keep the ball." So I went out there and kept the ball coming around the corner, thinking that the end is going to crash down when the guard pulls, but the end stayed up field and hit me, and I fumbled. Luckily, Rashad Bauman came back and made an interception that sealed the game for us. For all the great plays that the offense made through the years, all the points that we put up, it was Rashad and the defense that sealed that Civil War for us.

All I ever dreamt about was getting that Rose Bowl ring, so getting snubbed by the BCS for a spot in the national title game that year has always been a tough thing for me to get over. But that being said, the Fiesta Bowl by far is my greatest memory at Oregon. For all the mess of the BCS, and the disappointment and feelings of being left out or robbed, you couldn't have drawn up a better script for a way for your career to end. Everybody played phenomenally that day. Everybody. That was truly the best game we had ever played as a group. That was the best game that team had ever played, beating Colorado to win the Fiesta Bowl.

I still wonder what if we'd had a shot at the title, I really do. But I'm left with such an incredible memory of my career at Oregon because of that last game. Maybe it could be that much better had we won the Rose Bowl and won the national championship, but who's to say what would have happened in that game? That was a heck of a Miami team, and not to say we couldn't have beaten them. I think we would have, and that was just how confident and good we were, but when I look back on my career at Oregon, I think of that Fiesta Bowl. I think of the two Arizona State games and that Fiesta Bowl as my greatest memories on the field.

As far as what it means to be a Duck, I learned mostly about the ability to build a team with a bunch of people from very different backgrounds all shooting for a common goal. If you look at the collection of guys who made up that 2001 team, it's really crazy. We had a guy who was a finalist for the Rhodes Scholarship in Ryan Schmid. We had a guy who was born in Korea and moved around with a military family and came as a walk-on receiver and ended up as an All-Pac-10 linebacker in Wes Mallard. We had a guy from the tough part of Phoenix in Rashad Bauman. And we had me, a quarterback who played the stinkin' piano. It was just a very eclectic group of people who worked extremely well together and developed a great friendship.

> Joey Harrington was Oregon's first finalist for the Heisman Trophy, finishing fourth in 2001 after being named Pac-10 offensive player of the year and a second-team All-American. The Ducks were 25–3 in games he started, and 11–2 when they trailed or were tied in the fourth quarter. Also a first-team academic All-American, Harrington was the third overall pick in the NFL Draft by the Detroit Lions. In 2008 he spent his seventh pro season with the New Orleans Saints.

KEENAN HOWRY

RECEIVER

1999–2002

Out of high school, I wasn't really recruited that heavily by any other schools. The only schools I was really recruited by were Oregon, Washington State, Arizona State, Colorado, and Kansas. I was recruited by Oregon State as well, and was actually scheduled to take a recruiting visit to Oregon State, but right before that Mike Riley took the head coaching job with the San Diego Chargers, so I ended up not taking my recruiting visit.

My main thing coming out of high school was even though I felt like I was probably one of the more dominating receivers in California at the time, in high school everyone was telling me I wasn't fast enough for my size. That was the knock on me. I had great production but was too slow for my size. So I didn't get recruited by USC or UCLA, the hometown programs. It didn't bother me, just for the fact that I didn't really want to stay in Southern California anyways. I always kind of wanted to get away, because I was never one of the people that had to stay close to home, that I had to go to 'SC or UCLA because everything else was not good enough. I wanted to leave. I wanted to experience everything, so it was really no big deal to me that they didn't recruit me. But just knowing that I was better than everyone else who was getting recruited by those schools, that did kind of bug me a little bit.

I already knew a lot about Oregon because Tony Hartley was up there and went to my high school. He was a senior when I was a freshman, and I was the same age as his younger brother. I would always kind of keep up on what happened with him, and see how he was doing, just for the simple fact that we went to the same school. Tom Osborne recruited me for Oregon. He called me and told me they were interested and everything, and I would keep in contact with him and Chris Petersen, who is the head coach for Boise State now but was coaching receivers for the Ducks back then. I had constant communication back and forth with those guys.

I came on my recruiting trip, and Oregon was just the place I felt most comfortable. Even though the Ducks didn't necessarily throw the ball a lot, I liked the tradition they were building. Oregon had been consistent in everything they were doing. Since their Rose Bowl year of '94, they were always building toward something, going up, as opposed to places like Washington State or Oregon State, which didn't seem as consistent then. Oregon had always had good seasons, and it seemed like the next season was always better than the last. Plus there was the fact it always seemed like Mike Bellotti was comfortable with where he was at and wasn't going to be leaving anytime soon. Riley had left at Oregon State, and eventually Mike Price at Washington State ended up leaving, too.

When I committed, I knew that Tony Hartley was a senior and a returning starter who wasn't going anywhere, and Bobby Nero was coming back on the other side. Redshirting wasn't on my mind, but at best I figured I'd end up backing up Tony my whole first year. So I prepared myself to play before moving up to Eugene. I worked on getting faster and stronger and just trying to learn the playbook. I came up on my spring break for a couple days while they were having practice, and then came up permanently a month before any of the other incoming freshmen. I stayed in Oregon to try and get as much of the offense down as I could.

At the start of training camp in the fall of 1999, Bobby Nero ran into some trouble. Now they were down one receiver, and I had been playing so well in the freshman two-a-days, and then again in the regular two-a-days, that I was going to get an opportunity to play. Going into the first couple games, it was pretty much here and there, I'd play a little bit. By my third game, against Nevada, I was starting opposite of Tony, which was a big deal since I'd lived with him over the summer and come from the same high school. I just never would have imagined that happening. Right after the UTEP game, the week before Nevada, Coach Petersen asked me to stay in his meeting room after our meeting was over. He told me he was going to start me at "X" that week, so he needed me to focus on learning all of the "X" position's responsibilities. That was kind of a big shock to me. It was like, "Oh, wow. This is kind of a big deal."

My second start was a home game against USC, which we won in triple overtime. I had never experienced hearing a crowd that loud before. There was so much going on, so much up and down, just going back and forth in the fourth quarter. Nathan Villegas tore his ACL on the game-tying field goal, and we missed a field goal horribly in the first overtime that would have won it. But then 'SC missed the field goal as well, and both teams came back and scored touchdowns in the second overtime. In the third overtime, Josh Frankel came off the bench cold and kicked the game-winning field goal for us. It was one of those games that you never forget, and it was just fun to be a part of, especially when you're playing against people who you played with in high school.

Early on that season, A.J. Feeley was playing lights out at quarterback. He was pretty much the top-rated quarterback in the nation at the time. Then he started to have some arm issues, and by the UCLA game at midseason, you could tell there was something wrong. We came home and played Arizona State, and he was just not himself. We went in at halftime, and they said they were going to make the change, and in comes Joey Harrington. He came in there and had his own energy and his own stuff that he did best. We just went out there and clawed back, and I ended up catching a pretty big touchdown from Joey in the third quarter. With the way the season had gone to that point, with a heart-breaking loss to UCLA and as bad as we played against Washington, we needed a spark and something positive to go on. And he was that for us.

We played in the Sun Bowl at the end of the year, and I got hurt the week before we left to go. I actually hurt my groin so bad that I could barely get out of bed and move around, so I ended up having to take that last week off from practice. We came to El Paso, and I was starting to feel better, so I ended up playing. We weren't really doing anything offensively early in the game, and we finally put it together at the end. We were down quite a bit late, but I ended up catching a long pass down the middle, against the Jim Thorpe Award winner from Minnesota that year, Tyrone Carter. I just beat him really bad to catch that pass and get us down to the 1-yard line, and then Joey snuck it in for a touchdown.

Our final drive, we were methodically moving the ball down the field, and then I scored a touchdown to win the game, which was just incredible.

We had this play that was actually designed to go to the fullback, and he was supposed to go to the flat, while Tony and I lined up on the same side. Tony came in motion and he went in and picked the guy who was covering the fullback. I just ran a simple corner route, just to kind of get in the way. Well, as Tony came down, the guys who were covering Tony and me both slid down and left me completely uncovered, so I just released up the field and put my hand up, and Joey happened to see it. It wasn't the best pass Joey ever threw. Sometimes Joey got a little too excited, and it was a low ball I had to go down and kind of catch at my ankles. But that was one of the best memories I have from that whole year—catching that touchdown. It kind of pushed us forward to the next season and put us back on the map as a team that was going to be able to compete for the Pac-10 title.

The turning point in 2000 was back-to-back games against UCLA and Washington after we started 2–1. At the time, playing two teams ranked third in the nation in back-to-back weeks was kind of unheard of, at least for us. We went out there the first week and really did well against UCLA, and the next week we got no rest and again played well against UW. Personally, the Washington game was a landmark for me, simply for the fact I had a tremendous game returning punts. I think I had about 120 yards in returns called back by penalties, but I made an impression on the coaches. Michael Fletcher had done a great job there the year before, but he had graduated, and in 2000 the punt returner was kind of up in the air. I had gone back and forth for the job with other guys, and then I kind of separated myself from everybody else during that Washington game.

249

A few weeks later we headed down to Arizona State for a game that went into double overtime. That was a crazy game because we started off so horribly and then finally in the second half the light went on, and we started scoring at will. Everybody was just playing lights out in the second half. And then to have our game-tying drive end the way it did, with Justin Peelle getting stopped on the 1-yard line, was like, "Well, I guess it's not going to work out." Our defense stuffed them for two downs after that, and it was like, "All right, third down, here's our chance, give us one more chance on offense." Watching from the sideline, you saw the running back break through the line, and it seemed like it was over, but then the next thing you know the ball was out. We recovered a fumble that gave us new life, and we scored a touchdown on the very next play. It was just amazing. Your emotions were just on a rollercoaster.

So we headed into the Civil War needing a win for the Rose Bowl, and it wasn't to be. If you told somebody that this team was going to have five turnovers, and only lose 23–13, you might say, "Damn, you guys must have played really well despite those five turnovers." But we really didn't. We played really badly the whole game, even though our defense kind of held us in there. We had so much riding on that game. We kind of played uptight. We knew going into that game that if we won, we were going to the Rose Bowl. And, especially knowing how bad the Big Ten was that year, we knew we would have an opportunity to go in and win a Rose Bowl. I think we knew that, and especially Joey kind of tensed up a little bit. I think we all did. We all played bad that game.

Everybody realized that we let that great chance slip away, heading into the Holiday Bowl against Texas. We knew we couldn't play as bad as we did against Oregon State. I think everybody was really focused going down there, being that so many guys on the team were from California. Playing in San Diego basically felt like a home game to a lot of us. You look back, and the game would not have been as close as it was had we not let them return a kickoff for a touchdown. At the time, I think we were up 10 and we were shutting them down, and that kind of gave them new hope. But everybody played well. Joey played amazingly. Maurice Morris had 100 yards receiving and about 80 yards rushing, and the defense played lights out. It was one of those team efforts, and we needed it. You look at all the guys on that Texas team, and at every position they had first-round NFL draft picks. But we went out as a team and really stuck it to them.

The way the 2001 season unfolded, it was like everything we had worked for was paying off. It was like I said about the recruiting process, Oregon just seemed like it was building toward something. You didn't quite know what it was, but year in and year out they were building. My freshman year built toward how well we played in 2000, and then you say, "Okay, you played so well in 2000, which kind of crescendoed with the Holiday Bowl. How are they going to turn that over to 2001?" Going into that season, I think everybody had a lot of questions, not just in the Pac-10, but in the nation. Can they be as dominant as they were last year again? That year in the Pac-10, with the exception of Washington, everybody had pretty much everybody coming back. I think everybody from the outside looking in saw the conference as up for grabs. I think we might have been projected to win the Pac-10, but even then it was still up in the air.

Keenan Howry was a precise route-runner and sure-handed wideout, not to mention a game-changing punt returner.

We had a tough game against Wisconsin to open the season, and people were saying that if we struggled that much our first game, we were going to have a hard time once we reached the Pac-10. I think everybody just worked extremely hard in that offseason to where we were ready for the tough games. And you take away two blocked punts and an onside kick against Stanford, and we're undefeated and playing for a national championship.

Instead we had the one loss coming into the Civil War, and once again, everything was on the line. But this time it wasn't just that if we won the game we won the Pac-10 outright. Now there was also a really good shot that we could play for a national championship. Colorado had already beat Nebraska, Tennessee had lost to Florida in the SEC Championship game, and the only game left was Colorado versus Texas, and Texas was the only other team ahead of us. It was like, "You know what? If we can win, there's a good chance that we could make it to the national championship against Miami."

The weather was horrible that day, and we didn't play particularly well on offense. We struggled and were down 6–3 in the fourth quarter, so both teams were playing pretty badly. We needed a spark, and I was able to provide it with a punt return to make it 10–6. It kind of turned the tables for us. It was a big deal. It gave everybody life, and then the defense stopped them again, and we got down and scored another touchdown to go up 17–6. By that point, we kind of had the game in hand.

252

That punt return is something that everybody is going to remember me for, I'm sure. Being a return guy, 80 percent of it is relying on other people to do their jobs. It's not like being a receiver where if I run my route correctly I'll get open and hopefully the quarterback can get me the ball. It's more like being a running back. If everybody blocks well, I have a good chance of having a big play. You're back there all by yourself, and you've got 10 guys running full speed at you, and you're just sitting there hoping these guys block well enough for me so I can at least get something. The punter had been struggling with the bad weather all day. He kicked a low line drive right to me, so when I caught it, I had time to look and see where everybody was. I set up the block for Ty Tomlin. I kind of hesitated and hopped to the right so he could get his block, and right when I hopped to the right, it was just like nobody was there. Everybody had made perfect blocks, and all I had to do was run straight, and that's pretty much all I did. By the time I got 20 yards down the field, nobody was there. It wasn't even a footrace because nobody was chasing me. It was a big play and propelled us for the rest of the game.

We were on cloud nine and then came crashing back to earth when the BCS snubbed us. We looked at it like we'd done everything we needed to do, and everything had happened how it needed to happen, for us to finish No. 2 and play for the national title. We had been fourth or fifth the week before, we won, and the three teams in front of us lost. Honestly, I could understand how they could put Nebraska ahead of us, because they were 10–1, a good team. But how was it that Colorado also jumped ahead of us?

We had a big chip on our shoulder going into the Fiesta Bowl against Colorado, and a lot to prove going into that game. I think the coaches did a great job of not putting any pressure on us, because everything we had set to accomplish that year had already been done. We went out and, with the exception of Stanford, we won all our Pac-10 games. We won the Pac-10 outright, there was no sharing like the year before. We would have made the Rose Bowl under the new format, with a separate national title game. We had no pressure. We knew we were a better team than Colorado, and we knew that they couldn't compete with us. I think that the coaches took all the pressure off us and we went out there and played exceptionally well.

253

It wasn't the same my senior year. Disappointment is not even the correct word for that season. I can't even describe in one word that whole experience. Offensively we had a better team than the year before. Anytime you can have a backup, Onterrio Smith, rush for 1,000 yards, and you have three of your five linemen coming back, you figure that's not going to be a problem. You have your three starting receivers coming back, and your tight end in George Wrighster, who is more physically gifted than Justin Peelle, so you figure that's not going to be a problem. Then we had Jason Fife, who was more mobile and had a stronger arm than Joey, coming in at quarterback. So you're figuring that's not going to be a problem. And we figured we had a new offensive coordinator, Andy Ludwig, coming in who didn't have as good of talent at Fresno State, yet they're putting up numbers. We should be scoring 40 or 50 points a game.

I felt like that should have been our m.o. the whole year, because we lost both our starting corners from the year before. Even though we had some talent back in the front seven, the staple of the Oregon defense is that you have two corners who can play man-to-man without any help. Knowing that you don't have that anymore, you would think that our emphasis would have been trying to score as many points as possible, and I just didn't feel that our game plan week in and week out was to score as many points as we could. Not to take anything away from Onterrio, because he's my good friend and he's an awesome back, but I just think we put too much on him. Anytime you're playing Portland State and you have 30 carries for barely 100 yards, you have to think maybe we shouldn't be running the ball that much.

In our first three games we struggled against Fresno State, barely beat them. We played okay against Mississippi State, and then we beat Portland State. And then we beat Idaho, which is almost like another D-II school. I kept telling people that year, we're going to struggle once we get in the Pac-10 because we're going to struggle to score points. We hadn't allowed Jason Fife to do anything. We've been almost babying him along, so when it came to the point of him needing to take charge and drive us down the field and score points in a tight game, we haven't asked him to do that yet, so how would we expect him to do that five or six weeks later in the Pac-10?

I felt like when you have that much offensive firepower, I would have come out the gate and been throwing the ball 30 times a game, getting Fife ready to play later in the year. Because everybody knew that we had a first-year starter at quarterback, and Onterrio at running back, we were going to run the ball. Everybody was gearing up for that. But that's not how the season went. We went out there and played Arizona the first week, and even though we beat them, they weren't real good, and our defense got exposed as not being able to cover. I think their receiver had almost 200 yards receiving, and then the next week was the same thing. And I think we could have had the offense to still win games by outscoring people, but we hadn't prepared ourselves to do that in the early part of the season. We started 6–0 but ended up 7–6, and that was disappointing.

254

That couldn't diminish what we did the seasons before that, though. For me, to come out of that season and be the career receptions leader, the career touchdown receptions leader, to have all the records that I achieved throughout my whole time there, it was just a great accomplishment. I loved every minute of it. I can't sit here and let that senior year put a bad taste in my mouth about my experience at Oregon. It didn't. I accomplished so much, met so many great people. I completely loved my experience up there. I had a great time.

Keenan Howry finished his Oregon career with 173 receptions for 2,698 yards and 24 touchdowns, at the time school records for catches and touchdown receptions. He also held the Ducks' record for career punt return yardage, with 1,221, and was in the top 10 for average return at 11.7 yards. Howry was first-team All-Pac-10 as both a receiver and a punt returner in 2001, and again as a punt returner in 2002. He was invited to play in the East-West Shrine Game, then was a seventh-round draft pick of the Minnesota Vikings in 2002. Howry played three seasons in the NFL and is coaching high school football while continuing to train for a potential comeback.

KELLEN CLEMENS

QUARTERBACK

2002–2005

IF YOU LOOK AT MY BACKGROUND, coming from rural Eastern Oregon, going to an agricultural school might have made more sense. I wanted to stay relatively close to home, so I visited all four Northwest schools in the Pac-10, and things just clicked for me at Oregon. I knew that's where I wanted to be. Mike Bellotti's tenure with the Ducks speaks for itself, and the stability he brought to the program, you just don't see that everywhere. All four Northwest coaches told me during recruiting they'd be around my entire career, but Mike Bellotti's the only one who actually was. I think the other three may have all been gone by my sophomore year.

Coming from more of a conservative background, Eugene seemed very liberal when I first got there. Now I consider it a pretty small town, after having lived in New York. But for a young kid leaving home for the first time, it was great. My first fall, 2001, was a learning experience in all kinds of areas. In football, the playbook was obviously a lot thicker. I spent a lot of time picking Joey Harrington's brain, that being his final year. And what a great year to come in. Finishing 11–1 and winning the Fiesta Bowl was an awesome way to start a career.

I still stay in touch with Joey, and we'll talk about some of the plays we ran back at Oregon and the terminology we used. It's crazy to think about how many quarterbacks from the state of Oregon made it to the NFL in our generation. I see A.J. Feeley once or twice a year, either at games or wherever.

Joey, A.J., and I have the same agent, so we'll get together through that sometimes. I'll even get together with Derek Anderson sometimes, even though he's a Beaver.

My first touchdown as a Duck came against Portland State in 2002. The call was Right Ace 6 Stretch Right Boot Left, something like that. I'll never forget that play—a touchdown to Nate LiaBraaten. Then a few weeks later I threw an interception against Washington on my first play. That was just as memorable, but not for the same reason. And then where my career really got a jump start was getting to play extensively in the Seattle Bowl at the end of 2002. The result wasn't what we wanted, but that was valuable live action for me. It showed me I could play at that level. For a guy who was just 19 years old at the time, that was a pretty nice way to get your confidence going and to instill some trust by your teammates.

The fall of 2003 started out well. We beat Michigan and were 4–0, and then just got slaughtered the next week against Washington State. The biggest thing about that year was we lost a few games and were starting to slide like we did at the end of 2002, but this time we were able to pull out of it. We started out 6–0 the year before and were ranked in the top 10, just rolling, and then the wheels came off. It's definitely something you're aware of, saying, "We're not going to let that happen again." We went 7–6 in 2002, lost the last four. But then in 2003, even though we lost four of five in the middle of the year, we rallied back and made the Sun Bowl to finish up 8–5.

What can I say about 2004 other than, "Oh, my goodness." The Indiana game that started it off was just brutal. We had so many opportunities to get stuff done and just couldn't. Personally, I threw a couple of picks. That was a really tough way to get a season started, and then we went down to Oklahoma. They were highly ranked as usual, and after losing that one we just never got on track. Later on, we had Cal against the ropes and couldn't finish it off, and got beat in the Civil War to finish the season. It was just not a good year. We had some injuries that hurt us, which was tough. We had a pretty good streak of winning seasons and bowl games, and going 5–6 killed that. That stung.

We at least returned almost everybody in 2005, so the foundation was there to improve. That group had redshirted in 2001 and saw something special that the team had then, and we wanted to find that again for ourselves. We knew we had talent—Demetrius Williams, Tim Day, those guys were getting healthy. The addition of Jonathan Stewart was huge, and Dante Rosario

Kellen Clemens led
the Oregon offense
during its transition to
the spread attack.

showed up in a big way. Haloti Ngata was back and healthy. So the table was set. But the main thing was chemistry. We had a group of seniors plus Haloti, who was a junior, that had played a lot of football together. Coach Bellotti preaches to recruits the family atmosphere, how much we have each other's backs, and we had that in 2005, no doubt about it. That carried us through a lot of close games. We wouldn't always necessarily play outstanding football, and we played some tough opponents, but unlike past seasons, we made some big plays when we needed to, and that's because we all trusted each other.

My career ended at Arizona in the eighth game of the season. They were doing some things defensively we hadn't seen, so it was a tight game. I can still picture the play on which I was hurt. A guy came from my left side, and I didn't do a very good job of making him miss. He came down on my left leg, and it broke. It was all over. That was tough to get over.

But when I think about the five years I was a Duck, it's all in a very positive light. I was able to challenge for some school records, which was an honor. But the chemistry we had, the relationships with teammates, is more important than any records. I just would have loved to have finished that last year out on the field with my guys.

I wouldn't be where I am today if I hadn't gone to the University of Oregon. The flexibility of Coach Bellotti to change the offense my fifth year, that was a gutsy call, and obviously it paid off and then some. Bringing in Gary Crowton to run the offense was a great move. And I've got a pretty good business degree to hang on the wall, which is important, too.

259

Kellen Clemens led Burns High School to an Oregon state championship before joining the Ducks, and was on track to set a number of UO passing records before being injured as a senior. His eight career 300-yard passing games were one shy of Danny O'Neil's school record. Clemens was voted Oregon's most inspirational player in 2005, and was a second-round draft pick of the New York Jets the following spring.

NICK REED

DEFENSIVE END

2005–2008

OREGON WAS THE FIRST TEAM TO NOT ONLY recruit me heavily but offer me a scholarship. I didn't commit on the spot, but I had always been interested in Oregon from following college football closely as a kid. They caught my eye with all the cool stuff they had, the uniforms and such. As I went through recruiting, I was looking at more and more schools, but Oregon had been the first one there, and the Ducks were always in the back of my mind. For some reason, I just really liked Oregon even before I got the chance to visit Eugene. Once I finally visited, it was a pretty easy decision for me. The location was great because I like the outdoors, and the longevity of the whole coaching staff was really impressive. Most college coaches seemed to bounce around every four or five years, but Oregon had coaches that had been there for 20 or 25 years, and some of them had even grown up in Eugene and came back. So I thought there must have been something pretty special about Eugene and I wanted to be a part of it.

Being a Southern California kid coming to Oregon was a big shock. It was totally different. The first couple months I hated it, just like everyone else, but I got to know Oregon and the people in Eugene better, and my point of view changed. It's just a really special college town, big enough that you can have everything you'd want to do, but it's also a tight-knit community. You feel like any time you go to dinner or the movies, you might bump into somebody that you know. Even before I accomplished anything on the football field, I was having people coming up to me saying, "Oh, you're a freshman. I know you." People in Eugene are big fans, and that's just a cool experience—something I was never familiar with where I grew up.

I came up hoping I would play right away, but I didn't know what would happen, or even which position I'd play. I went through the same thing after my senior year at Oregon. Going from college to the NFL was just like going from high school to college, because everyone thought I was too small to be a D lineman and assumed I'd be a linebacker. I didn't want to play linebacker, I wanted to be a D end, but I kind of heard what everybody was saying when I got to college. So I came in and figured I'd at least make a push to be on special teams. I didn't want to redshirt, and I made that clear. I told them that, and I think they kept that in my mind. I think I demonstrated that I would be able to help out a little on the line. I did some pass rushing stuff, and I was definitely happy to have that happen.

My high school defensive line coach, Mike Piel, played end for the Rams in the NFL for a couple years. By the time I got to Oregon, the stuff that the Oregon coaches were teaching was stuff I had already done a hundred times with Coach Piel in high school. Getting off the line at the snap, getting the offensive lineman's hands off you and working the speed rush was stuff that some people may have had to learn, but I was really comfortable with it already.

Freshman year, I think I got my name in there as a hard-worker against Arizona State when I blocked a punt. That was kind of my claim to fame when I was a freshman. We were losing to Arizona State by a touchdown, and they were punting from around the 25-yard line. I blocked the punt at about the 15-yard line or so, and the ball was bouncing around, and if I was more of an athlete I would have scooped it and scored. But the ball was right on the 1-yard line, and I just jumped on it. People made fun of me for a long time for not getting into the end zone, being so close. So then, later in the season against Arizona, Haloti Ngata blocked a punt, and the ball was spinning around on about the 20-yard line. I had to run about 20 yards to get to it, and I was thinking, *I'm going to try and scoop and score right here.* It couldn't have been any better, because the ball was literally spinning on its top, so it basically was begging to be picked up. Well, I was running at full speed and tripped over the ball, and their punter recovered it and advanced it about one inch short of the first down. So we managed to keep the ball, but it was an embarrassing moment for me.

I also had a sack against Stanford, my only sack of the season. That was a big moment for me, too. The one thing I took away from that season, and I don't want to name any names because I don't want to put anyone down, was that even though we had a great team and went 10–2, and even though we did well despite Kellen Clemens getting hurt and went to the Holiday Bowl, which it was a cool experience, as a freshman I noticed that some of the older guys took practices off. They wouldn't practice on Mondays or Tuesdays or something. When I saw that, it was always my goal to not be like that as a senior. I took pride in participating in every workout I possibly could.

As a sophomore, I didn't start at the beginning of the season. They didn't trust me yet against the run. They moved Matt Toeaina out from tackle to end, and I was kind of pissed off at the beginning of the season because I wanted to be playing. I had a good game against Oklahoma in the third game of the season, and then we had a bye week.

That Oklahoma game was memorable to a lot of people because of its controversial ending, but what I remember best was tackling Adrian Peterson. I got the biggest bruises of my life on my left bicep from hitting him. Later on, I was in when we blocked the field goal that won the game, and in the film you can see me hopping around like a little girl. But I was talking to a coach from the Chicago Bears while I was at the Shrine Game in 2009, and he said Peterson is hands down the toughest guy he's ever had to play against.

After that was the bye, and I went out that weekend and goofed around and had a lot of fun. We came back the next Monday, and I wasn't feeling really well from having too much fun during the bye week, and I found out I was going to be starting my first game that Saturday. I was like, had I known that was going to happen, I would have spent the whole bye week watching film!

I did okay when I got my first start, against Arizona State—had three or four tackles, got some pressures. I didn't have a great game, but it was solid. I was competing with Dexter Manley for that starting spot, and Dexter actually had three sacks that game, so I thought right there my starting spot was gone. But they left me in there, and Dexter and Jeremy Gibbs and I all rotated at the two end spots, along with Darius Sanders. As the year went on, I got more comfortable. That's what that year was about for me, getting over the whole feeling of, okay, I'm on the field, what am I doing? I was just calming down, seeing the play and the tackles, and playing smart football.

My position coach, Michael Gray, was instrumental in that. He is a players' coach all the way. He had a lot of experience, so he took his experience and gave it to us, and he was a good coach in that regard. He could explain

Nick Reed recalled Oregon's blue-collar roots during a four-year career in which his work ethic resulted in a school record for quarterback sacks.

to us what we could and couldn't do, and he could tell our defensive coordinator, Nick Aliotti, who had these lofty goals for what he wanted us to do, what he could and couldn't expect from the D line. I got really close with the graduate assistants, Eddy Morrissey and Matt Dawson. They had a big role working with our position group.

The 2006 season ended on a rough note. The Arizona game, where we lost 37–10, was the most embarrassing game I've ever been a part of, until we played the Las Vegas Bowl two games after that. I felt like garbage about the season. I was glad I was coming back and had time to get back what I lost that year. I didn't think I had a bad year personally. I just felt like, as a team, we did not do very well. The whole team felt that way, and we had a big meeting in the offseason, and I think we addressed some of the problems, like people not practicing and not showing up to meetings. We tightened the screws on everybody, and I think it helped out quite a bit.

There was a new attitude coming into the fall of 2007. Toward the end of fall camp, the seniors always get up and talk to the players about what our expectations are. I wasn't a senior myself, but I was sitting there listening to the seniors talk about how we were going to have a great year, and I guess I wasn't sure at that point. Eric Steimer, the long snapper, got up and said, "My goal is a national championship. I think we can do it. We can win a national championship this year." I felt a little stupid later, but right then I thought maybe we should have been focusing on the Pac-10 or the Northwest. I didn't say it, but I was thinking, *Come on. That's ridiculous.* I would have never guessed that's how the season was going to go.

That was the year Dennis Dixon turned himself into a Heisman candidate, which was another development I didn't necessarily see coming. It's always so hard to gauge those things, especially because I don't play on offense and I don't know how our offense is going to be. I just remember hating—hating—playing against Dennis Dixon. He was so hard to play against. He made pass rushing seem useless. Because if you went right at the guy, he would just go outside, and if you went outside, he would just step up in the pocket and shoot through a gap. I'm sure Coach Aliotti had a lot of sleepless nights because of him.

The belief really started to set in after the Michigan game. They had already lost to App State, so we knew it was a game we could win. We had performed well in our own opener, but I think everyone had assumed the Michigan game would be a lot closer. Nobody expected us to beat them by as much as we did. I think after that we had an idea of what we could do. And then, after we beat 'SC at home, I really thought we could do something special. Before that we had lost to Cal at home, and I figured we were screwed as far as the national title goes. I don't like to be negative, and so I never ever said this to anyone, but losing a Pac-10 game early in the season isn't a good sign, and I figured we were done. But after we beat 'SC, it was a whole new turn of events. We were ranked, and the next week we played ASU at home, which I think was the biggest game I've ever been a part of, just because we were both ranked so highly and ESPN *College Gameday* was there and everything. Being a part of something like that was pretty cool.

But then Dennis hurt his knee, and everything went off track. Still today, we talk about "woulda, coulda, shoulda." Everyone talks about how Dennis was going to win the Heisman and we were going to go to the national championship. Even after we lost to Arizona there was still the Pac-10 chase to think about. Had a couple things here and there gone our way, we could have had it.

That didn't work out, but we rebounded to beat South Florida in the Sun Bowl. My first two years at Oregon, we lost bowl games, and everyone was kind of saying that Mike Bellotti didn't know how to coach bowl games, and that we were doing something wrong. Just up the road, the Beavers had won a million bowl games in a row, and they must have it right, that was the thinking. We never changed anything about our bowl practices from one year to the next. They were always the same, the same intensity, same amount of time, same time of day the four years I was there. I think it was just the players coming out ready to play on that day, compared to the Vegas Bowl the year before, in particular.

After that, I had serious national title hopes for the 2008 season. I was being optimistic because it was my senior year, and I started to understand where Eric Steimer was coming from the year before. It was my last shot. I knew we would have quarterback issues after Dennis graduated, but otherwise the offense played well, and our defense played okay. We had some issues getting everyone on the same page early on. Honestly, we started off really slow that year. We started 3–0, but after needing overtime to win at Purdue and then losing to Boise State, I was a little nervous about where the season was going to go. Obviously Boise State went off and had a good season, but we just played so poorly against both of them that I was nervous for the season. Maybe the defense didn't play as well as I had hoped. I wished the defense had helped the team out more, but as usual the Oregon offense got everything together, Jeremiah Masoli settled down at quarterback, and we ended up having a good year.

Our defense was really good against the run that year. That was our D-line focus, was to stop the run, and we had a great season at that. I was so glad to see Cole Linehan and Sonny Harris succeed at that. Coming into the season, a lot of people didn't have respect for them. They did great, and it was awesome to see. But overall, even though our defense always played hard, we always gave up more points than we should have. But as our offense figured it out and played better and better and better, not many people could stop the Ducks. Particularly in my last Civil War, when we won 65–38.

For me, the Civil War was fairly unique. I played high school football with a kid who went to OSU, Gregg Peat, and in the four years I was at Oregon I spent a lot of time hanging out in Corvallis. A lot of people aren't happy to hear it, but I spend a lot of time with a lot of Beavers. When I got here, I didn't know what the Civil War was about, but as I lived here longer and longer I understand that it's a huge rivalry in the state. The two years that we lost, it was kind of embarrassing every time I had to drive through Corvallis. Not so much seeing the players—nobody really said anything about the game too often—but it's just that feeling that you really do feel like you owned the state those years that you won the Civil War, and those two years that we didn't it kind of felt like I had to keep my head down driving through Corvallis. It made the Civil War so much more special for me, because I knew so many of the guys so well, as opposed to other games where if you lose you don't ever have to hear about it or look in their faces. But I spent so much time with those guys that it means a lot more to win that game.

I don't think I won a game back home in Southern California until the Holiday Bowl against Oklahoma State senior year. People used to ask me, "You were 0–3 down there, were you distracted, or what was going on down there?" I didn't feel distracted by having friends coming to the game, nothing like that. Just like the bowl games, I don't think there was any rhyme or reason for those losses other than the other team played harder that day.

There was a lot of people who said the Pac-10 stunk in 2008, and that the Big 12 was the place to be, and they were going to roll over everybody. I don't think anybody gave Oregon a chance. I remember one national poll in which about 80 percent of the fans picked Oklahoma State. But when our offense got rolling, we couldn't be stopped. We started off slow again, but we held their offense to a lot fewer points than they were probably used to. After halftime, our offense picked it up, and as usual they couldn't be stopped. I had a good senior year, but going into the bowl game that would have all been for not had we lost that game, because that's how everybody would remember us. That's kind of what I remember about my freshman year, was that we had such a good year, but it was all kind of soured by that loss in the Holiday Bowl. It was awesome to turn that around in my final game.

It's almost impossible to sum it up, what it means for me to be a Duck. The experience I had playing college football in Eugene was second to none. I don't think it could have been any better anywhere else. I think it was one of the best choices I ever made, just the friendships I made there and everything there was to do in Eugene. One of my favorite things to do in Eugene was to go floating down the river, which kind of had a sour note at the end with the tragedy involving Todd Doxey, but those other trips are going to be my favorite memories. [Editor's Note: Doxey, a redshirt freshman safety, drowned while on a river outing with teammates in the summer of 2008.] Football was a huge part of my experience as a Duck, but it wasn't all of it, and I think that's what I love more than anything—that I had my life in Eugene with all my teammates and we did so much fun stuff in Oregon like boating and floating and hunting. And then on top of that we had four really good seasons.

Nick Reed finished his career as Oregon's all-time leader in sacks and was voted the team's MVP and a Walter Camp first-team All-American in 2008. Reed was a two-time All-Pac-10 pick and a two-time Academic All-American, and as a senior he was awarded the Morris Trophy as the Pac-10's best defensive lineman. Following his senior season, Reed was invited to play in the East-West Shrine Game, and he was a seventh-round draft pick of the Seattle Seahawks.

From
Anna
Nickerson
Christmas
2011

ABOUT THE AUTHOR

Rob Moseley covered his first University of Oregon football game in 1997 and has written about the team extensively ever since. He became the primary beat writer for the Ducks at the *Register-Guard* newspaper in Eugene beginning with the 2007 season. Moseley graduated from the university's school of journalism and communications in 1999.

Monday Jan 2. 2012
Ducks beat Wisconsin
U of Oregon   Badgers
45 to 38
Last Duck Rose Bowl
win was 1917

ATERA · PHIL MCHUGH · JACK CRABTREE · NORM CHAPMAN · J

DAVE WILCOX · BOB BERRY · DENNY SCHULER · BOB NEWLAN

· DON REYNOLDS · STEVE GREATWOOD · VINCE GOLDSMITH · N

· ANTHONY NEWMAN · J.J. BIRDEN · BILL MUSGRAVE · DANNY

TON · DIETRICH MOORE · PETER SIRMON · MICHAEL FLETCHE

N HOWRY · KELLEN CLEMENS · NICK REED · JACK PATERA · PHI

ACHER · WILLIE WEST · MEL RENFRO · LARRY HILL · DAVE WILCO

E · TOM GRAHAM · TOM DROUGAS · DAN FOUTS · DON REYNOL

N · MICHAEL GRAY · DON PELLUM · CHRIS MILLER · ANTHONY

RUHL · ALEX MOLDEN · JOSH WILCOX · KENNY WHEATON · DIET

RASHAD BAUMAN · JOEY HARRINGTON · KEENAN HOWRY · KE

NORM CHAPMAN · JIM SHANLEY · DARREL ASCHBACHER · WILL

ER · BOB NEWLAND · KEN WOODY · BOBBY MOORE · TOM GRAH

E GOLDSMITH · NEIL ELSHIRE · GARY ZIMMERMAN · MICHAEL (

USGRAVE · DANNY O'NEIL · CHAD COTA · RICH RUHL · ALEX MO

MICHAEL FLETCHER · AKILI SMITH · SAUL PATU · RASHAD BAUMA

PATERA · PHIL MCHUGH · JACK CRABTREE · NORM CHAPMAN · J

DAVE WILCOX · BOB BERRY · DENNY SCHULER · BOB NEWLAND

DON REYNOLDS · STEVE GREATWOOD · VINCE GOLDSMITH · N